Pay Commissions of India

First Central Pay Commission (1947)
to
Seventh Central Pay Commission (2015)

PAY COMMISSIONS of INDIA

First Central Pay Commission (1947)

to

Seventh Central Pay Commission (2015)

Highlights and Summary of Each of the 7 Pay Commissions with Focus on Seventh Pay Commission

Compiled and Edited by

M.M. Sury

New Century Publications

New Delhi, India

NEW CENTURY PUBLICATIONS
4800 / 24, Bharat Ram Road,
Ansari Road, Daryaganj,
New Delhi - 110 002 (India)

Tel.: 011 - 2324 7798, 4358 7398, 6539 6605
Fax: 011 - 4101 7798
E-mail: indiatax@vsnl.com • info@newcenturypublications.com
www.newcenturypublications.com

Editorial office:
LG–7, Aakarshan Bhawan
4754-57/23, Ansari Road, Daryaganj,
New Delhi - 110 002

Tel.: 011 - 4356 0919

First Published: **2016**

ISBN: **978-81-7708-424-5**

Published by New Century Publications and printed at Salasar Imaging Systems, New Delhi

Designs: Patch Creative Unit, New Delhi

PRINTED IN INDIA

About the Book

The Government of India constitutes, as a matter of convention, a pay commission after almost every 10 years to review and make recommendations on the wage structure of Central Government civilian and armed forces employees and pensioners. A pay commission, depending on the terms of reference, examines various aspects—such as pay and allowances, retirement and death benefits, conditions of service, promotion policy and such other related matters—of the wage structure of employees and submits its recommendations to the Government. The Government, in turn, takes the final decision as to the implementation of the recommendations, which may be full or partial or amended or modified. The chairman and members of the pay commission are nominated by the Government.

A pay commission is not a constitutional body and therefore the Central Government has a lot of leeway about which part of the report to adopt and in what timeframe. Since India's Independence, 7 pay commissions have been set up, from time to time, to review and recommend wage structure for Central Government employees. Usually a pay commission is given 18 months time to submit its report.

A pay commission, before recommending the pay structure, analyzes voluminous data relating, inter alia, to the general economic conditions in the country, financial resources of the government, strength of the work force, and pay structure in public sector and private sector undertakings. Clearly, review and determination of the pay structure of Central Government employees and pensioners is a stupendous and complicated task. Reports of pay commissions provide glimpses of the events, challenges and perceptions of labour leaders and policy makers during the post-Independence period.

The present work provides highlights and summary of recommendations of each of the 7 pay commissions which have reported so far. The work is divided into two parts. Part I deals with the Reports of First to Sixth Pay Commission. Part II is exclusively devoted to the Report of the Seventh Central Pay Commission which was submitted to the Government on November 19, 2015.

About the Editor

M.M. Sury received his B.A. (Hons.), M.A., and Ph.D. degrees in economics from the University of Delhi. He taught economics in the same university for 42 years. Specialising in fiscal economics, he has published extensively on Indian fiscal system in recognised national and international journals, including *Small Industry Bulletin for Asia and the Pacific* (United Nations, Bangkok), *Bulletin for International Fiscal Documentation* (International Fiscal Association, Amsterdam), *Asian-Pacific Tax and Investment Bulletin* (Singapore), *Journal of the Indian School of Political Economy* (Pune), *Indian Economic Journal* (Bombay), and *Margin* (New Delhi). He was a Visiting Fellow at the International Bureau of Fiscal Documentation, Amsterdam (May 1989), a Fellow. at the Indian Institute of Advanced Study, Shimla (1991-92) and a Visiting Fellow in the Department of Law and Management, University of Mauritius, Mauritius (September-October, 2000). He was Economic Adviser, First Delhi State Finance Commission (1996-97).

Contents

Introduction

By the Editor

Labour is an active factor of production. Unlike machines, it needs incentives to do work. Hence, issues pertaining to wages and salaries, allowances, fringe benefits etc. feature prominently in the sound management of human resources of the government bureaucracy. The level of government remuneration affects the ability of the civil and defence services to recruit and retain personnel of the desired quality. While considerations other than remuneration also affect the performance of employees, it would be equally myopic to ignore the influence of financial rewards on staff motivation and performance.

Protection and Welfare of Labour in the Constitution of India

Indian Constitution provides an overarching framework for regulation of conditions of work as well as protection and promotion of livelihoods. The Constitution of India guarantees Fundamental Rights to every citizen including the right to life. According to Supreme Court of India, the right to livelihood is inherent in the right to life. Since the ultimate aim of social security is to ensure that everyone has the means of livelihood, it follows, therefore, that the right to social security is also inherent in the right to life.

Part IV of the Constitution of India contains Directive Principles of State Policy which lay down goal posts and direction of State policy. Articles 41, 42, 43 and 43A of the Constitution falling under Part IV pertain to labour and its welfare. These Articles read as follows:

"**41. Right to work, to education and to public assistance in certain cases**— The State shall, within the limits of its economic capacity and development, make effective provision for securing the right to work, to education and to public assistance in cases of unemployment, old age, sickness and disablement, and in other cases of undeserved want".

"**42. Provision for just and humane conditions of work and maternity relief**—The State shall make provision for securing just and humane conditions of work and for maternity relief".

"**43. Living wage, etc. for workers**—The State shall endeavour to secure, by suitable legislation or economic organisation or in any other way, to all workers agricultural, industrial or otherwise, work, a living wage, conditions of work ensuring a decent standard of life and full enjoyment of leisure and social and cultural opportunities and, in particular, the State shall endeavour to promote cottage industries on an individual or co-operative basis in rural areas".

"**43A. Participation of workers in management of industries**—The State shall take steps, by suitable legislation or in any other way, to secure the participation of workers in the management of undertakings, establishments or other organisation engaged in any industry".

The Directive Principles of State Policy, which though not justiceable, are 'fundamental in governance of the country' and it is 'the duty of the State to apply these principles in making laws'.

The Constitution of India recognises the right of women to employment and includes a number of Articles to give direction to the state policy. Article 14 lays down the equality before law of all citizens of the country, and Article 15 prohibits discrimination on the grounds of sex, religion, race etc. Article 15(3) empowers the state to make special provisions for women and children within the framework of the fundamental rights. Article 16 emphasises equality of opportunity in matters of public employment.

Article 39(a) states that the citizens, men and women equally, have the right to an adequate means of livelihood. Similarly, Article 39(d) directs equal part for equal work for both men and women. The objective of these provisions is to protect women from exploitation.

Labour policy of the Government of India derives its philosophy from the aforementioned provisions of the Constitution.

Classification of Labour

Labour being an active factor is the most crucial of all factors of production. Adam Smith (1723-1790), father of modern economics, termed labour as the source of all wealth. Labour population of a country is classified into the following groups:

- **Skilled Workers:** These include doctors, engineers, aircraft pilots and other highly trained persons. They receive education and training for a very long period of time.
- **Semi-skilled Workers:** In this category are placed workers who are moderately educated and trained to perform their jobs. Thus, truck drivers, nurses and airhostesses are semi-skilled workers.
- **Unskilled Workers:** This category includes workers of the ordinary type as, for example, sweepers, porters and watchmen.

The term wages has a variety of connotations.

Kinds of Wages

Payments made for the services of labour of any kind are called wages.

Money and Real Wages: Money or nominal wages refer to the amount of wages measured in terms of money. In economics, the term money wages is used to represent the labour cost of production of a commodity. Real wages refer to the amount of goods and services which a worker can buy with his money wages.

Piece Wages and Time Wages: Piece wages are paid on the basis of quantity of work done. A tailor may be paid a certain amount for each shirt stitched in a particular fashion. Piece wages are possible only where the work is uniform and the worker's output is easily measurable. Time wages are paid on the basis of length of time as, for example, monthly wages. Time wages do not bear close relationship between earnings and output as is the case with piece wages. Employers generally favour piece wages while employees prefer time wages.

Wages in kind consist of payments to the worker, not in the form of money, but in the form of commodities.

Reasons for Differences in Wages

Wages are the reward for the services of labour. However, wages of all types of workers are not the same. Differentials in wage rate are due to a host of factors.

1. Wages differ with the type of job. Generally, more risky jobs carry more wages than less risky jobs involving same skills. Coalminers get more wages than ordinary ditch-diggers.
2. Wages depend on the length of education and training required to perform a particular job. A surgeon gets more than a typist because the job of the former requires education and training for a much longer period than the job of the latter.
3. Wages vary with experience in a particular job. An airline pilot with 20 years experience gets more than a newly recruited pilot.
4. Wage differentials may exist due to sexual and racial prejudices. Very often women get less wages than men for doing the same job.
5. Wages also differ according to the structure of the labour market. In a competitive market, wages are less than in an imperfect labour market. Members of strong trade unions earn more than their less organised counterparts.

Labour Policy and Productivity

Labour enters the production process from the supply side as well as from the demand side. The focal point for both aspects is higher productivity because it is through higher productivity that higher real wages can be ensured, cost of production can be brought down and higher demand for products can be generated, which would lead to further growth. The role of labour has to be perceived in this broad perspective.

The success of labour policy has to be adjudged on the basis of the productivity standard that it helps the economy to achieve. While technical factors and the state of technology are crucial in determining productivity levels, there is no denying the fact that discipline and motivation of workers, their skill, the state of industrial relations, the extent and effectiveness of participation of workers, the working climate and safety practices are also of great importance. While maximising employment generation, requisite attention has to be directed to the improvement of labour productivity through the adoption of up-to-date technology in productive processes in major sectors.

Labour policy in India has been evolving in response to the specific needs of the situation in relation to industry and the working class and has to suit the requirements of a planned economy. A body of principles and practices has grown up as a product of joint consultation in which representatives of Government, the working class and employers have been participating at various levels. The legislative and other measures adopted by the Central and State Governments in this field represent the consensus of opinion of the parties concerned and thus acquire the strength and character of a national policy.

Under various laws, a comprehensive code has been developed to ensure satisfactory working conditions, safety of person and the provision of a variety of facilities to promote the welfare of the workers. Steps, however, have to be taken to make the implementation of the statutory provisions more effective. The improvement of working conditions can result in greater productive efficiency on the part of the workers.

Social Security for Workers

Economic growth alone cannot be relied upon to deal either with the promotion, or with the protection of living standards. Many view social security as a system of proper distribution of income and also a right mechanism of wage fixation. Social security is an essential ingredient in the protection, development and full utilisation of human resources.

Human development insists that everyone should enjoy a minimum level of security. In fact, a system should be built in which the State bears the responsibility for providing and ensuring an elementary or basic level of security, and leaves room for partly or wholly contributory schemes. This will mean that the responsibility to provide a floor will be primarily that of the State, and it will be left to individual citizens to acquire higher levels of security through assumption of responsibility and contributory participation.

Social protection could be instrumental in motivating the workers to work better and to increase productivity insofar as it would enable them to work free from domestic worries to a great extent. The concept of social security aims to provide a safety mechanism against stoppage or substantial reduction of earnings resulting from sickness, maternity, employment injury, occupational distress, unemployment, invalidity and old age. Broadly, social security should cover housing, safe drinking water, sanitation, health, educational and cultural facilities for the society at large. It is necessary to ensure living wages, distinct from the concept of minimum wages, which can guarantee the workers a decent life.

Currently, there are contributory and non-contributory social security laws in India. The contributory laws are those which provide for financing of the social security programmes by contributions paid by workers and employers and in some cases supplemented by contribution/grants from the government. Most workers under the organized sector are covered under the institutionalized social security provided through Employees' Provident Fund Organization (EPFO) and the Employees State Insurance Corporation (ESIC).

History of Pay Revisions in India

Till nearly the end of the 19th century, the Superior Services in British India were manned almost exclusively by Europeans most of whom belonged to what were known as the *covenanted services*. Public opinion was then pressing for the Indianisation of these Services and not much attention was paid to the *uncovenanted or subordinate services*. Indianisation of the higher services was desired for political, and financial reasons. It was felt that the proper thing was for the nationals of the country to have an increasing share in its administration. It was also considered that the scales of salaries fixed on the assumption that high scales were required to attract Europeans to service in India imposed an unnecessarily heavy burden on the finances of the country.

Aitchison Commission: Aitchison Commission (1886-87) made recommendations in respect of both the *covenanted* and the *uncovenanted* services. It suggested that from out of the appointments reserved for the Imperial Civil Services, some should be transferred to a local service to be called the Provincial Civil Service to be recruited in India in each Province. Further, below the Provincial Civil Service, a lower service to be called the Subordinate Civil Service should be formed. Dealing with the relations between the Imperial and the Provincial Civil Services, the Commission recommended that the salaries of members of the Provincial Civil Service should be fixed on independent grounds and should have no relation to those attached to appointments in the Imperial Civil Service. However, as regards status, the members of the Imperial and Provincial Civil Services should, as far as possible, be placed on a footing of social equity and, when holding similar offices, be graded together on the official precedence list. The recommendations of the Commission were not given effect to in the spirit in which, or to the extent to which, they expected them to be acted upon. Circumstances compelled further consideration of these and connected questions by the Islington Commission.

James Meston Committee: In 1908, a Committee presided over by Sir James Meston dealt with the pay and prospects of clerks in the secretariats of the Government of India and certain other offices. At that time, the clerical establishments of the secretariat were divided into two divisions, viz. first and the second; the former comprised all those clerks who were required to deal with the higher class of clerical work and the latter who were employed on work of a routine nature.

The Committee found that the cost of foodstuffs and other necessaries of life, house rents and wages of domestic servants had greatly increased by that time, that the standard of living had also advanced and continued to advance and that—except in the Finance Department from which clerks occasionally received promotion to the enrolled list—clerks in the Government of India secretariat had practically no hope of securing executive appointments such as were open to clerks in Provincial Secretariats and other offices under Local Governments. It accordingly held that the proper course would be to render the conditions of clerical service in the secretariat sufficiently good to offer to its members a career not appreciably less attractive than that which was afforded to men of equal educational qualifications in other branches of the public service.

The Committee felt that there was much to be said in favour of making the secretariat clerical service one to which its members would be proud to belong and of fostering an *esprit de corps*. In view of the cost of living and the need for attracting the proper type of men, they fixed the initial pay for first division clerks at ₹ 140. Having regard to the value of his work, his experience and standing, it held that a clerk of 25 to 30 years of service, who for no fault of his own had not risen to a superintendentship, should get a maximum pay of ₹ 400.

The second division clerks were regarded as standing on a different footing because their work was assumed to be of a simple or routine character. Their recruitment was, therefore, held to be subject to the ordinary laws of demand and supply. The Committee, therefore, fixed the initial pay for this category of clerks at ₹ 60 and the maximum at ₹ 200, adding a personal allowance of ₹ 25 or ₹ 50 after the 28th and 30th year of service. It was opposed to the incremental system and proposed that in each division there should be a considerable range of grades at short intervals of pay.

Referring to Registrars and Superintendents, it said, "It is a matter of high importance that both these classes of officers should be liberally paid not only on account of the responsibilities of their work but because these appointments are practically the only goals towards which the ambition of the first division clerk can press". It accordingly suggested ₹ 800 for the Registrar and three grades of ₹ 500,

₹ 600 and ₹ 700 for superintendents. In recognition of the responsibility of the work done by the superintendents—whom they described as the repositories of the experience and traditions of their departments, analogous to the senior members of the permanent Civil Service in England—the Committee recommended that they should be granted the rank of gazetted officers. It emphasised that the Secretariat stood on a footing of its own different from any other offices in India and that it required in its clerical staff a higher degree of intelligence, a broader outlook and a more discriminating critical faculty than would be expected in other offices.

Islington Commission: Islington Commission (1912-15) was asked to examine and report on the conditions of service, salary, leave and pension governing the Indian Civil Services (I.C.S.) and other civil services (Imperial and Provincial), the limitations that still existed in respect of the employment of non-Europeans and the working of the existing system of the division of services into Imperial and Provincial. The Commission's enquiry was limited to the higher services. Exploring the possibilities of wider employment of Indians in the superior services and the proper method of their recruitment, the Commission grouped the services under the following three heads:

1. Those which required a preponderating proportion of British officers (e.g. the Civil Service and the Police).
2. Those services in which it was thought desirable that there should be an admixture of both Western and Eastern elements (e.g. education, military, finance, medicine, telegraph engineering, railways and survey of India).
3. The scientific and technical services where they held that there were no special reasons for having a large number of officers recruited from Europe.

For the first, they decided that recruitment should continue to be exclusively in England. For the second, it recommended that Government recruitment might be made both in England and in India. For the third, it was of the opinion that it should be the aim eventually to recruit in India for their normal requirements.

The Commission expressed strong disapproval of the graded system of remuneration then in vogue and recommended the substitution of an incremental system subject to the proviso that no increment should be given as a matter of right. Even among time-scales, they expressed a preference for what they called the *compartment system* under which "separate scales are fixed for separate groups of officers in each department and a process of selection takes place before an officer can pass from one scale to another or from any scale into a selection post".

Recommendations of the Islington Commission were mainly responsible for the system of classification and pay scales obtaining in India at the time of the appointment of First Central Pay Commission in 1946. Though their report was signed in August 1915, its consideration had to be deferred for the duration of the

First World War. Final orders on their proposals were passed only during 1919-1920; and in doing so, the authorities took into account the further rise in prices that had taken place between 1912 and 1920.

Economic Crisis (1929-30): Between 1908 and 1928, all classes of public servants under the Central Government seem to have had their emoluments increased, in some instances more than once. When the economic crisis of 1929-30 set in, Government had to review the whole position. To meet the immediate emergency, certain percentage cuts were made in the salaries of most public servants for four years. On the suggestion of a Retrenchment Advisory Committee, the question of revision of rates of pay for future entrants was taken up. Recommendations in this behalf were made by certain sub-committees of the Retrenchment Advisory Committee and Sir Tenant Sloan was placed on special duty to examine the subject and make proposals.

War-time Measures: The new scales of pay of 1931-34—which were half-heartedly accepted by some sections of the services even at the time when they were introduced—proved inadequate to meet the conditions created by the Second World War. The Government of India had to formulate measures to protect their employees against the hardships caused by the rise in prices. About the middle of 1940, they sanctioned a scheme of *grain compensation allowance* for their lowest paid employees. Under this scheme, the Central Government employees stationed in the various Provinces received the same benefit as the respective Provincial Government employees and the scale of benefit was dependent on the actual market price of foodgrains.

In course of time, it was found that allowances based on Provincial schemes which lacked uniformity were unsuitable for employees of the Central Government whose conditions of service were more or less uniform. With prices continuing to rise, it was felt that the question should be tackled on an all-India basis, and in August 1942, the Government of India devised a scheme of dearness allowance which replaced the *grain compensation allowance* scheme with effect from August 1, 1942. As relief under the new scheme was granted even to the higher categories of public servants—whose cost of living was dependent on several factors besides the cost of foodgrains—it was considered no longer necessary to link the relief to the price of foodgrains. The whole country was divided into three areas (A, B and C) in accordance with the difference in the cost of living. The classification followed an existing arrangement adopted by the Posts and Telegraph Department for purposes of pay scales. Subsequently, a number of towns which showed a marked rise in cost of living were upgraded. The beneficiaries were divided into two classes, those receiving ₹ 40 per month and above and those receiving less. In view of the difference in the wage and standard of living between the two categories, a slightly lower rate of dearness allowance was adopted for persons drawing less than ₹ 40. This scheme of dearness allowance was also recommended to the Provincial Governments for adoption in respect of their staff.

As conditions of life became more and more difficult during the later years of the War, claims, representations and protests from several sections of the services increased. Final orders in respect of some of these matters were being deferred till after the termination of the War. Certain groups of employees who felt conscious of the strength of numbers and organisation threatened to go on strike. The ground for the appointment of the First Central Pay Commission was prepared. Thus, on February 7, 1946, the Secretary, Posts and Air Department, announced in the Legislative Assembly that Government intended to appoint "a Commission to go into the whole question of scales of wages, pensions and other conditions of service for the whole class of Central Government servants, suitable in post-War conditions, as also the question of setting up some machinery for negotiation between Government and its employees, somewhat on the lines of the Whitely Councils in the United Kingdom."

Central Pay Commissions

The Government of India constitutes, as a matter of convention, a pay commission after almost every 10 years to review and make recommendations on the wage structure of Central Government civilian and armed forces employees and pensioners. A pay commission, depending on the terms of reference, examines various aspects—such as pay and allowances, retirement and death benefits, conditions of service, promotion policy and such other related matters—of the wage structure of employees and submits its recommendations to the Government. The Government, in turn, takes the final decision as to the implementation of the recommendations, which may be full or partial or amended or modified. The chairman and members of the pay commission are nominated by the Government.

A pay commission is not a constitutional body and therefore the Central Government has a lot of leeway about which part of the report to adopt and in what timeframe. Since India's Independence, 7 pay commissions have been set up, from time to time, to review and recommend wage structure for Central Government employees. Usually, a pay commission is given 18 months time to submit its report.

A pay commission, before recommending the pay structure, analyzes voluminous data relating, inter alia, to the general economic conditions in the country, financial resources of the government, strength of the work force, and pay structure in public sector and private sector undertakings. Clearly, review and determination of the pay structure of Central Government employees and pensioners is a stupendous and complicated task. Reports of pay commissions provide glimpses of the events, challenges and perceptions of labour leaders and policy makers during the post-Independence period.

The months and years of establishment, months and years of reporting, and the names of chairmen of various Central Pay Commissions are given in the table below.

Chronology of Central Pay Commissions

Pay Commission	Month and Year of Appointment	Month and Year of Submission of Report	Name of the Chairman
First Pay Commission	May 1946	May 1947	Srinivasa Varadacharia
Second Pay Commission	August 1957	August 1959	Jaganath Das
Third Pay Commission	April 1970	March 1973	Raghubir Dayal
Fourth Pay Commission	June 1983	Three Reports submitted in June 1986; December 1986 and May 1987 respectively	P.N. Singhal
Fifth Pay Commission	April 1994	January 1997	S. Ratnavel Pandian
Sixth Pay Commission	October 2006	March 2008	B.N. Srikrishna
Seventh Pay Commission	February 2014	November 2015	Ashok Kumar Mathur

With regard to the number of members, there seems to be a declining trend. The First Commission had 9 members, the Second 6, the Third and the Fourth 5 each. The Fifth had only 3 members. The Sixth had 4 members and the Seventh 3.

Number of Members (including Chairman) of Various Central Pay Commissions

First Pay Commission	9
Second Pay Commission	6
Third Pay Commission	5
Fourth Pay Commission	5
Fifth Pay Commission	3
Sixth Pay Commission	4
Seventh Pay Commission	3

Pay commission is a peculiarly Indian institution today. Historically, it is a successor to the Royal Commissions set up during the British period for various purposes, including pay revision like the Aitchison Commission (1886-87) and the Islington Commission (1912-15). The practice of setting up of Commissions at intervals with the specific objective of revising pay and allowances of Government employees has been discontinued by most, if not all countries, of the world including the United Kingdom. India has the unique distinction of having a cumbersome and centralized system of determination of basic pays that remain unchanged for more than a decade at a time, reinforced by instalments of dearness allowance which are released every six months. Most countries have now switched over to negotiated pay settlements at the decentralized departmental level in which the salaries are revised every year after taking into account all factors including the change in the cost of living index.

Need for Pay Commission

A great many changes take place in the structure of emoluments of Government employees over a decade. It thus becomes necessary to modify the pay structure so as to enable Government employees to lead clean, honest and respectable lives at standards compatible with what their peers have meanwhile attained or what they themselves accept as reasonable at the standards of living to which they have become accustomed. Successive pay commissions have been set up in the past for evolving compensation packages for employees at intervals of 10 to 13 years. These pay commissions have examined various issues such as pay and allowances, retirement benefits, conditions of service, promotion policies etc. and submitted recommendations thereon.

The joint consultative machinery (JCM) was constituted by the Government in the year 1966 to promote harmonious relations and secure the greatest measure of co-operation between the Government in its capacity as employer and the general body of employees (belonging to Groups C and D) in matters of common concern. According to sub-clause (ii) of clause 20 of the scheme for joint consultative machinery and compulsory arbitration for Central Government employees, matters determined by the Government in accordance with the recommendations of a Commission of Enquiry are not subject to arbitration for a period of 5 years from the date of the recommendations. Thus, pay commissions are a device by which an independent body investigates the demands of Central Government employees and submits its recommendations which are binding on both Government and its employees. Conceptually, they fall short of a forum for collective bargaining, but they do provide an opportunity for a periodic review by an outside body in which both the Government and the employees have confidence.

Regarding the jurisdiction of the pay commission, Supreme Court has repeatedly held the view that equations of job evaluation of posts or equation of pay or determination of pay scales are the primary functions of expert bodies like the pay commission with which normally the Courts should not interfere except on any of the grounds of unjust and arbitrary state action or inaction or on any grave error having crept in while fixing the pay scales which may warrant the interference of the court.

Excessive Job Security for Government Employees

It is well-known that there is excessive job security for Government employees as enshrined in Article 311 of the Constitution of India and that cumbersome rules act as a hindrance to easy exit of Government employees. It is undeniable that Government jobs provide unparalleled job security, pension benefits, work-life balance and status. Further, the Government also provides a vast array of non-monetary benefits that can and should be monetized in order to correctly assess the actual compensation package available to the employees. Quantification of these benefits has other advantages as well. The aspirants for each category of Government job would know beforehand precisely what total package to expect, and could decide for themselves whether the Government job is sufficiently attractive vis-à-vis jobs in other sectors. This is all the more necessary because the salary packages offered in the private sector are on the basis of the cost to the company.

Quantification of non-monetary benefits will enable the Government, Parliament and the public to have a clear, comprehensive and accurate picture of the total expenditure being incurred on Government employees, since non-monetary perquisites scattered over many budgetary heads, mask the true picture of the expenditure incurred on the employees.

Moreover, under the present work culture, it is difficult to get work out of regular employees. It is well-known that permanent employees in Government offices, public sector undertakings (PSUs) and the organised private sector cannot be touched because they are highly unionised. They take unfair advantage of being unionised at the cost of temporary, ad hoc and daily workers who have to do the major portion of the workload of an organisation. It is true that the day a temporary government employee is made permanent, his attitude to his job becomes casual thereafter.

Do Pay Commission Reports Destabilize Government Budgets?

Wages and salaries have been growing primarily because of periodic revisions carried out on the recommendations of the pay commissions of the Centre, and the States falling in line, without due regard to the capacity of individual States to pay. The burden of pay revision is compounded by releases of dearness allowance (DA) twice a year by the Centre which has an effect on the States too. While it is the prerogative of the States to decide the size of their government, the total wage bill cannot be allowed to rise beyond a certain proportion of revenue receipts which represent the capacity to pay. How the implementation of the recommendations of the Fifth Pay Commission destabilized the budgets of the Central and State Governments is a well-known fact (for details, see section 5.1.3 of chapter 5 of this book).

In implementing the pay commission recommendations, the Central Government has been, in some respects, more generous than what the recommendations of the pay commission implied. Some States have gone even beyond those levels resulting in the rise of emoluments of the employees beyond what is warranted by their capacity to pay.

As the recommendations of the Central Pay Commission have an impact on the States, the terms of reference of the pay commission should be settled in consultation with the States. Similarly, the decision on the recommendations of the pay commission should be taken in consultation with the States.

Pensions have been the fastest growing item of budgets of Central and State Governments in recent years. At the rate at which pensions are growing, liability for pension payments is going to cast a very heavy burden on the budgets in the coming years. Several factors have contributed to the growth of pensions. One has been the generous rise in the pensions recommended by the Fifth Pay Commission.

Another factor has been the addition of the liability on account of pensions payable to retired employees of aided institutions and local bodies to the government's pension bill. The increasing longevity of people, though welcome, has also meant growing pension liability of governments.

A Case for Lenient Taxation of Salaries

In every country, there are some soft-to-tax and hard-to-tax sources of income. Wages and salaries are properly recorded and therefore it is easy to assess and collect taxes on them through the pay-as-you-earn system (i.e. tax deduction at source). Similarly, income from securities paid through banks can easily be subjected to deduction at source.

Contrarily, the three hard-to-tax classes of the non-corporate sector are: (a) unincorporated commercial and industrial units, (b) self-employed professionals, and (c) rich peasantry. The problem of taxing the first two categories relates to accounting difficulties while in the case of third category, it is essentially the lack of political will. Non-reporting and under-reporting of income is quite sizeable in these sectors. The growing small business sector is a tax haven. It is very difficult to enforce a reliable system of book-keeping to assess earnings of this sector. Pragmatically, a system of lump sum taxation may be tried in place of taxation of profits.

Earned versus Unearned Income: Earned income (or employment or labour income) is derived from actual work or service performed and includes wages, salaries, and income from professions. Unearned income (or capital or property income) is derived from investment, rent etc.

Should tax laws distinguish between earned and unearned income in order to accord a favourable treatment to the former? Lenient treatment of earned income is justified on various grounds. Employment earnings represent returns on current efforts whereas capital income is often the result of inherited wealth, monopoly power, capital gains, gambling wins, and property received through gifts and marriages.

Earned income is more uncertain than investment income. A human being is a depreciating asset which ceases to earn on retirement or death. Uncertainty of the human asset also arises from possible chances of suspension, dismissal, premature retirement from service, illness, unemployment, and accident. Contrarily, physical and financial assets have a tendency to appreciate in value with the passage of time, particularly in a growing economy. Uncertainties associated with business income are less grievous and can be insured against by making gilt-edged investments.

Possession of property, besides being a source of monetary return, confers certain other benefits on the possessor, e.g. ability to dissave, security, and independence. It may also be argued that expenditure incurred in connection with earning income from employment (including expenses on education and training) is far more than that incurred in obtaining investment income. Therefore, it is unjust to treat the fruits of one's own labour and windfall profits equally. [1]

J.E. Meade Committee Report on *The Structure and Reform of Direct Taxation* advanced the following four arguments as to why earned income should be treated *softly* vis-à-vis other income for tax purposes. [2]

1. Earned income is less permanent than investment income.
2. Earned income involves a sacrifice of leisure which is absent in the case of income from property, particularly from inherited property.
3. Earned income is the creation of a taxpayer's own skill, ability, and effort while unearned income may accrue through the luck of inheritance.
4. Prestige, security, independence and influence, generally associated with the ownership of wealth, are absent in the case of earned income.

It is also well-known that labour earnings are recorded more systematically and in most cases tax is deducted at source, leaving no scope for malpractice in tax payment. As Vito Tanzi has observed, "Income taxes on wages and salaries cannot be evaded, or at least it is much harder to do so, which provides a good ground for a lighter treatment of these incomes. In fact, if they are treated in the same way as other incomes, and if the assumption is true that taxes on them are difficult to evade, then a *de jure* non-discriminatory treatment of these incomes would amount to a *de facto* discrimination." [3]

It is not surprising that tax laws of many countries provide for relatively lenient tax treatment of earned income, e.g. earned income tax credit in the United States.

In the context of India, a serious lacuna in the present system of personal income tax is the non-discriminatory treatment of earned and other forms of income for tax purposes. Income of an assessee from various sources is pooled together for the purpose of computation of taxable income and tax liability determination. This so-called *global principle* of income tax does not differentiate between different sources of income.

It may be recalled that in 1945 a distinction between earned and unearned incomes was introduced when assessees were allowed to exclude from their earned incomes a fixed proportion subject to a maximum limit. However, this distinction, under which the earned income was treated leniently, was abolished from April 1, 1968. This decision was widely criticised as a retrograde fiscal measure.

The present law of income tax does recognise and tax different sources of income differently, though to a limited extent. Thus, long-term capital gains enjoy special concessions under the income tax law. It is ironical that preferential tax treatment denied to earned incomes is available to long-term capital gains which are purely accidental in nature and bear no relationship to efforts on the part of the recipient.

If the distinction between earned and unearned incomes is to be revived, it may take the form of: (a) reduction in the base of earned income (for example, exclusion from income of a fixed proportion subject to a maximum limit) and/or (b) lower rate structure for earned incomes.

Endnotes

1. One may argue that apart from the tax on return from it, capital itself may be subjected to wealth tax, gift tax, and estate duty. However, in most countries these taxes are not levied and wherever they are levied, the revenue is insignificant.
2. The Institute of Fiscal Studies, *The Structure and Reform of Direct Taxation,* Report of a Committee Chaired by Professor J.E. Meade, London: George Allen and Unwin, 1978, p. 372.
3. Vito Tanzi, *The Individual Income Tax and Economic Growth,* Baltimore: The John Hopkins Press, 1969, pp. 51-52.

Part I:
Central Pay Commissions: First to Sixth

1

First Central Pay Commission

1.1 First Pay Commission at a Glance

The First Pay Commission was constituted in January 1946 under the chairmanship of Shri Srinivasa Varadacharia. It submitted its report in May 1947 to the Interim Government of India. [1] The Commission was based on the idea of *living wages* to the employees. In this regard, it observed, "in no case should be a man's pay be less than a living wage".

Composition of the First Pay Commission

Sir Srinivasa Varadachariar	Chairman
Mr. Hossain Imam	Member
Mr. N.V. Gadgil	Member
Mr. Frank Anthony	Member
Dr. J.C. Chatterjee	Member
Sardar Mangal Singh	Member
Mr. N.M. Joshi	Member
Mr. Vadilal Lallubhai	Member
Mr. C.V.S. Rao	Member
Mr. K.R.P. Aiyangar	Secretary

The abysmal level of salary of the average Government employee prompted the establishment of the Commission. Hence, the appointment of the Commission was seen as a humane measure—a far cry from present times. The average salary of the employees, even after making allowance for the lower living standards of the day, ranged around ₹ 30.

The minimum basic pay for Class IV staff was raised from ₹ 10 to ₹ 30 and for Class III from ₹ 35 to ₹ 60 per month.

The recommendations were accepted and implemented in 1946. The pay scales prescribed by the Commission replaced the 1934 pay scales.

The First Pay Commission recommended that the age of retirement in future should be uniformly 58 years for all services and the scale of pension should be 1/80 of the emoluments for each year of service, subject to a limit of 35/80 with a ceiling of ₹ 8,000 per year for 35 years of service, which the Government of India while accepting the recommendation, raised to ₹ 8,100 per year which earned a monthly pension of ₹ 675 at the maximum.

1.1.1 Terms of Reference and Scope: The Resolution dated May 10, 1946 appointing the Commission required them to enquire into and report on the following:

1. The conditions of service for the Class I, Class II and Subordinate Central Services as well as establishments now designated as inferior who are subject to the Civil Services (Classification, Control and Appeal) Rules, or the Railway Services (Classification, Control and Appeal) Rules and Railway servants, as defined in paragraph 101, State Railway Establishment Code, Vol. 1 with particular reference to:

- The structure of their pay scales and standards of remuneration, with object of achieving rationalisation, simplification and uniformity to the fullest degree possible.
- The extent to which the present leave terms should be altered and simplified.
- Conditions of retirement and the extent to which the existing regulations in regard to pensions and contributory provident funds require simplification.

2. The machinery for negotiating and setting questions relating to conditions of service which may arise out of differences between Government and its employees.
3. The principles on which the remuneration of industrial workers and daily rated employees of Government should be based.

By a Resolution dated July 3, 1946, civilian Government servants whose pay was charged to the Defence Services Estimates were also brought within the scope of the reference. By a letter dated November 6, 1946, the Finance Department communicated to the Commission the desire of the Home Department that when submitting their report, the Commission should also make recommendations regarding the pay scales for the new all-India Administrative Service and all-India Police Service which it was proposed to form. A letter dated November 23, 1946, from the Department of Education asked for the advice of the Commission in regard to the fixation of scales of pay for the principal and vice-principal for the central training colleges to be set up in connection with the post-War development plan. By letter dated November 30, 1946, the External Affairs Department asked for proposals from the Commission in respect of a basic scale of pay for the proposed Indian Foreign Service.

At the first meeting of the Commission, a letter from the Government was placed before them suggesting that, if convenient, their recommendations in regard to the revision of pay scales might be made available to Government as early as possible, in advance, if necessary, of the recommendations on the other points included in the terms of reference. In answer to a query as to whether the Finance Department expected the Commission to fix the pay of each post which was charged to civil estimates, or it would suffice if their report indicated generally the rates of pay for different Services and for particular classes or categories of posts, the Chairman was informed that the Finance Department favoured the latter alternative, it being left to the administrative department to decide, in consultation with the financial authorities, the question of gradation, or classification of posts and their allocation to particular categories for which pay scales had been suggested by the Commission. This was confirmed by the Finance Department in their letter dated November 29, 1946, addressed to the Commission.

1.1.2 Scheme of the Report: The Report of the Commission was divided into three Parts.

Part I gave an account of the procedure adopted by the Commission, described the background of the enquiry, the steps leading to the existing pay structure and pay scales of the Central Services, the events which led to the appointment of the Commission and the circumstances in which they had to make their report.

Part II of the report dealt with the main aspects of the problem, so far as they were common to all departments of the Central Services. In particular, it dealt with questions like: (i) classification of the services, (ii) criticism of the existing pay structure, and (iii) the necessity for increasing the present rates of pay and the lines on which new scales of pay should be determined, including a discussion of various suggestions as to the minimum and the maximum pay to be fixed. Some typical scales of pay for the four main classes of the services were suggested. Claims for various allowances (including dearness allowance) were dealt with. A variety of matters suggested as coming under the general head of "conditions of service" were discussed. Amendments to the existing rules relating to leave, age of retirement and retirement benefits were considered and proposals for way and means to settle or prevent disputes between the services and the Government were also made. Part II concluded with some observations bearing on the question of the remuneration of industrial workers and daily rated employees of the Government.

Part III made detailed proposals in respect of the salaries to be paid to, and the redress of grievances of, the employees of each of the principal sections of the public service in the light of the general conclusions reached in Part II. A summary of the Commission's recommendations was given at the end.

1.1.3 Procedure Adopted: Immediately after the announcement of the appointment of the Commission, all public servants of the Central Government and all other persons interested were invited by a press note to communicate their views or suggestions on the topics covered by the terms of the reference to the Commission.

All Departments of the Government of India were asked to furnish for the information of the Commission full particulars regarding all appointments under their administrative control. Provincial Governments were also requested to afford the Commission every facility in the conduct of their enquiry.

In response to the public invitation above referred to, the Secretary to the Commission received more than 950 representations from service associations and individuals setting forth the lines on which (in their opinion) their pay and conditions of service should be improved.

The Commission assembled at Delhi on July 10, 1946 and at this meeting the main lines on which the enquiry was to be conducted were agreed on. During the sittings between July 11 to 15, 1946, a detailed questionnaire was prepared in the light of the representations that had been received from service associations and of other materials then available. As it was represented to the Commission that some public servants hesitated to send in their representations because of the restrictions imposed on them by the Government Servants' Conduct Rules, the Secretary was asked to address the Government in the matter; and the Government agreed to afford ample facilities to their employees to send in representations to, or give evidence before, the Commission on matters falling within the terms of their reference.

Between July 20 to 25, 1946, more than 1,500 copies of the questionnaire were sent to persons or bodies who had sent in representations to the Commission and to all associations of employees known to the Government. Copies were sent to the members of the Central Legislature and to prominent public men. Copies were also made available to the public and to the press. Replies to the questionnaire were received from more than 370 associations and individuals.

For further elucidation of the material points and at the instance of the Services themselves, the Commission decided to give—to some public men, to several heads of departments and to the representatives of numerous associations of service men—an opportunity of supporting, by oral evidence, the points stressed in their replies. Tentative programmes were prepared from time to time indicating the associations and persons to be called in to give oral evidence. To obviate any suggestion that certain groups or associations had been left out, opportunity of appearing before the Commission was given to all associations who had sent in representations or given replies to the questionnaire or had expressed a desire to be heard. To save time, all associations or persons with common interest were summoned to appear at the same time. Between September 9 and December 21, 1946, the Commission devoted more than 50 sittings to this part of their task and examined more than 400 persons including heads of departments or representatives of associations.

When the Provincial Governments were notified of the appointment of the Commission, they were informed that though the Commission's enquiry was to be confined to the Central Government employees, the findings of the Commission might be of use to the Provincial Governments also in the event of their undertaking any revision of the scales of pay of the Provincial Services. Such revision was, in fact, undertaken by several Provincial Governments and one of them desired that an opportunity might be given to it to lay its views before the Commission as it was desirable that the scales of pay for members of Services belonging to both the Central and Provincial Governments serving in the same area should, as far as possible, be correlated. The Commission decided that it would be best to hold an informal Conference with the representatives of the Provincial Governments so as to facilitate an exchange of views between the members of the Commission and the Provincial Governments. Eight Provinces responded to the Commission's invitation and the Conference was held on October 16-17, 1946.

1.2 Summary of the Recommendations of the First Central Pay Commission

Notwithstanding the argument against making any permanent revision of basic salaries in the present changing conditions, it would be safe to recommend scales of basic salary fixed on the assumption that prices may stabilize at a level which will give a cost of living index somewhere between 160 and 175 taking the pre-War index to be 100. So long as the cost of living continues to be substantially higher, some system of dearness allowance must continue in operation.

1.2.1 Classification of the Services:

1. The categories now classed as *subordinate* and *inferior* should be described as classes III and IV respectively. Class IV should include all posts whose maximum pay does not exceed ₹ 60 and which are not included under Class III.
2. The inclination of the majority of Members is that it is desirable to retain the two classes, I and II but in departments where the differentiation between the two classes is not necessary or possible either because of the mode of

recruitment or because of the difficulty of distinguishing between the importance and responsibility of the duties respectively performed by Class I and Class II officers, the two-fold classification may be dispensed with and the two groups may be treated as one gazetted service.

3. The present list of Class II services however requires revision.
4. It is not practicable to constitute all the scientific services into a single cadre for purposes of promotion. There is no objection to the posts in each of the four classes being sub-divided into *executive*, *administrative*, *scientific*, *technical*, *clerical*, *manipulative*, *artisan*, *messengerial* and so on, without such sub-divisions carrying any particular legal or material consequences.

1.2.2 Pay Structure:

1. Having regard to the present structure and in particular to the disparity between old and new entrants the scales suggested are considered fair remuneration for the several posts concerned. The case of old entrants raises a question of policy which is for the Government to decide.
2. For the scientific services a decent minimum or starting salary so as to attract men with high qualifications and a better time-scale to make up for inadequacy of chances of promotion would be appropriate.
3. Though Provincial Governments favoured the view that the pay of Central servants serving in several provinces should bear as close relation as possible to the pay of Provincial Government servants of the same category in the same area, the Commission recommended 'All-India scales', allowance being made for the higher cost of living in certain places in the form of local allowances.

1.2.3 Pay Rates and Pay Scales:

1. While accepting the broad principles laid down by the Islington Commission, attention was paid to more recent trends and the Commission recommended that so far as practicable a fair relativity should be maintained between the rates of pay of certain classes of civil servants and comparable outside rates, the parity being judged only with reference to long-term trends in wage levels in the country.
2. While accepting the limitations to the application of the minimum wages theory, it was recommended that the State must take some step forward in the direction of giving effect to the living wage principle in dealing with its employees who are virtually on the *poverty line*.
3. According to the majority view, ₹ 55 and ₹ 90 were recommended as reasonable living wages for a working class family and a middle class family respectively at a cost of living index of about 260. Of these sums, ₹ 30 and 55 may respectively represent the basic pays and the balance, dearness allowance

at the index level mentioned.

4. Recognising the present disparity between the minimum and the maximum of public salaries, the growing demand for personnel from private business and industry and the views on the one hand that the State should not compete with private enterprise in respect of prize jobs and on the other that adequate remuneration is essential for maintaining ability and integrity in the permanent services, it was recommended that as a first step it will be fair to fix ₹ 2,000 per month as the maximum salary of public servants in India for a few selected posts.
5. The continuance of the system of time scales with suitable efficiency bars is recommended.
6. The following typical scales were recommended:

- **Class I Services and the All India Police Service:**
  Junior scale: ₹ 350-350-380-380-30-590-E.B.-30-770-40-850 (19 years).
  Senior scale: ₹ 600 (6th Year)-40-1,000-1,000-1,050-1,050-1,100-1,100-1,150 (21 years).
  Junior administrative posts: ₹ 1,300-60-1,600.
  Senior administrative posts: ₹ 1,800-100-2,000.
  For posts intermediate in responsibility between junior and senior administrative post: ₹ 1,600-100-1,800.

  The scale of ₹ 1,800-2,000 is intended for the heads of the biggest departments and would normally be the highest point which a permanent civil servant could reach in his service. Posts now carrying a maximum salary of ₹ 3,000 must, as far as possible, be fitted into the selection grade of ₹ 1,800-2,000.

  The highest paid posts like those of secretaries, general managers of Railways, members of the Railway Board, members of Central Board of Revenue, chairman and members of the Public Service Commission, etc. should be fitted into scales between ₹ 2,000 and ₹ 3,000 preferably on four levels of ₹ 2,250, ₹ 2,500, ₹ 2,750 and ₹ 3,000.
- **All India Administrative Service and the Foreign Service:**
  Junior scale: ₹ 350-400-450-450-500-540-30-600-E.B-30-870-40-950 (19 years).
  Senior scale: ₹ 800 (6th year)-40-1,200-1,200-1,250-1,250-1,300-60-1,600 (24 years).
  Selection grade for posts like commissioner: ₹ 1,800-2,000.
  The highest administrative post may carry pay ranging between ₹ 2,000 and ₹ 3,000.

- **Class II Scale:** ₹ 275-25-500-E.B-30-650-E.B-30-800
  Where the entrant has already to spend some years in acquiring special qualifications for any particular job, he may be started on an appropriate salary higher up in the scale.
- **Class III:** This class should comprise not merely people with literary qualifications, but also skilled artisans. The following 12 typical scales have been suggested:
  (a) ₹ 55-3-85-E.B.-4-125-5-130
  (b) ₹ 60-5/2-75
  (c) ₹ 60-4-120-E.B.-5-170
  (d) ₹ 75-3-105
  (e) ₹ 80-5-120-E.B.-8-200-10/2-220
  (f) ₹ 100-5-125-6- E.B.-6-185
  (g) ₹ 100-8-140-10-200 E.B.-10-300
  (h) ₹ 150-7-185-8-225
  (i) ₹ 160-10-250- E.B.-10-300-15-450
  (j) ₹ 200-15-350- E.B.-15-440-20-500
  (k) ₹ 250-15-400
  (l) ₹ 300-20-500
- **Class IV:**
  Unskilled and unlearned employees (including peons and *daffadars*): ₹ 30-1/2-35.
  Jamadars and *Daftries*: ₹ 35-1-50.
  Skilled or semi-skilled workers: ₹ 35-1-50 and ₹ 40-1-50-2-60.

7. It is not proposed that the salary now drawn by any officer should be affected to his prejudice. But as regards the promotion of such officers, the question may arise as to the way in which they are to be dealt with if the promotion is likely to take them beyond the limits indicated by the scales that we have suggested. Such cases should be dealt with on the same lines as the Government may decide to adopt in respect of pre-1931 entrants.
8. When a person on the existing scales is brought on to the new scales, his initial pay should be fixed at the lowest figure arrived at by the following calculations:

- What he would draw if his entire service in the existing scale had been on the corresponding proposed scales of pay?
- Fix the initial pay at the stage in the proposed scale next above the pay he is drawing in his present scale and add one increment in the proposed scales for every three completed years of service.

- Add to the present pay, the sums stated below and fix initial pay in proposed scale at the stage next above the amount so arrived.

Salary (₹)	Amount to be added (₹)
Not exceeding 100	15
101-250	20
251-400	30
401-500	40
501 and above	50

1.2.4 Allowances and Other Benefits:

A. Dearness Allowance: The following slabs were recommended:

Pay Range	Cost of Living Index						
	280	260	240	220	200	180	160
Up to ₹ 50	30	25	20	15	10	5	---
₹ 51-100	40	35	30	25	15	10	---
₹ 101-150	45	40	35	30	18	---	---
₹ 151-200	55	45	30	30	20	---	---
₹ 201-250	60	50	40	30	20	---	---
₹ 251-300	75	60	45	30	25	---	---
₹ 301-500	85	70	55	40	25	---	---
₹ 501-750	105	85	60	40	---	---	---
₹ 751-1,000	125	100	75	50	---	---	---

1. The cost of living index should be an all-India number prepared by the economic adviser to the Government of India.
2. Allowance should be paid only on substantive pay (exclusive of overtime). During all leave with pay (half or full) it should be allowed on the substantive pay.
3. The slabs should be reviewed every six months and a change should be made only if the index figure for the previous three months for which index figures are available stood above or fell below the index figure for the next slab.
4. All allowances and concessions introduced during the War to meet the high cost of living (by whatever name they might have been called, including the good conduct pay in the Postal service and War allowance in respect of the higher ranks of the services) will cease hereafter.
5. As long as any concessions in the matter of supply in kind are allowed, their estimated money value shall be deducted from the dearness allowance

calculated in accordance with the Table mentioned. Any encouragement given at this juncture to co-operative organisations of public servants for the purchase of their supplies will be opportune.

6. Persons drawing pension up to ₹ 150 per month may be given dearness allowance at half the rates shown in the Table, treating pensions as pay for the purpose.

B. Housing or House Rent Allowance:

1. If a building programme should be undertaken, priority should be given to schemes for housing employees in the lower grades of the service.
2. The Commission do not recommend any general change in the present policy provision of rent-free accommodation nor any change in the practice whereby an employee to whom Government quarter is allotted, pays a concessional rent limited to the standard rent or 10 percent of the employee's pay whichever is less.
3. As the scales of pay recommended by the Commission are based on the assumption that in the costlier cities and special areas, the basic scale will be supplemented, by the grant of a suitable house rent or other allowance, a house rent allowance with certain restrictions as regards pay limits and areas is recommended on the lines indicated in the following table.

(in ₹)

Pay of Officer	Cities with Population of Over 1 Lakh	Cities with Population of Over 5 Lakh	Bombay and Calcutta
Below 55	5	7	10
55-100	7	10	15
101-250	-	15	20
Over 250	-	7½ percent of pay	10 percent of pay

C. Children's Education Allowance: It is recommended that a beginning may be made with a scheme for helping members of the subordinate grade in the services in the matter of the education of their children. In Rule 1101 of the State Railway Establishment Code, the words excluding the 'inferior servants' from the benefit of that chapter must be omitted. Persons drawing a salary of ₹ 100 or less per month may be paid by the State a contribution of 75 percent of the tuition fee in the case of the children of Class IV and 50 percent of the fee in the case of children of Class III employees. The contribution might be given up to the higher secondary stage or a corresponding stage of technical education.

D. Compensatory Allowance:

1. Local allowances should be limited to a few costly cities.

2. Government should review the conditions in other specially costly cities besides Bombay and Calcutta and decide to what extent similar benefits must be extended to staff serving in those cities.
3. Bad climate allowance: Provincial Governments' classification may be followed for areas where the allowance is admissible.
4. Frontier allowance: Complaints that these allowances were inadequate for service in non-family stations and the claim for parity of treatment in this matter with personnel paid from Defence Estimates are brought to the notice of Government.
5. Government should look into the grievance that in the Nilgiris, while hill allowance was being given to subordinate and ministerial staff, it was not allowed in the case of postmen and other lower grade staff.
6. For local allowances generally, the practice of the Provincial Governments is the matter of granting such allowances for their employees should be taken into account.
7. Field Service Allowance: No specific addition to pay need be made to cover the contingent liability to be called for military service but when such personnel are required to serve in field areas, they should be paid an adequate allowance.

E. Conveyance Allowance: The grant of conveyance allowance as a regular addition to pay to enable staff to meet expenditure on transport from their homes to their offices is not recommended. A liberal grant of interest free loans for the purchase of cycles is recommended.

F. Medical Aid: The attention of Government is invited to the claim that the nature and seriousness of the ailment should be the deciding factor and not the status of the patient in determining the grade of medical officer to whose aid the patient should be entitled. To the extent that free treatment is allowed to the employee himself, i.e. when in the opinion of the medical attendant owing to remoteness or absence of hospital facilities or seriousness of illness the patient cannot be moved out, the family of an employee may also be provided free treatment at his residence.

G. Travelling Allowance:

1. In view of increases recently sanctioned, no general revision is suggested in respect of mileage and daily allowance etc. the distinction whereby the inferior servants (now Class IV) are not paid additional fares for journeys on tour or transfer is discriminatory and may be removed as also the discrimination against the lower staff who do not receive travelling allowance for journeys made while going on leave for rest and recreation.
2. In view of the uniform scales of pay which have been suggested for the

railway employees and other categories of civil servants, the existing benefits which the former enjoys in the matter of pass privileges should be scaled down.

1.2.5 Hours of Work—Overtime and Holidays:

1. As regards employees of industrial or commercial departments (including All India Radio), hours of work must be regulated with due regard to the nature and conditions of work obtained in the particular department. In ordinary offices, the normal hours of attendance may reasonably be fixed at 38½ hours a week so as to provide for 6½ hours of actual work on each week day after allowing half an hour for lunch and 3½ hours of work on Saturdays. Any increase in the lunch interval should be met by a corresponding increase in the total number of hours of attendance.
2. Improvement in office accommodation and the introduction of canteen arrangements are recommended.
3. Early steps should be taken to review the staff strength required in each office or department. Detention in office beyond office hours should ordinarily be only under the written orders of some responsible officer. An ordinary method of compensation for overtime work in offices would be to give a day off in lieu of overtime worked for a number of days. Even in departments where overtime is unavoidable, e.g. Railways, Customs, etc. such work should be minimised. Pecuniary compensation for overtime may be at rates ranging from mere time rate to 1½ times; double the normal rate would be justified only where the work involves special strain or exceeds a certain limit or involves prolonged employment during night.
4. As the number of working days in most departments does not now exceed 260 days per year, the Commission recommend that every effort should be made to increase the total number of working days. The dislocation of work caused by communal holidays may be remedied by slightly increasing the number of casual leave days, if necessary, communal holidays being abolished altogether.

1.2.6 Differentiation on Ground of Race and Sex:

1. The principle of equal pay for equal work is accepted. The service of foreign experts for specialist services should be obtained on a contract basis and the need even for such engagements should gradually be eliminated by training Indians. Where a non-Indian is recruited to a post in one of the permanent cadres, it will be best not to alter the basic pay but to grant an allowance analogous to overseas pay.
2. In regard to employment of women, the practice in private industry where women are generally paid lower than men on account of their low output

cannot be ignored; but for certain kinds of work where the services of women are exclusively or preferably required, e.g. school-mistresses, lady doctors, nurses, telephone operators, etc. grant of more favourable terms is approved.

1.2.7 Conditions of Service:

1. Direct recruitment at different levels is approved in principle but in respect of none of the higher levels should direct recruitment be exclusive.
2. While the claim for reservation of a higher percentage of posts for promotion is not accepted, it is recommended that even where direct recruitment is the rule, persons already in service who possess the requisite qualification may be allowed to compete for such recruitment by a reasonable relaxation of the rules relating to age limit etc.
3. For jobs where academic qualifications are not of much importance, due consideration should be given to those in service who have the benefit of experience.
4. In applying the formula of seniority-cum-merit, the extreme view that seniority should prevail except when a person has been declared to be unfit is not accepted. For jobs in respect of which long familiarity with a particular type of work is itself adequate training, the rule of seniority should receive greater weightage but for the higher grades of service, considerations of fitness must have precedence over claims of seniority.
5. As the efficiency of the promotion system depends on the method adopted to determine the relative merits of candidates, it is recommended that where the F.P.S.C. agency is not used, selection by promotion boards consisting of independent officers may be adopted as widely as possible. It may be convenient to have lists prepared from time to time of candidates for promotions instead of taking a decision after a vacancy has arisen. Except where qualifying examinations are in vogue, examination tests as a means of selection for persons already in service at each stage of promotion are not recommended.
6. The personal rolls of the employee must generally contain observations regarding his qualities, capacity etc. The whole official record of a person must be taken into account when considering claims for promotion and not merely the latest entries. Employees must be informed wherever possible of the intention to record adverse remarks in their personal rolls and given an opportunity for explanation and improvement. They must in all cases be informed of adverse entries and their explanation, if any, must be recorded.
7. As regards the working of the disciplinary rules, the Commission is of the view that so far as the upper grades of the services are concerned, the safeguards provided by the rules are normally sufficient to discourage

victimisation or unfair acts. Attention is drawn to certain defects in the rules so far as these relate to employees of the lower grades. Many of the claims made by the service representatives proceeded on a mistaken identification of the steps taken for the dismissal of a public servant with the steps in a criminal trail. The officer exercising delegated powers in disciplinary matters is not in the position of a prosecutor acting also as judge. He should eschew personal considerations and determine such cases in the best interests of the service. An extension of the system of having personnel officers to deal with all disciplinary cases is recommended. It is neither desirable nor practicable to insist on the intervention of an outside body in all disciplinary matters. It would meet the ends of justice if persons dismissed or removed from service are allowed, in addition to the right of appeal, a right to petition the higher authorities for a review of their case and the right of lower authorities to withhold such petitions where no appeal lies is abrogated. An opportunity for personal appearance before the officer dealing with the appeal is also recommended.

8. Miscellaneous recommendations relate to avoidance of delay in dealing with staff cases, removal of restrictions in the matter of union officials helping in the defence of personal cases. Steps should be taken early to have the number required in each office or department (including industrial establishments) examined with some approximation to realities and after a certain length of service, say one year, even temporary employees should be entitled to most of the privileges of the permanent employees, in the matter of earned leave, medical aid, provident fund etc.
9. Supporting the demand for help and encouragement to public servants to educate themselves even after entering service, certain proposals adopted in the U.K. as a result of the Report of the Assheton Committee are recommended.

1.2.8 Leave Rules:

1. The existence of variety of rules and regulations governing various classes of public servants is recognised as a natural cause for dissatisfaction. The demand for extending the liberal provisions of Fundamental Rules to all services is not accepted. As leave rules should be framed with due regard to an employee's need for rest on the one hand and public interest on the other, the employees' age and length of service, the nature of his work, and the field of recruitment are all considered to be factors justifying differentiation between classes of employees.
2. Full pay leave: As regards employees belonging to the Class I, II and III services, the Railway Rules regarding earned leave should be brought into

line with the Revised Leave Rules, 1933 incorporating the changes recommended in the latter set of rules. In regard to Class IV services, both in the Railways and civil departments, employees should earn full pay leave at the rate of 1/22nd of duty during the first ten years of their service, at the rate of 1/16th from the 11th to the 20th year of service and at 1/11th of service from the 21st year onwards.

Certain relaxations on the limits of accumulation are recommended:

(a) extension of 90 day limit to 120 days generally, (b) the extension of the limit to 180 days if the leave is spent out of India and (c) the extension of the limit in the case of Class IV service to the extent that leave may be earned during four years.

3. Half pay leave: In place of the existing system under the Revised Leave Rules and Railway Leave Rules, it is recommended that half pay leave should also be earned like full pay leave. Members of Class I, II and III services should be entitled to half pay leave at the rate of 1/16th of duty throughout their service. Members of Class IV at 1/22nd of duty for the first 20 years and 1/16th thereafter.
4. When leave is granted on medical certificate, any public servant will be entitled to commute the half pay leave that he has earned into full pay leave for half of that period, such full pay leave on medical certificate not exceeding 6 months in the whole service.
5. Leave not due on half pay, subject to a limit of three months at a time and 6 months in all, such leave being debited to subsequent leave earned, may be allowed in the case of permanent employees who may require leave on medical certificate but have not enough earned leave at their credit.
6. Leave salary may be calculated as follows:

- For the first 30 days out of leave taken at a time, on the average of last 12 months' pay whether substantive or officiating; and
- For the periods of leave beyond the first month, with reference to the pay drawn or that would be drawn by the employee in the permanent post held by him substantively on the date preceding the commencement of leave.

7. Where temporary employees are kept on indefinitely, they could after completion of one year's continuous service earn leave on full pay as well as half pay on the same terms as permanent employees of the grade with a like right to commute half pay leave into full pay leave on medical certificate.
8. Study leave rules should be worked more liberally; they should not be limited to gazetted services nor should they be limited to studies abroad.
9. Maximum limit on leave salary should be removed in the case of those who

are governed by the new scales of pay recommended by the Commission.

10. The lifting of the ban recently imposed forbidding the grant of additional pay for officiating appointments of less than two months vacancies is recommended, such cases being governed by the pre-existing practice.
11. Attention is invited to certain anomalies in regard to the calculation of holidays for counting the limit of casual leave, grant of quarantine leave and in the application of the Revised Leave Rules.

1.2.9 Retirement Benefits:

1. Preference is indicated in favour of a combination of the benefits available under the Pension and Provident Fund systems and of remedying some of the defects in these systems.
2. The age of retirement in future should be uniformly 58 for all services, with an option to Government to retire an employee on grounds of loss of efficiency at 55 or to grant annual extensions thereafter.
3. The demand for extending the concession of voluntary retirement to all those who have put in 25 of years service is not accepted. Instead, abrogation of Article 465-A is suggested in case of new entrants.
4. The lower scales of pensions recommended in the case of new entrants, i.e. those not in permanent service as on April 1, 1938 should not be applied.
5. An overall maximum of ₹ 8,000 per year as pension would be provided in keeping with the salaries maxima proposed by the Commission.
6. The scale of pension should be 1/80 of emoluments for year of service subject to a limit of 35/80 and not exceeding ₹ 8,000 for 35 years of service.
7. Additional pensions may be abolished in the event of the above higher limits being adopted.
8. The scale of gratuity for non-pensionable employees in Railways may be raised to ½ of month's pay per year of service subject to a maximum of 15 months pay not exceeding ₹ 25,000 in the case of all grades.
9. The Commission does not recommend any departure from the principle that compensatory allowances as such should not count as reckonable emoluments.
10. The demand for a minimum pension as subsistence allowance for pensioners is not accepted.
11. For women employees generally (who may leave service on marriage) and other establishments who may not serve a full term, the contributory provident fund concession may be allowed instead of pension.
12. Minimum qualifying age for pensionary service should be 20 for Class I, II, III and 18 for Class IV services.
13. Employees may be permitted to commute lump sum payments under the

Provident Fund Scheme into annuity or pension.

14. Since a suitable 'appeals' procedure has been laid down, the Commission feels there is no risk of the power to withhold special contribution or gratuity being exercised arbitrarily.
15. Limitation of the power of assigning provident fund assets to other than wife and children is recommended.
16. No increase in the scale of Government contribution or bonus for railway employee appears justified.
17. To provide for free interchange of personnel (particularly in scientific and technical services) between government services and local bodies, the Commission suggests for consideration, the adoption of a scheme similar to the Federated Superannuation System for Universities in vogue in the U.K.
18. The Commission recommended the extension of the scale of benefits (bonus) allowed under the Railway Provident Fund Rules to employees in other Departments as well who are not in pensionable service, but not the gratuity or special contribution as in Railways.
19. There should be no differentiation between industrial and non-industrial employees in the matter of retirement benefits.
20. A scheme which has appealed to the Commission is the surrender by an officer retiring from service of a given amount of pension on retirement from service so as to obtain a capital sum or annuity to be paid to dependent beneficiaries on the lines of the Mysore schemes. A possible variant may be devised to enable the option to be exercised during service, i.e. before the pension actually accrues.
21. In view of the reduction in pension scale from 1/60 to 1/80 per year of service (which involves a surrender of 25 percent of pension), a gratuity of half a month's pay per year of service subject to a maximum of 15 months pay is recommended as a retiring gratuity or death benefit as the case may be.
22. As a measure of family protection, security to the employee himself and stability from the Government point of view, the pension system with necessary improvements is superior and option should not be allowed to pensionable employees to elect provident fund system.
23. The institution of family pension funds is not advocated for the services as a whole.
24. The Commission is opposed to the extension of the commutation of pension rules and the grant of commutation amounts without medical examination.
25. The institution of compulsory insurance is favoured, and is commended particularly in the case of employees whose conditions of service involve accidents and risks.

26. A compulsory insurance scheme outlined by Mr. Wilson, M.A.G., is recommended for further examination by the Government.
27. An option similar to that allowed under the U.K. Superannuation Act, 1935 is recommended in the case of persons in pensionable service.
28. In the case of non-pensionable employees, compulsory insurance may take the form of an option to take an annuity for a given period for a beneficiary instead of a pure life assurance cover.
29. The retiring benefit for every public servant should consist of two components: (i) a recurring monthly pension and (ii) an insurance cover the premia for which would be found by Government by making a reduction of 25 percent in the amount of pension.
30. A contribution by Government of about 3 percent of an officer's pay as it stands from time to time would be sufficient to liquidate Government's liability for one fourth of the pension. It is suggested that a postal endowment policy for this amount should be issued to each employee on confirmation. As the substantive pay increases, the policy amount will have to be augmented. In order to reduce the work connected with the revision, it may be made at longer intervals than a year and by making this group insurance scheme compulsory, the necessity for recurring medical examination may be obviated.
31. The amount of cover available will be paid to the party on retirement in the normal course or to his heirs if he should die before retirement.
32. The above arrangements could be applied to persons governed by the Railway Provident Fund Rules also by requiring the subscribers to forego a part of the Government contribution and gratuity.
33. Since the extension of the above schemes to persons in service might present difficulties, they may be given the following benefits:

- At their option to forego 1/4th of the pension that might accrue and in return to become entitled on retirement to a lump sum of 3/80ths of pay for each year of service subject to a maximum of 15 months pay.
- On death in service after completion of not less than 5 years service, a lump sum of one year's pay or 3/80th of pay for each year of service subject to a maximum of 15 months pay may be paid to the heirs.
- On death after retirement, if the money drawn by way of pension and lump sum is less than a year's pay, the balance of a year's pay may be paid to the heirs.

34. Where a Government servant who has rendered more than 25 years service dies in harness or shortly after retirement, the widow and dependent children

of the deceased should be allowed to draw in addition to the benefits last mentioned, a portion of the pension limited to half of the pension earned subject to a maximum of ₹ 150 per month for a maximum period of say five years. When such a Government servant dies before expiry of 5 years after his retirement and has drawn his pension for only a short period, the benefit of a similar limited pension may be extended to his family for the unexpired portion of the 5 year period.

1.2.10 Conciliation Machinery:

1. The Commission is not impressed with the argument that in the absence of organised associations of employees anything in the nature of the Whitley scheme cannot be usefully introduced. As associations with different degrees of stability and cohesion have latterly come into existence in this country, the very opportunity and experience of working something like the Whitley scheme will help to advance the organisation. The machinery should, however, be elastic, to suit the different grades of public servants and the varying groups among them. As regards organisation of staff associations, they may for some purposes be regional, for other purposes departmental while matters of common interest may be attended to by an all-India body.
2. Following the English practice, no special conciliation or adjudication machinery need be provided in the case of Class I Services. For Class II service, and certain non-industrial grade of Class II, an organisation on the lines of the Whitley machinery would prove useful. For Class IV services and certain grades of Class III in commercial departments since trade unions have come to stay, the experience of other countries indicates that notwithstanding the dangers and difficulties associated with certain stages in the development, it is best for the Government to deal with well-organised unions of employees.
3. In respect of arbitration, English opinion and practice have been against compulsion. In view however of the enactment of the Industrial Disputes Act, 1947, it is recommended, that experience of the working of the Act should be awaited before considering any other course in respect of classes of employees who come within the purview of the Act. In regard to Class II services and those sections of Class III service who have not organised on trade union lines, a resort to an ad hoc tribunal similar to the Civil Service Arbitration Board in England is suggested.

1.2.11 Labour Classification:

1. The main question regarding basic pay payable to unskilled labour has been discussed. A classification of the higher grades (including supervisory staff) into: (i) semi-skilled, (ii) skilled and (iii) highly skilled is recommended.

2. Persons of whom only physical or manual work, not requiring any intelligence, training or experience, is expected may be classed as unskilled labour. As regards tests to be adopted in determining the higher categories, the basis of differentiation may vary from industry to industry. Sometimes theoretical training may be more essential while in others apprenticeship or practical experience may be more important. Classification in the last resort must be based on trade tests. It will be convenient if each industrial establishment constitutes a Board, say of three of its officers, to determine the classification which should be reviewed from time to time.
3. In regard to remuneration, the minimum wage recommended by the Commission should be applied at the lowest level whether or not the principle is accepted in private industry. As regards the higher grades of labour, there is not much justification for suggesting that remuneration should be markedly higher in Government services than in private industry.
4. There is much to be said in favour of a system of paying efficiency bonus according to the outturn of each worker.
5. It will be best to leave the question of wage fixation to Wage Boards. Where wages have to be fixed by a Regional Board, it may not always be possible to give effect to the principle of all-India uniformity.
6. The daily-rated system for labour whether in Railway or other departments of Government should be reduced to a minimum.

Endnote

1. The Interim Government of India, formed on September 2, 1946 from the newly elected Constituent Assembly of India, had the task of assisting the transition of India and Pakistan from British rule to independence. It remained in place until August 15, 1947.

2

Second Central Pay Commission

2.1 Second Pay Commission at a Glance

The Second Pay Commission was set up in August 1957, 10 years after Independence. Justice Jaganndha Das was the Chairman of this Commission. It may be recalled that the First Pay Commission had recommended the setting up of a pay commission after 10 years. Moreover, it was also necessitated by the partition of the country and the need to restructure the bureaucracy accordingly.

Composition of the Second Pay Commission

Justice Jagannadha Das	Chairman
Shri V.B. Gandhi	Member
Shri N.K. Sidhanta	Member
Shri M.L. Dantwala	Member
Shrimati Maragatham Chandrasekhar	Member
Shri L.P. Singh	Member-Secretary
Shri H.F.B. Pais	Associate Secretary

The Commission finished its report within 2 years and submitted it to the Government. The recommendations of the Commission had a financial impact of ₹ 39.6 crore on the Government. The Commission reiterated the principle on which the salaries should be determined. It stated that the pay structure and the working conditions of Government employee should be crafted in a way so as to ensure efficient functioning of the system by recruiting persons with a minimum qualification.

The Commission revised the pay scales by merging 50 percent of the dearness allowance (DA) with basic pay and it recommended ₹ 80 as the minimum remuneration (basic pay ₹ 70 plus DA ₹ 10) payable to a Government employee.

The Commission rationalized the pay structures by reducing further the number of scales. It re-affirmed the view of the First Pay Commission that the age of superannuation should be 58 years for all classes of public servants but did not recommend any increase in the non-contributory retirement benefits and recommended that if in future any improvement is to be made, it was the considered view of the Commission that these benefits should be on a contributory basis.

2.1.1 Terms of Reference: These were as follows:

1. To examine the principles which should govern the structure of emoluments and conditions of service of the Central Government employees.
2. To consider and recommend what changes in the structure of emoluments and conditions of service of different classes of Central Government employees are desirable and feasible keeping in mind the considerations mentioned below.
3. To recommend, in particular, the extent to which benefits to Central Government employees can be given in the shape of amenities and facilities.
4. In making their recommendations, the Commission will take into account the historical background, the economic conditions in the country and the implications and requirements of developmental planning, and also the disparities in the standard of remuneration and conditions of service of the Central Government employees on the one hand and of the employees of the State Governments, local bodies and aided institutions on the other, and all other relevant factors.
5. The Commission may consider demands for relief of an interim character and send reports thereon. In the event of the Commission recommending any interim relief, the date from which this relief should take effect will be indicated by the Commission.
6. The Commission will devise their own procedure and may appoint such advisers as they choose for any particular purpose. They may call for such information and take such evidence as they may consider necessary. Ministries and Departments of the Government of India will furnish such information and documents and other assistance as may be required by the Commission. The Government of India trust that the State Governments, service associations and others concerned will also extend to the Commission their fullest co-operation and assistance.

The Commission was requested to make its recommendations to the Government as soon as practicable.

2.1.2 Procedure Adopted: The Commission met on September 9, 1957, and on September 11, 1957, issued a public notice inviting associations of Central Government employees and other organizations, institutions and individuals who might be interested, to send memoranda of their views on matters covered by its terms of reference, not later than October 10, 1957. At the request of some service associations, the date was extended first to November 10, and then to December 10, 1957.

In the last week of September 1957, it addressed all Ministries and other agencies of the Central Government requesting them to furnish factual information, as on June 30, 1957, in regard to the various services and posts under their administrative control. As its terms of reference required it to take into account, among other factors, the disparities in the standard of remuneration and conditions of service of the Central Government employees on the one hand, and of the employees of the State Governments, local bodies and aided institutions on the other, it simultaneously addressed the State Governments requesting them to supply to it essential information regarding the remuneration and conditions of service of their own employees and those of local bodies and aided institutions.

In response to the public notice, it received about 5,000 memoranda, of which more than 800 were from service associations etc. and in a considerable number of these memoranda, the question of interim relief had been raised. The Commission accordingly devoted its attention for some weeks mainly to the examination of that question. On December 14, 1957, it submitted a Report to the Government, recommending grant of an increase in dearness allowance which was to continue until it made its final Report.

On January 14, 1958, it issued a questionnaire drawn up on the basis of its preliminary study of the matters entrusted to it for enquiry, and in the light of the issues raised in the memoranda received till then. The Commission invited replies by February 20, 1958 but on the request of many service associations, and others interested, extended the date to March 10 of the same year. It received more than 700 replies from service associations, State Governments, Public Service Commissions, public men, economists, and retired and serving civil servants.

With minor exceptions, the basic information sought from the Central Government was received by the end of April 1958. Information from many of the State Governments was received piecemeal, but by November 1958 the Commission had furnished practically all the information regarding the employees of the State Governments.

At the request of the Commission, the Ministry of External Affairs addressed Indian Missions in certain countries in October 1957 requesting them to forward to the Commission with information regarding the civil services of those countries likely to be of assistance to it in its enquiry. Apart from the Indian Missions abroad, the Commission received valuable information regarding emoluments and conditions of service of Government employees in certain countries through the good offices of the International Labour Office, Geneva.

The Central Government permitted its employees generally to send to the Commission, in their purely personal capacity, any views and suggestions which they might wish to.

As regards Secretariat officers of and above the rank of under secretary and heads of departments, the orders of Government were: (i) that secretaries were free to express to the Commission their personal views formed in the light of their knowledge and experience, (ii) that other secretariat officers and heads of departments should be permitted to give evidence to the Commission orally or in writing on matters coming within their respective spheres of work; but (iii) that such permission was not necessary in the case of those who wished to give evidence on behalf of service associations with which they were connected.

With a view to studying on the spot the working conditions in different classes of Government offices, and also to have an idea of the kind of residences provided by Government for lower grades of staff, the Commission visited a number of Railway and Posts and Telegraphs offices in Delhi during February 1958, and spent about a fortnight in Calcutta in April-May of the same year.

2.2 Summary of the Recommendations of the Second Central Pay Commission

2.2.1 Principles of Pay and Conditions of Service:

1. The structure of emoluments and conditions of service should be so designed as to ensure recruitment at different levels of persons with requisite qualifications and abilities and to keep them efficient.
2. The social position which a Government servant is traditionally expected to maintain should not in itself be a factor in the determination of his remuneration.
3. While the *model employer* principle, as commonly understood, is not suitable for determination of remuneration, the social principles and standards which Government have laid down for, or commended to employers, generally should be taken into account. Further, in the matter of conditions of work and employment practices generally, the Government may become the pace-setter—a model employer.
4. The minimum wage or salary should not be determined only on economic considerations, but should also satisfy social tests. Even above the minimum level, the Government should remunerate their employees fairly.
5. In the present circumstances, the principle of fair comparison with rates of remuneration in outside employment is not suitable for full and detailed application; but it is one of the important factors to be taken into account.
6. Once the demands of efficiency of the public service are satisfied, social

considerations require limitation of disparities between the highest and the lowest salaries, and their reduction as far as possible.

7. With the minimum and maximum salaries having been determined on a combination of social and economic considerations, sound and equitable internal relativities constitute the most important single principle to be followed in the determination of the intermediate salaries.
8. Except in the broad sense of being an indicator of the level and the state of the economy, and thus of the resources which the Government can draw upon for their needs, the trend of national productivity cannot be accepted as a factor in itself relevant to the determination of salaries and wages of Government servants.
9. The level of consumer prices is among the factors relevant to the determination of rates of remuneration of Government servants.

2.2.2 Economic Conditions and Developmental Planning:

1. Fluctuations in prices have occurred during the last twelve years, but the general trend, especially since 1955, has been upward. The growing tempo of investment in the economy and the relative shortage of foodgrains are the main factors responsible for the prince increase.
2. Production and national income have increased over the last few years; the economic situation today is better and more promising that it was in 1947-48.
3. Indications are that there may not be a serious instability of prices in the near future, but a slow rise of prices is likely; hence the need for caution.
4. There has been a growing shortage of internal resources needed for financing development plans. Rapid economic development requires restraint on consumption consistent, as far as possible, with the social objectives of planning.

2.2.3 Disparities between Central Emoluments and those under State Governments, Local Bodies etc.

1. In the context of our constitutional structure, the issue of disparities is a highly complex one and tangled with other matters; it is not one that can be resolved in a simple way.
2. The suggestion that the Central Government employees posted in different States might be remunerated at the rates prescribed for the State employees, or, that, in the alternative, the dearness and other allowances alone might follow the State rates is not sound or feasible.
3. A scheme of recruitment to the non-gazetted posts under the Central Government by transfer of selected personnel from the appropriate services of the State Government may be considered.
4. The disparities should be regarded as a factor calling for restraint but not one

that would justify the denial to the Central Government employees of the minimum improvement in remuneration which otherwise appears to be fair and desirable.

2.2.4 Minimum Remuneration:

1. With the present magnitude of unemployment and under-employment in the country and the low levels of income, the present minimum of ₹ 75 is sufficient to attract recruits of the right type.
2. The present minimum remuneration of ₹ 75 in Central Government compares favourably with the average minimum rate in organised private industry.
3. A need-based minimum wage of the order of ₹ 125 per month proposed by the employees is not feasible, economically and financially.
4. A diet capable of providing 2,600 calories and other nutrients of the requisite order would cost ₹ 52 per month for a family of three consumption units. Adding the requirements of clothing, housing etc., a need-based minimum, permissible within the limits of the country's present output of foodstuffs would cost about ₹ 80.
5. With the consumer price index at 116, a remuneration of ₹ 80 would restore the real income of employees on the lowest pay to the level at which it was fixed on the recommendations of the First Pay Commission.
6. While it is necessary to keep inflationary pressures in check, a modest increase in minimum remuneration is called for on social considerations and in the interest of contentment of the staff. It is only as an element in an integrated economic and social policy that a sacrifice can reasonably be asked for from the lower grades of staff.
7. The minimum remuneration payable to a Central Government employee should be increased from ₹ 75 per month to ₹ 80 per month.

2.2.5 Highest Salaries: Keeping in view the necessity of maintaining a high standard of recruitment to the superior services, and the erosion of the real income which has taken place, reduction of the salaries at present prescribed for the highest grades is not recommended.

2.2.6 Dearness Allowance: While an upward tendency in prices is likely to persist, the possibility of a fall in the price level cannot be ruled out in view of likely fluctuations in agricultural production and other possible causes.

Dearness allowance should, therefore, continue as a separate element in the remuneration of Central Government employees. It should, however, be limited for the present to employees whose salaries are below ₹ 300 per month.

Judging from the recent trends in prices, the consumer price index (1949=100) is not likely to drop below 100. The basic salaries of the lower paid employees should, therefore, be fixed in terms of the requirements at an index level of 100. No downward adjustment in basic salaries should, however, be made even if the index falls to 90.

The entire remuneration of the higher paid employees should be in the form of salary with no separate dearness allowance.

In future adjustments of the dearness allowance to meet rise in prices, employees in the pay-range of ₹ 300 and above but below ₹ 400 should, however, be grouped with those in the pay-range below ₹ 300.

Should the consumer price index continue to rise, the case of employees in the pay-range of ₹ 400 and above but below ₹ 1,000 for grant of dearness allowance may be considered in the light of all the relevant circumstances at the time.

There should not be automatic adjustment of dearness allowance with the price index. A substantial and persistent rise in prices, however, normally creates a prima facie case for compensation and it should be the Government's endeavour not to allow the standard of living of their employees in the lower range of remuneration to fall.

For the present, employees drawing pay below ₹ 300 per month may be granted dearness allowance at the following rates:

- Basic pay below ₹ 150: ₹ 10 per month
- Basic pay of ₹ 150 or above but below ₹ 300: ₹ 20 per month

There should be marginal adjustments for employees drawing a basic pay of ₹ 300 or above but below ₹ 320.

These rates of dearness allowance should be taken as related to the consumer price index 115 (1949=100) and should continue unless the index falls below 100. If during a period of 12 months the index remains on an average, ten points above 115, the Government should review the position and consider whether an increase in the allowance should be allowed, and if so, at what rate. If thereafter the index falls by the same margin, and for the same period, the position may be similarly reviewed and appropriate adjustments made.

The benefit of dearness allowance should, in future upward adjustments, be extended to all employees drawing a basic pay below ₹ 400 per month in such a way that the total of basic pay and dearness allowance paid to any employee in the pay-range of ₹ 300 to ₹ 400 does not exceed ₹ 400.

2.2.7 Pay Scales: On promotion to a higher post, up to and inclusive of those from the present Class II level to Class I, the pay of an employee should first be increased by one increment in the lower scale and then fixed in the higher scale at the stage next above. No distinction should be made for this purpose on the ground that the lower post was held in a quasi-permanent or temporary and not permanent capacity.

Selection grades without functional differentiation are necessary in certain cases in order to provide incentives to employees who have no outlets, or very limited outlets, for promotion to higher posts.

The following typical scales of pay are recommended for Class I, II and III services and posts.

Typical Scales of Pay Recommended for Class I

(in ₹)

Supertime scales and fixed rates	3,000
	2,750
	2,500
	2,250
	2,000-125-2,250
	1,800-100-2,000-125-2,250-2,000
	1,800-100-2,000
	1,600-100-1,800
	1,300-60-1,600-100-1,800
	1,100-50-1,300-60-1,600-100-1,800
	1,300-60-1,600
	1,100-50-1,400

Time Scales:

Indian Foreign Service	
Senior scale	900-50-1,300-1,300-60-1,600-100/2-1,800
Junior scale	400-400-500-40-700-30-1,000
Class I (non-technical) services	400-400-450-30-510-700-40-1,100-50/2-1,250
Scientific Services	
Senior scale	700-50-1,250
Junior scale	400-40-800-50-950
Engineering and Some Other Services	
Senior scale	700-40-1,100-50/2-1,250
Junior scale	400-400-450-30-600-35-950
Medical Services	
Senior scale	850-45-1,300-50-1,400 (consolidated scale) or 675-35-850-40-1,050-50-1,150 plus non-practising allowance
Junior scale	575-25-600-30-750-40-1,150 (consolidated scale) or 425-25-450-30-600-35-950 plus non-practising allowance

Typical Scales of Pay Recommended for Class II

(in ₹)

Standard scale	350-25-500-30-830-35-900
Accounts department	590-30-830-35-900
Station superintendents (Railways)	590-30-830-35-900
Medical services	475-25-650-30-950 (consolidated) or 325-25-500-30-800 plus non-practising allowance
Programme executives in All India Radio, Grade III of the Central Information Service, stores officers etc.	350-25-500-30-800
Research assistants/technical assistants etc.	325-15-475-20-575
Assistants in the Central Secretariat	210-10-290-15-530

Typical Scales of Pay Recommended for Clerical Staff

(in ₹)

Supervisory grade I	425-25-575
Supervisory grade II	350-20-450-25-475
Supervisory grade III	335-15-425
Supervisory grade IV	210-10-290-15-380
Upper division clerk	130-5-160-8-280-10-300-130-5-160-8-280
Lower division clerk	110-3-131-4-175-5-180
Stenographers	320-15-530 210-10-290-15-425 150-5-160-8-280-10-300 130-5-160-8-280-10-300

2.2.8 Headquarters Organisation of the Government of India: The two grades of section officers should be amalgamated into a single grade carrying the standard class II scale.

A slightly higher remuneration than that recommended would be justified for lower division clerks if Government considers it necessary to have for the secretariat, a superior class of recruits even at that level.

Direct recruitment to the upper division grade should be stopped and promotion to a proportion of posts which are now being filled by direct recruitment should be made on the basis of a written examination conducted by the Public Service Commission.

2.2.9 Office Staffs Outside the Secretariat: Classification of offices into attached and subordinate offices should be made on a functional basis.

The secretariat and attached offices may be combined into a single headquarters organisation with a common office.

Definite criteria should be laid down for determining as to what offices should be included in the Central Secretariat Service Scheme.

The question of direct recruitment above the level of lower division clerk at the Armed Forces Headquarters should be examined.

The necessity for continuing the posts of assistant-in-charge should also be examined.

Posts of upper division clerk now filled by direct recruitment should be filled by promotion on the basis of a limited competitive test, except where for any special reason a university degree is considered an essential qualification for the posts.

10 percent of the posts of lower division clerks should be in a selection grade in cadres in which the proportion of promotion posts is less then 50 percent of the lower division posts.

There should be a selection grade for upper division clerks in the Indian audit and accounts department and the defence accounts department.

In the railways, typists should not be retained as a separate cadre but should be merged in the general clerical cadre.

In the railways, the system of employing clerks as telephone operators may continue, but the necessity for, and the rates of, special pay granted to them should be reviewed.

The arrangement for employing upper division clerks on supervisory duties on their grade pay plus a special pay is not satisfactory. If the duties are fully supervisory, it should be considered whether posts of head clerk should not be created.

Lower division clerks in non-secretariat offices may be permitted to compete for appointment to the grade of lower division clerk in the secretariat and may be allowed suitable age relaxation for this purpose.

Stenographers and steno-typists in non-secretariat offices may be permitted to compete for posts in the lowest grade of stenographer in the secretariat and may be allowed relaxation of age limit for this purpose.

2.2.10 Class II Services and Posts: The existing arrangement of having both class II services and a junior branch of the class I services may continue.

Government may decide in which services promotion from class II to class I should be considered to the senior scale of the latter.

2.2.11 Scientific Staff: All new recruits to class I junior scale should be given up to two advance increments—one increment for every year of approved research before entering service.

In view of the pay structure and the nature of work in the scientific services, it is recommended that the grade structure in research and development organizations should be such as to provide for a much larger proportion of posts in the senior and the higher grades together than in the junior grade.

A scheme of special merit promotion, providing for the creation of ad hoc posts outside the normal strength of a grade, in the scale of ₹ 700-1,250 or in a higher scale depending on the circumstances of each case, should be introduced for outstanding research workers.

A Scientific Civil Service on the lines of the all-India and some of class I Central Services is not feasible. But to ensure uniformity in the management of the different scientific services, and to facilitate occasional interchange from one such service to another, when this is in the interest of scientific work, a standing committee of representatives of various scientific departments and organizations may be set up.

2.2.12 Medical and Public Health Staff: Doctors who are in the whole-time employment of the Central Government for providing medical attendance and treatment of Government servants should not be permitted private practice.

2.2.13 Class IV Staff: Excluding: (a) categories peculiar to the railways and the Posts and Telegraphs Department, and (b) a few other categories for whom new scales have been specifically recommended, all class IV staffs on the existing scales mentioned below should be brought on to the new scales noted against each. Class IV staffs on scales other than those mentioned below may be fitted into one or the other of these new scales.

Existing Scales (₹)	**Proposed Scales (₹)**
20-½-25	55-1-60 (for under-age employees)
30-½-35	70-1-80-EB-1-85
35-1-40	75-1-85-EB-2-89
35-1-50 35-1-40-2-50	75-1-85-EB-2-95
40-1-50	80-1-85-2-95
35-1-50-2-60	75-1-85-EB-2-95-EB-3-110
35-1-40-2-60 40-1-50-2-60	80-1-85-2-95-EB-3-110
40-2-60	85-2-95-3-110
50-1-60	95-3-110

Including unskilled staffs in workshops, there are about 7 lakh employees in the scale of ₹ 30-½-35. Their total remuneration including pay and dearness allowance at present ranges from ₹ 75 to ₹ 80 per month. Their revised scale will be ₹ 70-1-85, which with a dearness allowance of ₹ 10 will raise their minimum remuneration to ₹ 80 and the maximum to ₹ 95 per month.

2.2.14 Workshop Staff: The following scales of pay are recommended for workshop staffs in general.

(in ₹)

Unskilled	70-1-80-EB-1-85
Semi-skilled and Un-skilled supervisory	75-1-85-EB-2-95 75-1-85-EB-2-95-3-101-EB-3-110 85-2-95-3-110 95-3-110
Skilled	85-2-95-3-110 85-2-95-3-110-EB-3-128 100-3-130 100-3-130-EB-3-142 110-3-131 110-3-131-4-143 110-3-131-4-143-EB-4-155 110-3-131-4-143-EB-4-171-EB-4-175-5-180 125-3-131-4-155 125-3-131-4-163-EB-4-175-5-180 140-5-175 150-5-180
Highly skilled	130-5-175-EB-6-205-7-212 150-5-175-6-205 150-5-175-6-205-EB-7-240 175-6-205-7-240 205-7-240

Unskilled staffs in the workshops whose work is exceptionally heavy, or whose normal duties involve special risks, should have, in addition to pay, a special pay of ₹ 3 per month.

There should be proper classification of jobs, but no particular system of job-evaluation in preference to others is recommended.

The system of "basic tradesmen" in the railways should be worked so as to provide a channel through which, in trades where there is no semi-skilled grade, unskilled workers may advance to the skilled grade and posts of basic tradesmen created with this object should not be set off against posts in the skilled grade.

A suitable system of payment by results should be introduced wherever feasible; but the basic time-wage for the period worked should be guaranteed, and the piece rate be determined after scientific studies and in consultation with the workers.

The task of fitting the workshop staffs in the new pay scales should be entrusted to specially constituted bodies consisting of two experts and a neutral chairman. The recommendations made by various bodies should be coordinated by a common chairman or a joint meeting of the chairman of all the bodies.

2.2.15 Railways: A bonus scheme for running staffs as an additional incentive for punctual running of passenger trains and expeditious movement of goods trains has been suggested for consideration.

An ad hoc committee may be set up to review the pay structure of marine staff.

2.2.16 Posts and Telegraphs Department: The age limit of 45 years for promotion to the postal superintendents' service class II should be raised.

The basic pay for task work messengers should be the same as for other telegraph messengers, and a new system of additional payments related to output above the prescribed standard may be evolved.

The strength of the cadre of boy messengers/peons, and qualifications for their recruitment, should be so determined as to provide for their absorption in vacancies of messengers/peons as soon as possible after they have reached the normal age of recruitment to Government service.

2.2.17 Union Territories: Excepting Delhi and Andaman and Nicobar Islands, the rates of remuneration of the employees of a Union Territory should be fixed with reference to those of the employees in the neighbouring State. If, however, the Central Government finds that the emoluments as in the neighbouring State fall below rates that would be fair on a consideration of the totality of the relevant circumstances, a suitable higher rate should be fixed.

The emoluments of the employees of the Union Territories should be so adjusted between basic pay and dearness allowance that they conform to the general pattern recommended for Central Government employees.

2.2.18 Special Pay: There should be a periodical review of special pays to ensure that a special pay is not granted except when the necessary conditions are satisfied and that special pays are not so large or granted so freely that they distort the pay structure.

2.2.19 Fixation of Pay in New Scales: The initial pay may be fixed in the new scale on a point-to-point basis, subject to specified limiting conditions.

2.2.20 Allowances:

A. Rent Free Quarters and House Rent Allowance: Rent free residence should be provided only if duties or conditions of work are such that a higher remuneration would be granted but for this concession.

Class IV staffs already enjoying thc concession may continue to do so.

Railway employees who are provided with residence in future should pay rent as employees in other departments.

Present classification of localities on basis of population should continue, but grant of house rent allowance in special cases may be considered on merits.

The revised rates of house rent allowance should be as follows.

(in ₹)

	Class of Cities		
Pay	A	B	C
Below 75	10	7.50	5
75 and above but below 100	15	10	7.50
100 and above but below 200	20	15	7.50 for those drawing below 150
200 and above	10 percent of pay	7½ percent of pay	Nil

Where application of these rates results in reduction of house rent allowance being drawn at present, the reduction may be spread over three years or so.

The condition of residence within the limits of the qualifying cities for the purpose of house rent allowance should be abrogated for both gazetted and non-gazetted staffs.

Employees whose place of duty, though outside, is in the proximity of a qualified city, and who, of necessity, reside within the city, may be given the house rent allowance admissible in that city.

B. Compensatory Allowance: The present basis, and general scheme of the city compensatory allowance does not call for revision; but the rates should be modified as follows.

(in ₹)

Pay	Class of Cities		
	A	B	C
Below 150	10 percent of pay subject to a minimum of 7.50 and a maximum of 12.50	5 percent of pay subject to a minimum of 5 and a maximum of 10 for all persons drawing below 500 per month	Nil
150 and above but below 300	8 percent of pay subject to a minimum of 12.50 and a maximum of 17.50	---	---

300 and above	6 percent of pay subject to a maximum of 75	---	---

Where the application of the proposed rates would result in reduction of the amount being drawn at present, the reduction may be spread over 3 years or so.

In Shimla and Shillong, compensatory allowance may be allowed at the following rates to employees drawing pay up to specified limits.

1.	House rent allowance	At the rate for B class cities
2.	Compensatory allowance	At the rate for A class cities
3.	Winter allowance	For 5 months, at half the compensatory allowance rates

In deciding whether a place should be declared a hill station for the purpose of allowances, classification made by the State Governments should generally be followed, but the rates may be different.

The existing scheme of hill allowances (except at Shimla and Shillong) may continue, with the adjustments in rates and slabs on the patterns of those in the compensatory and house rent allowances etc. for cities.

In the case of remote locality allowance or bad climate allowance, no change is necessary except for adjustment in rates and slabs.

No allowance in the nature of a permanent addition to pay should be given for field service liability as such, as distinguished from actual field service.

The discrimination against clerks and store keepers under the Ministry of Defence, recruited before 1948, who are liable to lose their seniority if found physically unfit for field service, should end.

C. All India Transfer Liability: No special monetary concession or compensation is called for all-India service liability.

D. Travelling Allowance: The basis for sanctioning and the rates of fixed conveyance allowance should be revised.

The daily allowance rates, and the rates of allowance for incidental expenses in connection with tours, should be reviewed.

Certain categories of posts and telegraphs staff, who are now governed by special rules, should be granted travelling allowance under the ordinary rules, except for regular journeys on their fixed beats.

Postmen and linemen should be entitled to an allowance when they have to spend the night away on duty.

Railway staff may not transport free to cost more personal effects than is permitted to other staffs, but they should be allowed incidental charges at the standard rates.

The present rates of allowance for incidentals for journey on transfer should be halved, but in lieu of the other half, an employee should be allowed half a month's pay subject to a limit of ₹ 150.

A retiring Government servant under certain conditions, or one invalidated from service, may be allowed travelling allowance for journey to his home town.

Work charged staffs in all establishments should be entitled to travelling allowance under the normal rules.

E. Transport between Place of Work and Residence: Loans for purchase of conveyance may be granted liberally.

No change is necessary in the present policy of not granting an allowance for travel between residence and place of work. But grant of transport concession in some form or other may be considered under certain exceptional circumstances.

Steps should be taken to ease the extreme transport difficulties of employees working in big cities.

2.2.21 Hours of Work, Weekly Off, Public Holidays, Overtime Allowance, Casual Leave and Special Casual Leave: Weekly hours at present prescribed for various categories of staffs may continue. Working hours of office staffs are on the low side and an increase would be justified, but an attempt should first be made to obtain better output within the present hours.

Uniformity in weekly working hours among various groups of employees is not necessary or feasible.

The railway administration should examine whether the basis on which certain categories, such as gatemen, have been classified for the purpose of working hours has changed on account of increased traffics etc., necessitating reclassification.

In establishments in which industrial and non-industrial staff work together, the latter should observe the same hours as the former when the nature of their duties are such that their presence throughout is necessary for efficient working of the industrial staff.

When night duty is such as to require continuous application, it should be allowed weightage of 10 minutes for every hour worked, except when weighage for night duty is in effect provided in the shape of reduced weekly working hours.

Split duty should not ordinarily be required to be performed in more than 3 spells. Where the employee's residence is not close to the place of work, 7 hours of split duty should be treated as equal to 8 hours of normal duty.

For office staff who at present work five-and-a-half-days a week, alternate Saturdays should be full working days, and full holidays. Offices which have continuous dealing with the public should, however, continue to have a five-and-a-half, or a six-day week, as the case may be.

No change is recommended in the present arrangements for a weekly break for other employees, except that in the case of *operating* staff the weekly off should be such as to allow a full night's rest, and it should not, as a rule, be less than 30 hours.

The staff on call duty should have at least a fortnightly off and this should generally be possible by internal adjustment of duties. Where, however, there is a single employee on call duty and such an arrangement will not be possible, he should not ordinarily be kept at a one-man station or section for more than 3 to 6 months at a time.

A fortnightly, if not a weekly, break should be allowed to cooks, waiters etc., by some suitable arrangement.

For *chowkidars* who have active duties requiring continuous alertness, a weekly off should be allowed. Chowkidars of different departments stationed at the same place might be treated as a single group for the purpose of enabling them to have a weekly or a fortnightly off by rotation.

To office staffs and other employees for whom a compensatory holiday is not obligatory under the law, such holiday need not be allowed for occasional work on Sunday, which should not, however, become a regular feature.

To operating staff generally, compensatory break should be allowed for work on an off day as soon as possible, and not later than 2 months.

An employee who is required to work on his off day should normally have compensation in the form of another day's break. But where, in exceptional cases, monetary compensation has to be paid for such work it should be at one and a half of the time rate. In no case should both, a compensatory break and a monetary compensation, be allowed for work on a weekly off day or on an authorised holiday.

A. Public Holidays: The number of public holidays should be reduced to 16 where they exceed that number.

Staff who do not at present, enjoy any public holidays should be considered entitled to the 3 national holidays, viz., Mahatma Gandhi's Birthday, Independence Day and Republic Day; and since, with some exception, they cannot be relieved of their duties on those days, they should be compensated by payment at one and a half time the normal rate.

No change is recommended in the existing number of holidays for workshop staffs, except that it should not in any case exceed 16.

Non-industrial staff employed in industrial establishments should have the same number of public holidays as the industrial.

For work on a public holiday to which an employee is entitled, overtime allowance should be paid at one and a half of the time rate, except when he becomes entitled to a higher rate under the Factories Act, 1948, or under any other law.

B. Overtime Allowance: Overtime allowance should be granted only to non-gazetted staffs drawing pay not exceeding ₹ 500 per month under specified conditions, and with the proviso in the case of office staffs (whose hours of work are relatively short) that claim to overtime allowance will arise only for duty in excess of 45 minutes beyond the prescribed hours on any working day.

In the case of workshop staffs who work for less than 48 hours, the overtime allowance for work in excess of the prescribed working hours, but not in excess of 48 hours, should be determined by common criteria so that only such divergencies may be retained as have a rational basis.

Non-industrial staffs in workshops whose hours of work are the same as those of industrial workers should be governed by the same orders regarding overtime payment as are applicable to the letter.

Overtime allowance should, in all cases, be calculated on the basis of pay and allowances, but excluding house rent allowance.

The rate of overtime allowance should be determined on certain specified general principles. An inter-departmental committee may review the present arrangements and work out a detailed scheme in the light of the general principles recommended.

Overtime allowance of railway staffs should not be calculated on monthly basis. If there are practical difficulties in calculating it on weekly basis it may be calculated on half-monthly basis.

Cases in which overtime earnings are a regular supplement to pay, and where pay has been fixed taking this factor into account, a complete stoppage or substantial reduction of overtime earnings should be compensated by suitable adjustment of pay.

C. Casual Leave: Casual leave should be reduced to 12 days in a year for office staff; operating and other similar staffs who have either no public holidays or a restricted number of public holidays may have 15 days; and workshop and other industrial staff 7 days in a year.

Facilities for special casual leave for work connected with service association etc. broadly modelled on those provided by the Department of Posts and Telegraphs or the Ministry of Defence to their civilian employees, may be extended to other employees representing recognised service associations.

Earned leave should be admissible to non-industrial staff at the following rates.

During the first 5 years of service	1.75 days for each month of service
During the next 10 years of service	2.25 days for each month of service
After 15 years of service	2.5 days for each month of service

Workshop employees in the railways may continue to earn leave at the rates applicable to non-industrial staff. However, if casual leave is allowed to them there should be a proportionate reduction in the rate of earned leave.

Leave entitlements of industrial staff in departments other than railways should be as follows.

Earned Leave:

During the first 5 years of service	1 day for each month of service
From the 6th to 15th year	1.25 days for each month of service
Above 15 years	1.75 days for each month of service

Leave on Half Pay: 10 days for each completed calendar year of service, subject to a maximum of 30 days at a time, and 180 days during the entire service.

Extraordinary Leave: Up to 3 months, at a time, but extendable up to 18 months if suffering from a disease requiring prolonged treatment.

Sick Leave on Full Pay: 10 days in a calendar year, non-cumulative.

Heads of departments, offices etc. must plan their work in such a way as to permit employees to take a certain amount of leave annually, and a longer leave after some years, or according to any special necessity.

There should not be a monetary limit on leave salary when an employee has to take leave because of sickness, or when he is allowed longer leave for pursuing an approved course of study otherwise than on study leave terms.

While the normal limits of accumulation of earned leave should be reduced to 120 days, additional accumulation of up to 60 days should be permitted at the discretion of the sanctioning authority when leave applied for is refused in the public interest.

Hospital leave should be admissible to all low-paid employees, as also to those class III employees whose duties involve the handling of dangerous machinery, explosive materials, poisonous drugs etc. or the performance of hazardous task.

Industrial staff should also be eligible for hospital leave up to 3 months on full pay, or 6 months on half pay, in a period of 3 years.

Maternity leave admissible to industrial staff should be approximately the same as that admissible to non-industrial staff. In the case of temporary and officiating service also, the period of maternity leave should count for purposes of increments.

Study leave may be granted for a study tour in which a Government servant may not attend a regular academic or semi-academic course; and for studies which may not be closely and directly linked with a civil servant's work but which will improve his capability etc. as a civil servant. Study leave should be liberally granted, particularly to scientific, technical, and administrative staff, and in suitable cases the staff should even be encouraged or advised to have such leave. Ordinarily, it may not be necessary to extend the standard study leave terms to industrial staff, but the question of providing them facilities for training and technical education may be considered.

The rates of leave salary during 'departmental leave' should be reviewed. Staff subject to 'departmental leave' should, while on duty, earn leave at the same rate as other staff, and not at a lower rate.

Leave salary may be calculated on the basis of the average of the rates of pay admissible during each of the 10 months in which an employee was on duty immediately prior to the month in which leave commences. However, in the case of employees who proceed on leave from posts, the maximum pay of which does not exceed ₹ 100 per month, leave salary may be based on the rate of pay drawn immediately before proceeding on leave.

An employee granted leave beyond the date of superannuation, or on the expiry of a period of extension of service, should not retain a lien on his permanent post during the leave, or count the leave as pensionable service.

The adequacy and basis of calculation of leave reserves should be reviewed.

2.2.22 Age of Superannuation: The age of superannuation should be 58 years for all classes of public servants, including those for whom the retirement age at present is 60. However, persons already in service may continue up to the age of 60, if they are at present entitled to do so.

Scientific and technical personnel may ordinarily be retained in service up to the age of 60 by grant of extension or re-employment for 2 years.

2.2.23 Retirement Benefits: Industrial staff, on being made permanent, should be brought under the standard pension scheme; those already in service, however, being given the option to continue under their existing retirement benefit schemes.

The right to withdraw the whole or a part of a pension should be restricted to certain very exceptional, specified contingencies, and even then the power should be exercised, and where the original order is passed by a subordinate authority the appeal against it decided, only in consultation with the Union Public Service Commission.

The rate of gratuity should be changed so as to make the maximum amount available on completion of 30 years of qualifying service.

Temporary service, when followed by permanency, whether in the same or any other post, should count in full for pension. Extraordinary service of certain employees in defence establishments should count as half and not as one quarter as at present.

Leave taken out of India should count for pension to the same extent as leave taken in India.

When the total period of qualifying service exceeds completed years by more than 6 months, an additional benefit of half a year's pension may be allowed for the purpose of determining the quantum of pension.

Officiating, special, and personal pay may continue to count in full in cases in which it so counts at present, but in other cases such pay drawn during the last 3 years of service should be taken into account in full or in half according to specified circumstances.

Non-practising allowance of doctors should count for pension.

Government may consider the question of granting some relief to persons whose pension does not exceed ₹ 200 per month, when there is an increase in the cost of living.

The minimum gratuity admissible to the family of a permanent employee who dies before completing 5 years of qualifying service should be equal to 6 months emoluments, except in cases in which death occurs in the first year of service, when the minimum may be 2 months emoluments.

The family of an employee who is a subscriber to a contributory provident fund should be granted gratuity equal to the difference between the amount that would have been admissible had he been on pensionable establishment and the Government's contribution to his provident fund with accumulated interest. If such an employee dies before becoming eligible for admission to a contributory provident fund, the gratuity should be the same as for purely temporary employees.

A widow's and children's pension benefit scheme, on a contributory basis, should replace the existing family pension scheme.

Scientific employees of semi-Government institutions, financed from cess or Government grants, when appointed to permanent Government service, should be permitted to count in full their service, in those institutions as qualifying service for pension, provided their previous employers are willing, in lieu of their contribution to the contributory provident fund, to pay to the government pension contribution for the period of service with them.

To facilitate freer interchange of scientists and technologists between the Government and the universities, the pensionary contribution which the latter have to pay when they borrow the service of a Government servant should be restricted to the rate at which the university contributes towards the provident fund of its other employees.

2.2.24 Leave Travel Concessions: The travel concession allowed to different classes of railway employees should be uniform, and in all cases reduced to one set of free passes and two sets of privilege tickets orders (PTOs).

For other employees, the present concession should be liberalised as follows: (a) it should be extended to such industrial and work-charged staff as are entitled to regular leave, (b) employees who leave their families in their home towns may have the concession for themselves only, annually, (c) for employees unable to avail of the concession in a block of two years, the next block should count from the end of the first year, and (d) an employee whose home place is not connected by rail, should be allowed the concession also for journeys between his home and nearest railway station.

3

Third Central Pay Commission

3.1 Third Pay Commission at a Glance

The Third Pay Commission was set up in April 1970 which gave its report in March 1973. Shri Raghubir Dayal was the chairman of the Commission. The Commission took almost 3 years to submit its report. The main demand of the employees for a need-based minimum wage—as per the norms of 15th Indian Labour Conference—was accepted in principle, though the Commission evolved its own concept of need-based wage.

Composition of the Third Pay Commission

Shri Raghubar Dayal	Chairman
Professor Niharranjan Ray	Member
Professor A.K. Das Gupta	Member
Professor V.R. Pillai	Member
Shri H.N. Ray	Member-Secretary

The Commission recommended a minimum remuneration of ₹ 185 per month. Taking into account the views of the employees, Government raised the minimum wage from ₹ 185 per month to ₹ 196 per month.

The Commission added three concepts of inclusiveness, comprehensibility, and adequacy for pay structure to be sound in nature. Pay fixation formula was also made more liberal. The recommendations of the Commission cost the Government ₹ 144 crore.

The Commission went beyond the idea of minimum subsistence that was adopted by the First Pay Commission. The Commission opined, "the true test which the Government should adopt is to know whether the services are attractive and it retains the people it needs and if these persons are satisfied by that they are getting paid".

The Commission was the first pay commission without military representation on it. It recommended that military pension be de-linked from military service conditions to conform to civil pensions. On the basis of this recommendation, the Government of the day took an *ex-parte* decision and terminated one-rank, one-pension (OROP)—the basis of military pensions till then. The termination of OROP proved unpopular with the armed forces, and provoked unprecedented public protests by armed forces veterans.

One of the terms of reference of the Third Pay Commission was death-cum-retirement benefits of Central Government employees. The Commission did not examine the question of relief to pensioners because in its view, unless the terms of reference were suitably amended it would not be within its jurisdiction to examine this question and on a reference by it, the Government of India decided not to amend the terms of reference. With regard to the future pensioners, the Commission, while reiterating that the age of superannuation should continue to be 58 years, further recommended that no change in the existing formula for computing pension was necessary. The only noteworthy recommendation was that the existing ceiling of maximum pension should be raised from ₹ 675 to ₹ 1,000 p.m. and the maximum of the gratuity should be raised from ₹ 24,000 to ₹ 30,000.

3.1.1 Terms of Reference: Terms of reference for the Commission were as follows:

The Commission was required to enquire into and make recommendations on the following:

1. The principles which should govern the structure of emoluments and conditions of service of Central Government employees.
2. What changes in the structure of emoluments and conditions of service of different classes of Central Government employees are desirable and feasible?
3. Death-cum-retirement benefits of Central Government employees.
4. The structure of emoluments and conditions of service, including death-cum-retirement benefits, of personnel belonging to the All India Services.
5. The structure of emoluments including benefits in cash and kind and death-cum-retirement benefits of personnel belonging to the armed forces, having regard to their terms and conditions of service.
6. The structure of emoluments and conditions of service, including death-cum-retirement benefits, of employees of Union Territories.
7. While enquiring into the level of minimum remuneration, the Commission may examine the Central Government employees' demand for a need-based minimum wage having regard to all relevant factors.
8. The Commission will make its recommendations having regard, among other relevant factors, to the economic conditions in the country, the resources of the Central Government and the demands thereon such as those on account of developmental planning, defence, and national security, the repercussions on

the finances of the State Governments, public sector undertakings, local bodies etc.

9. In case, in view of the increase in cost of living, the need for consideration of relief of an interim character arises during the course of deliberations of the Commission, the Commission may consider the demand for relief of an interim character and send reports thereon. In the event of the Commission recommending any interim relief, the date from which this relief should take effect will be indicated by the Commission.
10. The Commission will devise its own procedure and may appoint such advisers as it may consider necessary for any particular purpose. It may call for such information and take such evidence as it may consider necessary. Ministries and departments of the Government of India will furnish such information and documents and other assistance as may be required by the Commission. The Government of India trusts that the State Governments, service associations and others concerned will extend to the Commission their fullest co-operation and assistance.
11. The Commission will make its recommendations as soon as practicable.

3.2 Summary of the Recommendations of the Third Central Pay Commission

3.2.1 Principles of Pay Determination:

1. A pay structure, if it is to be sound, should satisfy the tests of *inclusiveness*, *comprehensibility* and *adequacy*. It should also be fairly simple and rational.
2. Beyond the minimum subsistence level, the adequacy or otherwise of the Government's pay structure is to be judged by the level of salaries that obtain in alternative occupations. Considerations of supply and demand necessarily play a part, but are subject to certain over-riding considerations. In the intermediate ranges, the limit is set by what the economy can afford. In the upper ranges, the limit is set by considerations of social acceptability.
3. The principle of *equal pay for equal work* may be considered in the limited context of Government employment, or it may also be assumed to have general applicability. Almost all memoranda received have drawn attention to the more favourable terms admissible to employees in the organised private sector than those admissible to the Central Government employees doing comparable work. The demand has been for *fair comparison*.
4. The present wage and salary structure prevailing in organised industry may not represent the structure that would have evolved as a result of the operation of market forces under conditions of near perfect competition, because of the sheltered position enjoyed by the Indian industry. There are many distinguishing features, which are peculiar either to Government service, or to

private trade and industry, with regard to pay, emoluments, conditions of service etc. in the two sectors.

5. In fixing scales of pay, whether in public sector undertakings or under the government, disproportionate importance should not be given to private sector salaries. The uncritical use of comparisons between Government salaries and salaries in organised trade and industry, without considering the work content and the totality of the prevailing circumstances, would be unjustified. The Government as the dominant employer will have to take note of its dual role, both as employer and as the supreme authority responsible for the governance and development of the country. The Central Government should formulate its pay policy having regard to the profound influence that the pay scales adopted by the Central Government exert on State Governments, quasi-governmental institutions etc.
6. The Government, however, should not ignore the fact that if the organised private sector is consistently able to offer higher wages and salaries than those offered by the Government for comparable work, then there would be a progressive deterioration in the quality and calibre of persons entering Government service. The first requirement is an efficient administration, and this will not be secured without a reasonable pay system which reflects changes in the pattern of remuneration in the outside world. Government service should attract and retain not only a high proportion of persons of average calibre but also a sufficient number of persons of the highest ability and competence to provide leadership and to strengthen the administrative and technical machinery.
7. Too large a disparity between wages and salaries in the Government sector, and those in organised trade and industry, for broadly comparable work should not be permitted, as it is likely to react adversely on the efficiency of the public service in the long-run. At the start of a career, the emoluments and other advantages under the Government should approximate fairly closely to what a person with similar qualifications, aptitude and training can obtain from a good employer in the private sector. A greater degree of divergence, however, between the total emoluments in the private sector and under the Government would be feasible and acceptable later in a person's career.
8. A common wage policy should be evolved for public sector undertakings, and an effective co-ordinating machinery should be established, charged with the responsibility of ensuring that pay scales of public sector undertakings should be fixed with the due regard to possible repercussions on other public sector undertakings, and on the Government's own scales of pay. It should ensure that no single unit goes seriously out of line. This mechanism should respond

flexibly to changes taking place in the economy as a whole.

9. A cautious adoption of job evaluation techniques over a limited sphere, particularly for industrial and fairly standardised jobs, seems to be indicated as an experimental measure.
10. There are intractable difficulties in directly relating pay with productivity for the bulk of the Government employees. However, the Government can, and should, forge stronger links than are prevalent now between the performance of a Government employee and the pay he draws.
11. The concept of model employer is open to such diverse interpretations that no precise guidelines of practical value are provided.
12. The Government being the dominant employer should formulate its own principles of wage determination as suited to its needs. Accordingly, it has been found advisable to bear in mind several principles and conditions in recommending scales of pay rather than rigidly adhering to a single principle. The true test of any set of principles to be adopted by the Government is whether the Government service is attracting and retaining the persons it needs and whether they are reasonably satisfied with the pay and other conditions of service taken as a whole.
13. For the majority of posts, the principle of *equal pay for equal work* taken broadly to cover the range of a time scale is generally unexceptionable, when considering the Central Government alone as a separate entity. In the absence of any distinguishing features, employees of the Central Government in different branches should be paid equally if their work is adjudged to be of equal value according to certain well-established criteria.
14. The pay of a post should be related to the duties and responsibilities attached to that post, to the difficulty and complexity of the task to be performed, to the degree of supervision exercised, and to the qualifications prescribed.
15. Simplification and rationalisation of the pay structure has been attempted to the extent possible. In devising a sound pay structure, equitable relativities have been sought to be established not only vertically but also horizontally. There are limitations, however, to the extent to which the existing pay structure can be simplified and rationalised, e.g. a drastic reduction in the number of grades may result in curtailment of promotion opportunities, and may prove unduly costly.
16. When making horizontal comparisons, it will initially be possible only to go by a broad overall assessment of the duties and responsibilities of various posts, and to allocate appropriate pay scales accordingly. Such an approach suffers from possible deficiencies and shortcomings. For this reason, the adoption of job evaluation techniques, first on an experimental basis and later,

if found successful, on a continuing basis is being suggested.

17. The principle of determining the pay of a post according to the duties and responsibilities etc. attached to that post can be extended for fixing the pay of the members of a regularly constituted service. In the latter case, it is possible only to take a broad overall view of the duties and responsibilities of the separate posts encadred in the service, and of the difficulty and complexity of the functions required to be performed by its members. The underlying assumption is that the more experienced officers will be assigned the more difficult and complex jobs, so that by and large there is correlation between the stage reached in the time scale and the duties and responsibilities of the posts likely to be held at that stage.
18. Persons required to possess specified post-graduate qualifications or to undergo highly specialised professional training for the due discharge of their official duties should be adequately remunerated and their pensionary benefits safeguarded keeping in view the additional time and money spent in acquiring these qualifications and the relatively shorter period of their effective service.

3.2.2 Minimum Remuneration:

1. There is much to be said for the view that if additional funds could be made available to the Central Government by various economy measures or by additional taxation and economy in non-Plan expenditure, these should first be used for the amelioration of the people who are unemployed or under-employed rather than for ensuring a minimum wage related to certain norms set by the 15th Indian Labour Conference (I.L.C.) for a section of the community.
2. Fair comparison with the private sector or with the public sector cannot be accepted as a sound basis for fixing minimum remuneration under the Central Government. If there is to be a comparison with the level of wages outside the government, it cannot be confined only to the organised private or public sector.
3. With the development of the country and increase in national income, the Government employees should, in the fullness of time, be entitled to the need-based minimum wage according to the norms laid down by the 15th I.L.C. However, in the present context, the Central Government employees should not be treated as a specially privileged section of the community and guaranteed a need-based minimum wage according to these norms when the Government is not able to provide even the barest essential to millions of their less fortunate compatriots.
4. Even though the fringe benefits result in some saving of expenditure on the part of the recipients or in mitigating the hardship to which they would

otherwise have been exposed, no deduction should be made on account of these from the computations of minimum wage.

5. Since a Central Government employee at the beginning of his career is not usually expected to be responsible for the maintenance of 3 adult consumption units including himself, the starting salary should be so fixed that at the end of 5 years, he should automatically receive a sum equal to the need-based minimum remuneration, according to the Commission's concept.
6. Having regard to the low per capita income of the country, the acute unemployment situation, the state of finances of the Central Government and the likely repercussions of a high minimum wage on the finances of the State Governments, it is supremely important that the maximum restraint should be exercised in devising the new pay structure. Accordingly, the minimum remuneration for the whole-time Central Government employee at the start of his career should be fixed at ₹ 185 per month at the 12-monthly index average of 200 (1960=100).
7. The special pay for certain categories of class IV staff, whose work is exceptionally heavy or involves special risks, health hazards or employment in unpleasant or uncongenial occupations, should be raised from ₹ 3 to 10 per month. Government should take action either to lay down uniform criteria or to prepare illustrative lists of categories for which this special pay should be admissible.

3.2.3 Starting Salary of Class I Services and Maximum Salary under the Government:

1. The starting salary in the class I services, including the all-India services, should be ₹ 700 per month.
2. No change need be made in the present ceiling of ₹ 3,500 per month on the maximum salary under the Government.

3.2.4 General Recommendations on Pay Structure:

1. With the attainment of higher levels of development, marginal differences in skills are of little significance for pay fixation. As a general rule, posts in different departments which are broadly comparable and for which equivalent qualifications have been prescribed should be placed on the same scale of pay unless there are over-riding administrative considerations to the contrary. It was, in certain cases, found necessary to let the consideration of internal harmony over-ride the need for external parties.
2. While recommending the continuance of most of the existing allowances and the abolition of some, no new allowances have been recommended nor any demands for increasing the quantum of the existing allowance have been endorsed except where it was found to be absolutely justifiable on strict and

critical scrutiny.

3. Posts in the various departments which are substantially comparable as rcgards duties and responsibilities, mode of recruitment and qualification standards have been grouped into common category posts.
4. The existing system of time scales has generally been retained with provision of fixed pay at certain higher levels.
5. Long pay scales have generally been recommended for entry/career grades, especially where promotion outlets are limited. For posts filled by promotion, relatively shorter pay scales have been considered appropriate.
6. Except in the case of blind alley categories, a solution to the problem of stagnation should be sought in revising cadre structure and reforming cadre management.
7. Continued progression on long scales running from 15 to 20 years or more should depend on periodic assessment of the employee's performance. One efficiency bar has, therefore, been provided in 10-15 years scales and two efficiency bars in the still longer scales.
8. There should be a more effective application of efficiency bars than has been done hitherto. Measures should be taken to ensure that crossing the efficiency bar is no longer a routine matter and that those who do not pull their weight are denied further increments. Government should also make more frequent use than they have done in the past of the grant of advance increments to persons who have done specially good work and deserve recognition.
9. It is not practicable to adopt any pre-determined ratio between the minimum and the maximum or a rigid time span. In recommending the quantum of increments in different scales, the following broad principles have been followed:

- The increases in the rates of increment, being proposed on account of the erosion that the value of increments has suffered have necessarily had to taper off with increasing levels of pay.
- As far as possible, the same size of increment has been suggested for the same pay range except that wherever in a series the lower scale posts are feeder posts for those in the higher scale, an increased rate of increment has generally been suggested in the higher scale in order to provide incentive for promotion.
- A higher rate of increment has been provided not only in a higher scale but even within the same pay scale towards the end.
- The almost universal feature of annual increments in the existing pay structure has not been altered, the only exceptions being the posts at the top

levels for which the pattern of fixed pay or of biennial increments has been proposed.

10. In future, an increment should be granted from the first of the month in which it falls due.
11. The existing system of over-lapping scales has been continued.
12. In all cases of pay fixation under F.R. 22-C, where an employee is drawing pay at the maximum of the lower scale, he should be allowed a notional increment above the maximum of the lower scale (equivalent to the amount of the last increment in the scale) and the pay then be fixed at the next above stage in the higher scale.
13. In all cases of promotions from one class I post to another class I post, the pay in the higher scale should be fixed at the stage next above the pay drawn in the lower scale irrespective of whether the lower post was held in a substantive, officiating or temporary capacity.
14. The benefit of concordance tables should be available to all organised class I services which have the characteristics of an 'established' service. The benefit may continue in the scientific and technical services where it exists at present. The same arrangement should be adopted for fixing the pay of promotees in services which have a junior and senior scale even though lateral induction takes place at the senior scale level also. The admissibility of this benefit should be widely publicised at the time of inviting applications for recruitment as this is likely to enhance the attractiveness of these services.
15. The device of special pay should be used as sparingly as possible although it cannot be discarded in the case of posts where persons have to be attracted for a fixed tenure from other cadres and departments. The existing practice of granting special pay to officers brought on deputation to the secretariat, or to posts at the headquarters of the departments should continue.
16. The existing rates of special pay in respect of posts in the Central secretariat should continue. As the nature of work in the headquarters' organisations of the Central services class I is broadly comparable to that performed at the levels of under secretaries and deputy secretaries in the Central secretariat, the posts in the headquarters' organisations of these services held by the senior scale officers should carry a special pay of ₹ 200 per month and those held by officers in the junior administrative and intermediate administrative grades should carry a special pay of ₹ 300 per month.
17. The field posts in the Central services class I to which special pay is attached, should, if held by a senior scale officer, carry a uniform special pay of ₹ 100 per month and those held by the junior administrative and intermediate administrative grade officers should carry a special pay of ₹ 200 per month.

18. In the technical and scientific departments also, the grant of special pay for posts at headquarters should be adjudged on the basis of the same criteria as applicable to posts in the headquarters of non-technical departments and special pay be granted where it is justified on merits. By and large, the rates of special pay attached to the posts at comparable levels should be uniform in different departments.
19. The system of special pay be continued in the intelligence agencies and police and security organisations in view of the special requirements of these organisations.
20. The system of granting deputation (duty) allowance is necessary where personnel have to be attracted to hold posts for a relatively shorter duration or for undertaking duties which are not similar to those entrusted to them in their regular line of work. No change is necessary in the existing provisions in this regard. The extent of application of the system of deputation allowance should, however, be limited to essential cases only. The cadre controlling authorities should strictly follow the principles laid down for processing cases of deputation in order to avoid discontent among the staff. They should also keep a check on the number of persons from their departments serving outside on deputation at any point of time so that the needs of the department do not suffer.

3.2.5 Promotion Policies:

1. The existing promotion prospects of class III as well as class IV cadres need further improvement. The specific recommendations in this behalf are as follows:

- Study leave rules may be extended to class IV staff (and in certain cases class III staff) to enable them to improve their educational or technical qualifications. Serving employees may be encouraged, by sponsoring their names and if necessary, by subsidising the fees, to pursue the requisite training courses after office hours, either by entering the industrial training institutes or by joining any other duly recognised institute. Those who are willing to undergo approved courses of training may be given suitable bursaries. In all these cases, however, the extension of the concession should be subject to suitability as judged by the department and should not be claimed as a matter of right.
- Employees who add to their qualifications in this manner may be allowed to compete with relaxed age limits, along with the outsiders, for higher posts. It may also be desirable for the benefit of such candidates to include in the selection tests, certain papers or tests relevant to the duties of the posts

considered, in lieu of certain marginally relevant academic papers or tests.

- There is a sizeable amount of routine clerical work which in certain departments is assigned to posts of record keepers etc. in the grade of ₹ 105-135. Efforts should be made to identify such work and create similar posts in other departments also. These posts may be set apart for the promotion of class IV officials.
- Cases of direct recruitment which are now occurring at certain intermediate levels in class III in some departments should be reviewed to see whether their continuance is justified. In any case, the serving employees who possess the requisite qualifications should also be made eligible to compete by relaxing the age limits, if necessary.

2. For enabling the brighter employees in class II and class III to get quicker promotion, it would be advantageous to introduce a large number of limited competitive examinations. If necessary, the existing promotion quotas should be increased.

3.2.6 Lateral Entry:

1. Persons outside the Government who have gained experience in various avocations, or who possess specialised qualifications relevant to the tasks in hand should be inducted into the middle management levels of the civil services. The procedure for such lateral induction may be as follows:

- In all the class I services (including the Indian Administrative Service but excluding the Indian Police Service and the Indian Forest Service), 10 to 25 percent of the vacancies arising each year in the junior administrative grade or its equivalent grade should be filled by direct recruitment.
- The actual percentage of vacancies to be filled in each service in this manner should be decided after a review of the cadre composition and the requirements of each service.
- Suitable age limit for competing at the selection should be laid down in respect of the outside candidates. Similarly, appropriate qualification requirements and duration of experience should also be stipulated. The experience referred to should be in positions comparable to posts in the Government just below the junior administrative grade or its equivalent.
- In order that suitable serving officers are also considered, they should be allowed to compete with the outsiders for the vacancies set apart for being filled by direct recruitment. The number of serving officers who should be permitted to offer themselves for selection should be roughly the same as the number included in the zone of selection for normal promotion through the departmental promotion committees, not more than 5 to 6 times the

anticipated number of vacancies including the quota set apart for direct recruitment.

2. These recommendations do not refer to services in respect of which separate recommendations have been made at relevant places of this report.

3.2.7 Selection Grades:

1. Selection grades serve a useful purpose by moderating the disparities which might exist in promotion prospects for comparable cadres in different departments. In class IV and class III cadres, the selection grade should generally be introduced on the basis of the following criteria:

- Generally, selection grades should be provided for the posts which are filled by direct recruitment where the number of higher posts to which employees in a particular cadre can seek promotion is less than half the strength of that cadre.
- The number of selection grade posts should not be less than 10 percent but should not exceed 20 percent of the posts for which they serve as the selection grade. For the purpose of calculating the number of selection grade posts, all the posts which have been in existence for 3 years should be taken into account whether the posts are permanent or temporary. The percentage of selection grade posts should be in inverse proportion to the percentage of higher promotion posts available.
- The selection grade should not be granted to an employee until the incumbent has covered three-fourths of the span of the main scale.
- The number of selection grade posts as also the need for their continuance in a particular cadre should be reviewed every 3 years and the selection grade posts be varied or discontinued, as the case may be.

3.2.8 Headquarter Organisations of the Government of India:

1. It would not be advantageous on the whole to shut out direct entry to the section officer's grade.
2. The existing quota of 10 percent of the posts in grade II of the CSCS reserved for the class IV personnel should be enhanced to 15 percent.
3. A regular opportunity should be provided to the stenographers in the non-secretariat organisations for entering the cadre of secretariat stenographers. Out of the five vacancies filled by direct recruitment in the present grade II of the CSSS, one should be reserved for the stenographers working in non-secretariat offices.
4. In the CSSS, a non-functional selection grade should be provided above the present grade of ₹ 350 (500)-900. The proposed selection grade should carry the scale of ₹ 900-40-1,100-50-1,400 and its strength should be 25 percent of

the strength of the existing grade of ₹ 350-(500)-900.

3.2.9 Office Staff in Non-secretariat Organisations:

1. An early comprehensive review should be carried out in order to remove the anomalies in the existing classification of offices into attached offices and subordinate offices.
2. Lower division clerks should be recruited on the basis of open advertisement and a competitive test instead of through the employment exchanges.
3. The existing quota of 10 percent of the vacancies in the lower division clerk's grade reserved for the class IV personnel should be increased to 15 percent.
4. The present system of granting advance increments to direct recruits or promotees to the upper division clerk's grade in the audit department on their passing the confirmatory test should be discontinued.
5. The position regarding selection grade upper division clerks in subordinate offices should be reviewed and only such posts of selection grade upper division clerks should be continued as to fulfil the conditions existing in the accounts offices, viz., substantial direct recruitment to the grade of upper division clerks and having to pass a departmental examination to earn future promotion.
6. Government should review the need for continuing posts of assistants in the subordinate offices after all the offices outside the secretariat have been reclassified.
7. Except for very small organizations, there should not be less than two or more than three clerical supervisory levels. The highest supervisory grade (clerical) should be allowed only in the large offices.
8. A selection grade of ₹ 550-750 should be allowed to the stenographers who are presently in the scale of ₹ 210-425.

3.2.10 All India Services:

A. Indian Administrative Service (IAS):

1. While it is for the Government to devise in consultation with the Union Public Service Commission (U.P.S.C.), the scheme of examination to suit the requirements of the different services, the pay scales cannot be related only to the standards of the recruitment examination.
2. It would neither be practicable nor desirable to dispense with the long senior scale for the I.A.S.
3. It would not be a feasible proposition to have identical scales both for the I.A.S. and the Central class I services. There is, however, a case for narrowing the existing disparities.
4. The strength of the selection grade in the I.A.S. should be equal to 20 percent

of the senior posts under the State Government with the provision that no officer should be promoted to the selection grade before he has entered the 14th year of service.

5. While the existing system of special pays should continue, the number of posts in the I.A.S. carrying special pay should not exceed 75 percent of the senior posts under the State Government (excluding those in the super-time scale).
6. The Central Government should lay down guidelines for the rates of special pay for various levels of posts in the State secretariats. It should not be obligatory to attach a special pay to all posts of deputy secretary in the States.
7. In each State, one or two posts should be given the scale recommended for the additional secretary to the Government of India.
8. The existing equation between the chief secretary and the secretary to the Government of India should continue. In the case of the newly-created smaller States, the equation should be with the additional secretary.
9. The chief secretary, Delhi should be equated to an additional secretary to the Government of India.
10. The Central Government should, to the extent possible, relieve promotion blocks in the affected States by selectively drawing in from such States, a greater number of officers in the super-time scale to the Centre.

B. India Police Service (IPS):

1. The existing relativity between the I.P.S. senior scale and that of the Central class I Services should be retained.
2. The strength of the selection grade in the I.P.S. should be increased from 15 percent to 25 percent of the total number of senior posts in the State with the stipulation that selection grade will not be admissible earlier than the 14th year of service.
3. Special pay should be allowed to the superintendents of police of those districts which are deemed to be more important and difficult. The number of posts in the I.P.S. carrying special pay should not exceed 75 percent of the senior posts under the State Government (excluding those in the super-time scale).
4. The Central Government should take a relatively larger number of senior I.P.S. officers on tenure deputation from those State cadres where the promotion to the deputy inspector general's rank is relatively slower.
5. The amount of initial grant for uniforms should be raised from ₹ 1,000 to ₹ 1,200 and that of the renewal grant, payable after an interval of every 7 years, should be raised from ₹ 800 to ₹ 1,000.

6. A kit maintenance allowance of ₹ 40 per month should be provided to all I.P.S. officers irrespective of rank so long as they are working at posts which require them to put on and maintain uniforms.

C. Indian Forest Service:

1. The scheme of pay scales devised for the Indian Forest Service should broadly conform to the pay structure devised for the Central class I engineering services.
2. A selection grade of ₹ 2,000-₹ 2,250 should be introduced for the conservator of forests on the same principles as recommended for the selection grade in the Central class I engineering services.
3. The Central Government should examine the system of special pays in the Indian Forest Service and, in consultation with the State Governments, list out certain posts on a uniform basis which should carry special pays in all the States.

3.2.11 Central Services Class I:

1. The integrated time scale of pay at present applicable to six of the Central class I services,, should be broken up into separate junior and senior scales of pay.
2. Recruitment to all the Central services, class I, should be so regulated as to enable the officers in the junior scale to generally get promoted to the senior scale after completion of not more than 5 years of service. Proper cadre management and career planning are essential in all these services.
3. The junior administrative grade for these services should be in the scale of ₹ 1,500 (14th year or under)– ₹ 2,000, the maximum being the same as recommended for the maximum of the senior scale of the Indian Administrative Service. This grade should be in replacement of the existing scales of ₹ 1,300-₹ 1,600 and ₹ 1,600-₹ 1,800. If, however, any of the departments consider it administratively more expedient to retain the existing two separate levels, the two segments could be ₹ 1,500 (14th year or under)– ₹ 1,800 and ₹ 1,800-₹ 2,000.
4. The pay of officers on promotion to the junior administrative grade in the Central services class I, should be fixed as per a concordance table. If the application of the condition of 14th year or under for promotion to the junior administrative grade creates difficulties or operates harshly in respect of the officers promoted from the respective class II cadres, Government should examine and adopt a formula which would be equitable and also legally tenable for regulating their pay.
5. The pay scale of the posts of heads of departments in the Central services class I deserve to be considerably improved, having regard to the duties and

the span of responsibilities etc. On the basis of the accepted criteria of workload as reflected in terms of staff strength, jurisdiction, number of sub-offices and other relevant considerations, it should be possible to differentiate between the various changes at this level in the different services and the posts upgraded to the level of joint secretary on a selective basis.

6. While the scale of ₹ 2,250-₹ 2,500 should apply to the majority of the posts of heads of departments in these services in replacement of the existing scales of ₹ 1,800-₹ 2,250 and ₹ 2,000-₹ 2,500, a minimum of 33⅓ percent of the posts in these grades should be placed in the scale of ₹ 2,500-₹ 2,750. If, for administrative and other considerations, it is thought necessary by any department to place some more posts in the higher grade (subject to the number not exceeding 50 percent of the posts in the existing senior administrative grade), such proposals should require the prior concurrence of the Ministry of Finance. No special pay should be attached to any of the post of heads of departments in these services in addition to the proposed scales.
7. The existing restrictions on the pay plus special pay of the officers of the Central services class I, in the posts of under secretary and deputy secretary in the Central secretariat do not serve much public purpose and merely act as an irritant, should be discontinued.

3.2.12 Class II Services and Posts:

1. Having regard to the different roles assigned to the class I and class II services, and to the need for building up cadres to man the senior administrative posts, the existing division into class I and class II services should be retained.
2. The distinction made at present between the class II and the junior class I grades is justified and it is not repugnant to any particular principle. The class II cadre should, therefore, continue as a separate entity.
3. On the demand for a large quantum of reservation for promotion to the class I cadre, there cannot be any common pattern, as the practice differs a great deal depending largely on the needs and organization of the different services.
4. As regards weightage for the service rendered in the class II on the subsequent promotion to class I, some weightage should be accorded at least in those class I services where promotion from class II is, for all practical purposes, to the senior scale of class I, and the extent and the conditions governing the weightage should be decided by the departments.
5. The class II service should be conceived as primarily, providing a promotion avenue for the class III staff, and from the point of view of improving their promotion chances, it would be desirable to avoid direct recruitment to class II, wherever possible. The choice should however, be left to the individual departments, since the decision would have to depend on the size of the class

II cadre and the quality of the class III base from which promotion takes place.

3.2.13 Dearness Allowance:

1. The supply of essential commodities to Central Government employees at subsidized rates is not a feasible proposition. A periodical revision of pay as compensation for rise in prices would also be a highly cumbersome process. The employees should, therefore, continue to be compensated for the increase in prices by the grant of dearness allowance.
2. Dearness allowance should be treated as a compensation to the wage earners and salaried employees against a possible rise in prices over the index level to which the pay structure is related.
3. The All India Average Consumer Price Index Number for Industrial Workers (General) with 1960 base published by the Labour Bureau should be adopted for the purpose of granting dearness allowance to Central Government employees in future.
4. The existing formula where under the changes in the cost of living are measured in terms of changes in a fixed number of points over a period of 12 months should continue. However, adjustments in dearness allowance should be made when the 12 monthly average of the index (1960=100) changes by 8 points.
5. Government should not be bound to automatically sanction an increase in dearness allowance according to any given formula even when the circumstances require that restraint should be exercised on wages and incomes. However, in case a policy of restraint on wages and incomes is adopted, it should not be confined to Government employees alone but should cover the entire organized sector.

3.2.14 City Compensatory Allowance (CCA):

1. The existing restriction that the place of duty of a Government employee should be within a distance of 8 kilometres of the municipal limits of a city for the purpose of determining his eligibility for C.C.A. should be relaxed. The allowance should be made admissible to all employees whose place of work falls anywhere within the 'urban agglomeration' of a city or town as adopted for the population Census of 1971. An 'urban agglomeration' should be treated as one unit of population for the purpose of determining the class to which the city belongs and C.C.A. at the rate recommended for that class be granted to all employees whose place of duty falls within the agglomeration.
2. A city or town which for any special reason may be abnormally expensive but does not qualify for grant of C.C.A. on the basis of population, should be given special consideration on merits.

3.2.15 House Rent Allowance:

1. The Government should take houses on long lease and make residential accommodation available to its employees on payment of 10 percent of their pay.
2. Government should lay down appropriate rates of house rent allowance for different cities and towns not on the criterion of population but on the basis of the prevailing levels of rent. Alternatively, notional rents for different types of accommodation meant for employees in specified pay groups should be laid down for different cities and towns. The difference between the actual rent paid and 10 percent of the pay should be reimbursed provided the actual does not exceed the notional rent; where it does, the extent of reimbursement will be limited to the difference between the notional rent and 10 percent of the pay.
3. Production and verification of rent receipts should be made compulsory in all cases. However, the employees who are at present drawing house rent allowance without production of rent receipts should be allowed this facility so long as they claim the same amount as house rent allowance as they are receiving at present. This concession should apply to fresh entrants also.
4. In hill stations and unhealthy and remote localities where a house rent allowance is now admissible under special orders, it should continue to be paid.

3.2.16 Leave Travel Concessions:

A. Railway Employees:

1. The present rail travel privileges of railway employees should, as a first step, be reduced to the level recommended by the Estimates Committee (Fourth Lok Sabha). The number of passes of the gazetted officers should be reduced to the level admissible to the non-gazetted officers at present. The number of PTOs should be reduced from 6 to 3 per year for both gazetted and non-gazetted officers. The facility for taking attendants on first class 'A' and first class passes should be abolished, but lady officers including lady health visitors and nurses may be allowed to take one attendant provided they are not accompanied by their husband or other male relative. Only those members of the family should be eligible to travel on free passes and PTOs as are covered under the travelling allowance rules for journeys performed on transfers.
2. All railway employees of class I, class II and class III who retire after having rendered more than 20 years of service should be allowed one set of free passes every year. No change need be made in the provisions concerning the travel concession available to retired railway servants of class IV.

3. The present limits for entitlement to different classes of persons should be reviewed to avoid a situation where a very large number of railway employees become entitled to a first class pass on the introduction of the revised scales of pay recommended by us. Those who are today entitled to a second class pass should not become entitled to travel in the first class on the abolition of the second class passenger compartment considering the liberal standard already adopted in the grant of first class passes.

B. Central Government Employees Excluding Railway Employees and Armed Forces Personnel:

1. The existing provision as regards journeys to home-towns once in a block of two years should be continued with the modification that once in a block of four years, every Government employee should be allowed to avail of the LTC for journeys to any place in India subject to other prescribed conditions.
2. The definition of family for purposes of the LTC should be the same as under the travelling allowance rules.
3. The employees should be permitted to avail of the LTC for journey performed during casual leave also without specifying any minimum period of absence.

C. Armed Forces Personnel:

(a) Service Officers:

1. The existing concessions should continue and the limit of 965 kilometres should not apply in the case of journeys undertaken to home-town. Dependent children should be allowed the same travel concessions as the officer's wife once in a block of two years. For travel concessions, the definition of family should be the same as for the civilian employees of the Central Government. The extra leave travel privileges enjoyed by officers engaged in flying and submarine duties should be continued.
2. The use of Form D concessions should be limited to 3 sets in a year, a set covering both the outward and the return journey. This facility should, however, be available in excess of this number for certain specific purposes like children going to a boarding school and returning to parents, journeys in connection with the medical treatment in military hospitals etc.

(b) Personnel below Officer Rank:

1. For journey to home station once every year, the free concession voucher should cover the serviceman's wife and children also and in every alternate year, he along with wife and children should have the option to travel to a leave station with Government bearing the cost of the outward and the return journey up to a distance of 965 kilometres each way. For travel concessions, the definition of family should be the same as in the case of service officers.

The expenditure on account of half the rail fare in respect of family members that is being borne today by the servicemen should be reimbursed to them.

3.2.17 Death-cum-Retirement Benefits:

1. The age of superannuation of Central Government employees should continue to be 58 years.
2. Government should look into the lack of uniformity in regard to the age of superannuation of class IV employees in the railways and in other Government departments and remedy the position as circumstances permit.
3. There should be no change in the existing age of superannuation of police personnel in the Border Security Force and the Central Reserve Police under the relevant Acts.
4. The retirement of Government servants should take effect from the afternoon of the last date of the month in which they attain the age of compulsory retirement instead of the afternoon of the actual date of their superannuation.
5. The existing provisions for the compulsory retirement of Government employees before they have reached the normal age of superannuation which are directed towards maintaining the efficiency and integrity of the public services are salutary and should continue.
6. No change should be made in the existing provisions relating to voluntary retirement of Central Government employees.
7. The benefit of pro-rata pension and gratuity at present admissible to scientific employees on absorption in autonomous organizations like Council of Scientific and Industrial Research (C.S.I.R.), Indian Council of Agricultural Research (I.C.A.R.), Central Universities, etc. should be extended to various categories of technical personnel also on similar absorption in these organizations.
8. The existing arrangements under which class I and some of the class II officers are required to take permission from Government before taking up commercial employment within two years of their retirement should continue. These restrictions should also be made applicable to the employees governed by the contributory provident fund rules and to those who are allowed to retire voluntarily under the existing rules.
9. The existing provisions, under which pension can be sanctioned and continued only if certain conditions, mainly related to safeguarding the efficiency and integrity of the Government service, are satisfied, should continue.
10. Emoluments for purposes of pension should continue to be calculated over a period of 36 months as at present.
11. No change is considered necessary in the existing formula for computing

pension. However, the maximum qualifying service for pension should be increased from 30 years to 33 years.

12. The upper pay limit for the grant of pension should be raised from ₹ 1,800 to ₹ 2,500 per month. The existing ceiling on maximum pension should also be raised from ₹ 675 per month to ₹ 1,000 per month.
13. Death-cum-retirement gratuity should continue to be calculated on the existing basis. The qualifying years for earning gratuity should, however, be increased from 30 years to 33 years, and the upper pay limit for earning gratuity should be raised from ₹ 1,800 to ₹ 2,500 per month. The maximum amount of gratuity should also be raised from ₹ 24,000 to ₹ 30,000. The exemption limit on gratuity for purposes of tax liability should be increased from ₹ 24,000 to ₹ 30,000.
14. The maximum amount of death gratuity should also be raised to ₹ 30,000.
15. The existing provisions regarding service gratuity do not need any change.
16. Government should fix the special contribution admissible to the railway employees governed by the State Railway Provident Fund Scheme as they deem fit, keeping in view the improvements recommended in pension and gratuity in the case of other Government employees.
17. The existing arrangements under which the Government employees are required to contribute partly towards the financing of the family pension scheme should continue. While the contribution of the employees should continue to be equal to two months emoluments, the maximum amount of contribution should be raised from ₹ 3,600 to ₹ 5,000.

4

Fourth Central Pay Commission

4.1 Fourth Pay Commission at a Glance

The Fourth Pay Commission was constituted in June 1983 under the chairmanship of Shri P.N. Singhal. Its report was given in three phases within four years and its recommendations were implemented with effect from January 1, 1986. ₹ 750 was the minimum pay recommended by the Commission. Recommendations of the Commission imposed a financial burden of ₹ 1,282 crore on the Government.

Composition of the Fourth Pay Commission

Justice P.N. Singhal	Chairman
Professor M.V. Mathur	Member
Shri J.P. Kacker	Member
Dr. Gopal Das Nag	Member
Shri. A.K. Majumdar	Member-Secretary

There was a huge difference in basic pay between the lowest and the highest grade in the pay scales of Fourth Pay Commission. The basic pay of the lowest grade was ₹ 750, whereas the highest grade was ₹ 9,000. The pay of top most grade was 12 times higher than the pay of Group D employees.

The Commission recommended to the Government to constitute a permanent machinery to undertake periodical review of pay and allowances of Central Government employees which was not implemented.

4.1.1 Terms of Reference: The Finance Minister made an announcement in his budget speech in the Lok Sabha on February 28, 1983, about the appointment of the Fourth Central Pay Commission. He stated that the government employees had suggested "some time ago that the government may appoint a pay body for revising pay scales". He referred to the change in the conditions since the report of the Third Pay Commission in 1973, the steady growth of employment under the Central Government, the changes in the relativities in the emoluments of the employees of departments inter se and also vis-à-vis other employees, the revision of pay scales and other benefits of State Government employees, and expressed the feeling that it would be appropriate to appoint the Fourth Central Pay Commission. He wanted to consult representatives of the employees before settling the terms of reference of the Pay Commission and stated that the membership of the Commission and the terms of reference would be announced as soon as possible.

Third Pay Commission Scales versus
Fourth Pay Commission Scales

(in ₹)

S. No.	Third Pay Commission Scales	Fourth Pay Commission Scales	Increase (X) Times
1.	196-3-220-EB-3-232 200-3-212-4-232-EB-4-240 (SG)	750-12-870-EB-14- 940	3.8
2.	200-3-212-4-232-EB-4-240 200-3-206-4-234-EB-4-250	775-12-955-EB-14-1,025	3.8
3.	210-4-250-EB-5-270 210-4-226-EB-4-250-EB-290	800-15-1,010-EB-20-1,150	3.8
4.	225-5-260-6-EB-6-308	825-15-900-EB-20-1,200	3.7
5.	260-326-EB-8-350	950-20-1,150-EB-25-1,400	3.7
6.	290-6-326-EB-8-350 260-6-290-EB-6-326-8-366-EB-8-390-10-400	950-20-1,150-EB-25-1,500	3.4
7.	260-8-300-EB-8-340-10-380-EB-10-430	975-25-1,150-EB-30-1,540	3.7
8.	330-8-370-10-400-EB-10-480	1,200-30-1,440-EB-30-1,800	3.6
9.	330-10-380-EB-12-500-EB-15-560	1,200-30-1,560-EB-40-2,040	3.6
10.	380-12-500-15-530 380-12-500-EB-15-560	1320-30-1560-EB-40-2,040	3.5
11.	380-12-440-EB-14-560-EB-20-640 425-15-530-EB-15-560-20-600	1350-30-1440-40-1,800-EB-50-2,200	3.5
12.	425-15-560–EB-20-640 425-15-500-EB-15-560-20-700 455-15-560-20-700	1,400-40-1,800-EB-50-2,300	3.3
13.	425-15-500-EB-15-560-20-640-EB-20-700-25-750 425-15-500-EB-15-560-20-700-EB-25-800 470-15-530-EB-20-650-EB-25-750	1,400-40-1,600-50-2,300-EB-60-2,600	3.3
14.	550-20-650-25-750 550-20-650-25-800	1,600-50-2,300-EB-60-2,660	2.9
15.	500-20-700-EB-25-900 550-25-750-EB-30-900	1,640-60-2,600-EB-75-2,900	3.1
16.	650-30-740-35-800-EB-40-960 650-30-740-35-880-EB-40-1,040 700-30-760-35-900 775-35-880-40-1,000	2,000-60-2,300-EB-75-3,200	2.8

17.	650-30-740-35-810-EB-880-40-1,000-EB-40-1,200	2,000-60-2,300-EB-75-3,200-100-3,500	3.0
18.	840-40-1,040 840-40-1,000-EB-40-1,200	2,375-75-3,200-EB-100-3,500	2.8
19.	650-30-740-35-880-EB-40-1,040 650-30-740-35-810-EB-35-880-40-1,000-EB-40-1,200	2,000-60-2,300-EB-3,200-100-3,500	3.0

This was followed by a statement of the Finance Minister on July 26, 1983, in the Lok Sabha that, after consultation with the staff side of the Joint Consultative Machinery, the terms of reference of the Fourth Central Pay Commission were to be as follows:

1. To examine the present structure of emoluments and conditions of service, taking into account the total packet of benefits, including death-cum-retirement benefits, available to the following categories of Government employees and to suggest changes which may be desirable and feasible:

- Central Government employees—industrial and non-industrial.
- Personnel belonging to the all-India services.
- Employees of the Union Territories.

2. To examine the present structure of emoluments taking into account the total packet of benefits in case and kind including death-cum-retirement benefits available to armed forces personnel and to suggest changes which may be desirable and feasible, having regard to their terms and conditions of service.
3. To examine the variety of allowances and benefits in kind that are presently available to the employees in addition to pay and to suggest rationalization and simplification thereof with a view to promoting efficiency in administration.
4. To make recommendations on the above having regard, among other relevant factors, to the prevailing pay structure under the public sector undertakings, State Governments, etc., economic conditions in the country, the resources of the Central Government and the demands thereon such as those on account of developmental planning, defence and national security.

There was some difference in the terms of reference of the Third and the Fourth Pay Commissions. One such difference was that while the Third Pay Commission was specifically required to examine the demand of the employees for a need-based minimum wage based on the recommendations of the 15th Indian Labour Conference, there was no such mention in the terms of reference of the Fourth Pay Commission. The other difference was that while the Third Pay Commission was required to enquire into and make recommendations on the principles which should govern the structure of emoluments and conditions of service of Central Government employees, there was no such provision in the terms of reference of the Fourth Pay Commission. The Commission took the view that the omission did not mean that it should proceed to examine the problem without determining or evolving such principles. It, therefore, enquired into and evolved the principles or what it called the *factors for pay determination* for its guidance.

Unlike the Third Pay Commission, the Fourth Pay Commission was specifically asked to examine the variety of allowances and benefits in kind that were then available to the employees in addition to pay, and to suggest rationalization and simplification thereof with a view to promoting efficiency in administration. The Third Pay Commission all the same examined this aspect of the matter, but the Fourth Pay Commission took specific note of the requirement and made an effort to rationalize and simplify the allowances and other benefits of government employees. It may also be mentioned that while the Third Pay Commission was required to make its recommendations having regard, among other relevant factors, to the repercussions of its recommendations on the finances of the State Governments, public sector undertakings, local bodies etc., the Fourth Pay Commission was required to make its recommendations having regard, among other relevant factors, to the prevailing pay structure within the public sector undertakings and State Governments etc. This variation was taken note of by the Commission in its deliberations.

Further, unlike the Third Pay Commission, the Fourth Pay Commission was specifically required, under the terms of reference, to examine the pension structure for pensioners, both past and future.

Summary of the Recommendations of the Fourth Central Pay Commission

4.2.1 Principles of Pay Determination:

1. There are differences in the packet of total benefits and emoluments of Central Government employees vis-à-vis public sector employees. It is therefore difficult to compare the emoluments of Central Government employees and those working in the public sector undertakings. It raises several conceptual issues.
2. The public sector undertakings have been created by government for specified purposes, and have adopted their own pay structure. The nature of work there and the conditions of service are different. The pay structure and the conditions of service of the Central Government employees have to be determined on their own merits. The structure of emoluments in public sector undertakings is relevant and has been kept in view.

3. The structure of pay and emoluments of State Governments has evolved over a period of time and efforts have been made to rationalise it. This has been kept in view while formulating the recommendations.
4. Even though there is no mention about principles of pay determination in the terms of reference, it is necessary to set out certain principles.
5. The principle of model employer is difficult to adopt as a concept for determining pay of Central Government employees. There is, however, no reason why the State should not play the role of a good employer in the field of pay determination.
6. It is necessary to revise the pay scales periodically. The aim of such revision is not only to take note of changes that may have taken place in the relevant facts and circumstances bearing on pay scales, but also to fill any errors or omissions that may have occurred in the earlier pay determination.
7. It cannot be gainsaid that the requirement that pay should be equal to the value of the work, is a truism which should hold the field.
8. As observed by the Megaw Committee, civil service is a "very different" kind of organization and the pay determination system for that service must differ in important respects from those prevailing in the private sector. Comparisons are hard to make, because of the difficulty of comparators.
9. Another consideration in determining pay is the level of productivity of the post or service. There is considerable difference in the nature of employment in the private sector, the public sector and the government. So, a method of pay determination which is suitable for one type of employment may not suit the other. The concept of productivity linked wages may not suit an employment under the State which is governmental in the sense of being unrelated to a large extent to industrial or commercial output.
10. Pay structure of employees has to be correlated to the nature and culture of the employment, the degree of satisfaction it generates—both to the employees and to the others—the totality of what it takes and what it gives to the employees, the resources of the employer, public assistance and satisfaction that the service renders etc. All in all, the factors which go in the determination of pay have to be reasonable if the result is to be satisfactory to all concerned.
11. The pay of a post should be such as to attract persons of the required qualifications and calibre to fill it. But the element of pay would not, by itself, be decisive of what government has to offer at the counter. Fringe benefits along with other conditions of service like security of tenure, welfare measures adopted by the government for the employees etc. all together make up the pay packet. Even the social status which the employment carries in

society may weigh with a candidate in making his choice.

12. The pay should be sufficient and satisfactory enough to motivate the employee for the efficient performance of his duties and responsibilities with a sense of rectitude.
13. The salary should be satisfactory enough to retain the employee in his job and encourage him to seek his promotional career in his service.
14. The salary structure should be coherent and should adequately reflect the substantial difference in the nature and responsibilities of the various posts. It should provide satisfactory incentives to performance and promotion.
15. A satisfactory structure of emoluments should also enable the employee to lead a simple life at a level or standard considered satisfactory by him and his likes and the society where he belongs.
16. The pay scale should not give rise to a sense of frustration in the employee. Efforts should be made to provide, as far as possible, comparable emoluments for comparable work.
17. It is necessary that the comparators should be chosen carefully and the benefits should be quantified and an overall and just judgemental view taken.
18. The sum total of all the direct and indirect benefits and not pay alone, should be added up to work out what an employee gets.
19. The effort should be to generate in the employees, a pervading feeling that he is serving an employer which has a genuine desire to look after him not only during the tenure of his employment but thereafter also.
20. The employee should be assured that his emoluments will not erode by increase in the cost of living and government will make an effort to provide as much relief as possible when the degree of tolerance is exceeded.
21. Earlier pay commissions had reduced the number of pay scales. It is desirable to pursue the effort of earlier pay commissions in reducing the number of scales of pay.
22. Pay scales may not always be enough to fit in every kind or category of employment. A suitable system of 'special pay' or allowances can take care of such cases. But the benefit should be kept to the minimum.
23. There should be a system of performance-related pay at all but the most senior levels of service. Increments in scales of pay may be admissible only to those who give fully satisfactory service.
24. An employee who gives consistent excellent performance should be considered for a limited number of non-pensionable cash benefits or increments at double the rate.
25. A suitable and defined criterion may be formulated for performance evaluation including such factors as improved output, efficiency, quality of

work, reduction of paper work, saving in cost, timing of performance, achieving of targets, etc.

26. Government can, and should, forge stronger links between the performance of a government employee and the pay he draws.
27. There should be a pronounced, objective and well-defined policy of promotion.
28. Proper consideration should be given to well established, rational and coherent internal relativities and to uphold them where necessary. However, where an effort is made to reduce the scales of pay, that may sometimes affect internal relativities.
29. Where relief to an employee is not likely to be available under the existing rules or regulations, suitable remedial action has to be taken even if it relates to an individual.
30. Proliferation of high level posts on considerations other than public interest is not acceptable.
31. When more posts are necessary, action should be taken to increase the cadre strength.
32. The capacity of the employer to pay its employees is a factor to reckon and should be given due importance and consideration.
33. Fairness of payments to government employees has to satisfy a double test. It has to be fair from the viewpoint of employees as well as the people they serve.
34. Relativities between major cadres or categories of posts based on functional differentiations have to be continued.
35. Due to the broad-banding of scales, some cases require readjustment to maintain the existing relativities.
36. The revised scales of pay recommended should apply to all posts other than those for which specific recommendations have been made.
37. The revised scales of pay recommended have been elongated with efficiency bars, wherever necessary.
38. There is a need for standardization of designations of posts on the basis of duties and responsibilities.

4.2.2 Rationalization of Pay Scales:

1. As a result of rationalization of pay scales, 153 pay scales have been reduced to 36 ranging from a pay of ₹ 750 to ₹ 9,000 p.m. The proposed scales adequately reflect distinct differences in responsibility at various levels. It should be possible to place any post created in future in one or the other scale.
2. In the case of promotion from the post of under secretary to deputy secretary, the minimum increase may be raised from ₹ 150 to ₹ 250.

3. The special allowance given to Parliament assistant may be increased from ₹ 200 to ₹ 300.
4. The procedure of recruitment to the posts of LDC other than by promotion in the secretariat and other offices may be streamlined to reduce the time lag between the examination and the issue of letter of appointment.
5. It will be desirable to merge grades A and B of the CSSs so as to bring about parity with CSS at this level. To provide further satisfactory promotional avenues for the members of CSSS, posts of private secretaries to secretaries to Government of India and equivalent officers may be upgraded.
6. It may be desirable to prescribe that the existing qualifications for direct recruitment to grade C of CSSS, which is matriculation/SSC with proficiency in stenography, may be raised to graduation with proficiency in stenography.
7. The State Governments should ensure that pay scales of feeder services are not higher than those of all-India services.
8. To remove difficulty in pay fixation of promoted officers, the pay drawn in the feeder service may be protected as personal pay on promotion to all-India service without adjusting it against future increments until such time as the officer is promoted to the suppertime scale.
9. An IPS officer should be a member of the cadre review committee for IPS.
10. (a) Compensation may be paid for the price increase above the twelve monthly index average of 608 (1960=100), to which the pay scales are related; (b) Compensation may be sanctioned twice a year payable with the salary for March and September; (c) In the proposed pay scales, employees drawing basic pay up to ₹ 3,500 may be allowed 100 percent neutralization, those between ₹ 3,501 and ₹ 6,000 may be allowed 75 percent and those above ₹ 6000 may be allowed 65 percent, subject to marginal adjustments.

4.2.3 House Building Advance:

1. The maximum limit for grant of house building advance was raised to ₹ 1.25 lakh in April 1984. This is inadequate and the amount of advance should be related to the prevailing cost of construction of the accommodation to which an employee is entitled. The scheme of advances should be reviewed periodically.
2. Funds available for house building advances are inadequate. Considering the magnitude of the problem, the provision of funds should be commensurate with the requirement of employees who want to acquire or build house of their own. Priority should be given in allocating sufficient funds in the budget for this purpose.
3. The present ceilings on financial assistance available from different sources for house building may be reviewed by government in view of the revision of

pay scales and thereafter as and when necessary to make them realistic.

4. Government's decision to utilize the funds under the Central Government employees group insurance scheme to augment the amounts available for house building is a step in the right direction. Government should also provide facilities by way of allotment of land at concessional rates at different places and allocation of cement and steel through special quota at controlled rates to employees or their group housing societies.
5. While providing financial assistance to government and quasi-government agencies engaged in house-building activities, it should be stipulated that a reasonable percentage of houses constructed by them shall be reserved for allotment to Central Government employees on ownership basis.
6. Government should introduce a scheme whereby employees are encouraged to make some savings for acquiring a house. Accumulations in the fund under the proposed scheme should carry a rate of interest one percent more than the interest on accumulations in GPF and government should contribute another one percent on the total amount at the time of final withdrawal.
7. The Third Pay Commission's recommendation for taking houses on long lease for allotment to government employees is reiterated.

4.2.4 House Rent Allowance (HRA):

1. Existing system of payment of HRA with reference to classification of cities based on population may continue and cities may be grouped into the existing three classes viz. A, B1 and B2, C and unclassified cities. There is a genuine need for granting HRA in unclassified cities/towns where it is not admissible at present.
2. Payment of HRA to government employees should be related to the type of government accommodation to which they are entitled on the basis of pay ranges. The amount of HRA will not change until there is a change in the employees' entitlement of accommodation. This will simplify the procedure for granting HRA and also be more rational.
3. For granting HRA, the employees may be placed in six revised pay ranges based on current entitlement to government accommodation. There should be three different rates of HRA based on classification of cities.
4. HRA at the rates recommended should be paid to all employees, other than those provided in government owned/hired accommodation, without requiring them to produce rent receipts. Employees residing in their own houses should also be entitled to HRA.
5. Steps should be taken to increase the level of satisfaction for government accommodation to as high a percentage as possible through phased programme of construction on high priority.

6. Provision of hostel accommodation should be made on a much larger scale in various cities/towns. Such facilities should be extended to all places where there is concentration of Central Government employees.

4.2.5 Children's Education Allowance:

1. In addition to the scheme for payment of hostel subsidy, the assistance under schemes of reimbursement of tuition fee, children's educational allowance and subsidy for purchase of books may also be given to all employees without any pay limit.
2. Reimbursement of tuition fee as defined under the existing rules may be made at flat rates of ₹ 20 per month per child for class X and below and ₹ 25 per month per child for classes XI and XII. Such reimbursement may also be made in cases where children are studying under the recognized open school system. In the case of physically handicapped or mentally retarded children of government employees, the ceiling of ₹ 20 per month where applicable may be raised to ₹ 50 per month.
3. In case of transfer from one station to another, if the employees have to keep their children at the old station for examination in the interest of continuity of their studies, they may be paid children's educational allowance without insisting on any other condition.
4. For administrative convenience and simplicity in accounting, children's educational allowance may be paid at a uniform rate of ₹ 50 per month per child for primary, secondary and higher secondary classes.
5. The hostel subsidy may be paid from the effective date of transfer even if the children of the employee are already admitted to the hostel of a residential school. The existing rate of ₹ 60 per month per child may be raised to ₹ 150 per month per child.
6. The subsidy for purchase of books may be raised to ₹ 120 per child for secondary/higher secondary classes and to ₹ 50 per child for other classes.
7. In consonance with the national objective of a small family, the benefit of all the schemes of educational assistance, whether separately or in conjunction, may be admissible for two children only.
8. Government should open more *kendriya vidyalayas* to meet the educational needs of transferable Central Government employees and the vidyalayas should continue to give preference to the children of such employees and members of all-India services and should admit other students only when the seats are surplus. Where a government employee is transferred in the middle of an academic session, all possible efforts should be made by the kendriya vidyalayas to accommodate his children. The number of kendriya vidyalayas with hostel facilities should be increased and wherever necessary hostels for

girls may be opened by the Kendriya Vidyalaya Sangathan.

4.2.6 Medical Facilities:

1. The CGHS should be streamlined, improved and expanded by providing additional funds.
2. The government may examine the feasibility and modalities of an insurance scheme for government employees in lieu of the medical reimbursement scheme.
3. A fixed medical allowance of ₹ 25 per month may be granted for outdoor treatment to all employees covered by medical reimbursement scheme.
4. The income limit for dependency may now be fixed at ₹ 500 per month.

4.2.7 City Compensatory Allowance (CCA):

1. There is need for rationalization and simplification of the existing system of payment of CCA.
2. A composite allowance inclusive of the present hill compensatory allowance and winter allowance should be allowed throughout the year at all places where those are admissible at present.
3. There is need for rationalizing the rates of special compensatory allowances to bring about some uniformity in them for places with broadly similar local difficulties, conditions etc. These allowances should be paid at flat rates as proposed.

4.2.8 Travelling Allowance (TA) and Dearness Allowance (DA):

1. It will be desirable to make the groupings of pay range simple and uniform for purposes of TA and DA.
2. Revised rates of daily allowance have been suggested.
3. DA at full rates may be paid up to 180 days where the employee has to be outside the headquarters for a continuous halt either on tour/temporary transfer or on training.
4. Rates of conveyance allowance may be revised.
5. Rate of cycle allowance may be raised to ₹ 20 per month subject to existing conditions.
6. Rates of mileage allowance may be revised by government with due regard to the rates prescribed for Delhi by the competent authority.
7. Entitlements for journey by rail on tour and transfer may be revised.
8. Additional secretary to the Government of India and officers of equivalent rank may be allowed to travel by air in the executive class within the country.
9. For carriage of personal effects by road between places connected by rail, the government employee may be reimbursed the actual expenditure on transhipment by road or 125 percent of the amount admissible on transportation by railway, whichever is less.

10. The existing rates of reimbursement for transportation of goods between places not connected by rail may be doubled.
11. An employee may be allowed an additional fare by the entitled class for both onward and return journey, in addition to the normal transfer TA entitlement, if he has to leave the family behind due to non-availability of government residential accommodation at the new place of posting.
12. Revised lump sum transfer grant and packing allowance will be as proposed.
13. The existing scheme of travel assistance for children of Central Government employees during approved vacations may continue except that the present restriction of 150 kilometres may be dispensed with.
14. The rationalized and revised TA/DA rates may be reviewed and revised by the government as and when necessary.
15. The rules of LTC to home town and anywhere in India as modified by the government are suitable and do not require any change.

4.2.9 Retirement Age:

1. The existing age of superannuation of 58 years may continue.
2. A comprehensive review of factors like the lowering of the age of the retirement, reduction in the upper age limit for recruitment, remustering in different grades after proper training, deployment pattern between difficult and other areas etc. should be made in respect of personnel of the central police organisation and other similar forces like BSF, ITBP, CRPF, Coast Guard, etc.
3. The existing rules for voluntary retirement are adequate and do not call for any change.

4.2.10 Provident Fund and Insurance:

1. The provident fund scheme may continue to be compulsory for all employees at the existing rate of contribution. It is necessary to tighten the rules for advances and withdrawals from the provident fund account so as to reduce administrative and accounting work.
2. Pass books should be issued to all employees showing the up-to-date position of their provident fund account.
3. Funds available under the Central Government employees' insurance scheme should be so managed as to earn higher return on investments, comparing favourably with that of the army scheme and the resultant benefits passed on to the employees.
4. The rates of subscription and the insurance cover under the Central Government employees' group insurance scheme may be increased by 50 percent.
5. Government should look into the shortcomings and deficiencies of

productivity linked bonus schemes.

6. As regards ex-gratia payment, while there is nothing to prevent the government from making such a payment if it so desires, it is in the nature of concession arising out of goodwill and cannot be claimed as of right.

4.2.11 Stagnation Relief:

1. To provide relief to those who reach the maximum of their scale of pay, one stagnation increment on completion of every two years at the maximum of the respective scales may be given. A maximum of three such increments may be allowed. The scheme of stagnation increment should be applicable to all cadres in groups B, C and D and also for posts in group A up to the senior time scale level.
2. In respect of group A central services, the present condition regarding stagnation at the maximum of the junior administrative grade for two years for promotion to the selection grade, may be removed.
3. Government may, after a proper review of the system of *flexible complementing* and *merit promotion,* consider extension to other scientific organizations where it is not applicable at present. It is necessary to ensure that the system is based entirely on an objective assessment of merit and that it is not used merely to provide for career progression on a time-bound basis.
4. There is need for granting special pay for compensating certain genuine cases, but it is necessary to limit the number of posts for grant of special pay.
5. Government may suitably determine the rates of deputation allowance with reference to the revised scales of pay. Deputation allowance may be given at fixed rates and not as a percentage of pay.

4.2.12 Women Welfare:

1. Grant of extraordinary leave should be considered sympathetically for women employees who desire re-entry in government jobs after a prolonged absence due to family reasons. For entering into government service, relaxation of age limit by ten years, i.e. up to the age of 35 years may be given for widows, divorcees and legally separated women.
2. Government should construct single working women's hostel in all major centres of employment. Priority may be given to women in allotment of residential accommodation.
3. Special transport facilities including chartered buses on payment wherever possible may be provided to women employees.
4. Child care services including crèches may be provided in the neighbourhood of place of accommodation of women employees or if this is not possible in or near the office.
5. The existing limit of 180 days on accumulation of earned leave as also its

encashment at the time of retirement may be raised to 240 days.

6. In consonance with the national objective of a small family, maternity leave may not be allowed to women employees having two children.
7. Women employees may be allowed to avail any kind of leave to which they are entitled up to a maximum period of one year in continuation of maternity leave. The facility should, however, be allowed for two children.

4.2.13 Armed Forces:

1. To provide pay progression to all commissioned officers in army, navy and air force, an integrated pay scale (₹ 2,300-₹ 5,000) has been recommended for all officers up to the rank of brigadier and equivalent in place of existing separate scales of pay.
2. In addition to pay in the integrated scale, service officers up to the rank of brigadier and equivalent may be given a rank of pay ranging from ₹ 200 to ₹ 1,200.
3. Separate pay scales have been recommended for officers of the rank of major general and above and equivalent.
4. Army commanders and equivalent and vice-chiefs in the three services may be given pay of ₹ 8,000 (fixed).
5. Officers of the AMC, ADC and RVC may be given higher start in the integrated scale of pay.
6. For officers of MNS, a separate pay structure has been suggested.
7. The officers passing the specified courses for infantry, artillery and armoured corps may be given qualification grant.
8. The starting pay of an infantry soldier may be ₹ 900 per month.
9. The rates of classification pay admissible to servicemen in army may be doubled.
10. The rates of appointment pay admissible to servicemen in army may be doubled.
11. The service officers posted to field areas may be paid an amount at prescribed rates if their families are not occupying government owned/hired accommodation.
12. The rates of compensation in lieu of quarter (CILQ) for personnel below officer rank have been rationalized and composite rates including compensation for furniture, water and electricity/kerosene have been suggested.
13. The rates of outfit allowance admissible to service officers may be increased.
14. The facility of free rations in peace areas may be extended to officers of the rank of major general and above and equivalent.
15. The existing separation allowance (peace) of ₹ 200 per month admissible to

officers of the rank of major general and above and equivalent may be discontinued.

16. The rates of specialist pay for the AMC/ADC/RVC may be improved.
17. The rates of N.P.A. for officers of the A.M.C., A.D.C. and R.V.C. may be revised.
18. The rates of good service/good conduct for personnel below officer's rank in three services may be improved.
19. The rates of flying pay may be revised.
20. The rates of submarine pay for officers and sailors may be improved.

4.2.14 Miscellaneous Recommendations:

1. Study leave rules may be modified to make the position clear regarding the eligibility of employees who have put in more than 17 years of service in government and study leave subject to the existing limits may be permitted in two spells where necessary.
2. Government may suitably revise the leave rules to remove the disadvantages faced by employees who have already accumulated leave to the full extent.
3. The working hours of office staff may be reviewed by government and increased suitably keeping in view the need to maintain and improve the level of productivity.
4. The number of holidays for operative and industrial staff may be the same as for others.
5. The present system of payment of overtime in government offices is not satisfactory and is not conducive to efficiency in administration. It may be discontinued.
6. All employees may be allowed a non-interest bearing advance equal to half a month's basic pay once a year without linking it to any specified purpose. This may replace the advance for festival, purchase of table fan, warm clothing and for meeting expenses on legal proceedings presently admissible under general financial rules.
7. Government may consider favourably the suggestion regarding reservation of certain percentage of seats in professional colleges and other institutions of higher learning for the children of government employees having all-India transfer liability and provide reservation of seats wherever possible.
8. Government may consider the advisability of transferring a Central Government employee with all-India transfer liability to his home state during the last 3 years of his service.
9. The subsidy on the cost of establishment may be raised to 100 percent from the existing 70 percent of departmental canteens.
10. The position regarding temporary employees should be regularly reviewed so

that no more than 10 percent of them remain temporary for more than ten years.

11. Rules regarding use of uniform may be strictly enforced and if necessary further supply may be discontinued if an employee is found to be attending to his duties without wearing the uniform regularly.
12. All industrial employees should have the same leave entitlement and encashment as admissible to industrial employees of railways. All other kind of leave available to industrial employees at present but not available to non-industrial employees may be discontinued.
13. Government may consider whether the present scheme of JCM and compulsory arbitration should be modified as to require that reasons for the recommendation of the Board of Arbitration should be given as far as possible.
14. As far as possible, comparable posts in UT should have similar pay scales.
15. An initial uniform grant of ₹ 1,200, a renewal grant of ₹ 1,000 every seven years and a kit maintenance allowance of ₹ 40 per month for all UT police services may be given.
16. The training of government employee is a matter of great importance and should be arranged whenever necessary, in accordance with the requirements of each department or office. A system of training manuals may be introduced where it may not be possible to depute the employees for training.
17. Government should undertake rationalization of designations of such posts in a co-ordinated and well-considered manner so that inter-departmental differences, which are sometimes called anomalies, may be kept to the minimum if not eliminated.
18. Government may consider constituting a cadre of personnel officers and advisers in major departments.
19. Government may consider expanding the facilities of departmental libraries so that many more officers may be able to utilize them.
20. Some incentive should be given to employees who acquire qualifications which are useful for their work and efficiency.
21. Encouragement and recognition may be provided to professors/consultants who have done outstanding work in high level institutions of teaching and research.
22. Government may consider amending the service rules suitably to facilitate mobility of scientific and technical personnel between government and autonomous institutions and universities, etc. in those services and for those posts where it is likely to be useful.
23. It is desirable that group A officers should undergo a minimum of two

extensive training courses to be suitably spaced in their career. It is fair and reasonable that some of these officers are exposed to generalist posts suitably equipping them by such training as may be necessary so that after successful completion of their training, they may be considered for appointment to the higher posts. For that purpose, a procedure may be devised for empanelling the best officers without regard to the service to which they belong. This will ensure proper utilization of the best personnel for higher posts under the government.

24. Arrangements may be made to provide in-house training facilities for group D employees so that they may acquire multi-functional skills suitable to the requirements of their office or organization. They may be allowed to compete for departmental examinations if they otherwise become eligible for higher posts, and the question of relaxing the age limit may also be examined where necessary.
25. Lack of integrity should be considered a serious defect and treated as such. A sense of self-respect, integrity and patriotism should be generated and developed in a Government employee and one way of doing so is to recognize integrity as an important factor for career progression and to give it a very high weightage while selecting officers for promotion.
26. It is suggested that government may set-up a permanent body which should be responsible for maintaining and updating the basic data on pay and allowances of government employees and to review the pay scales and rates of allowances and other related matter.
27. The principles of fixation of pay of employees in the proposed scales of pay have been suggested.
28. It would be administratively convenient to give the benefit of the proposed scales of pay from the beginning of the current financial year.
29. The immediate additional expenditure on the recommendations is estimated to be about ₹ 1,280 crore per annum. This burden is likely to be reduced to some extent as there will be increased contribution to provident funds, Central Government employees' group insurance scheme, and increase in the recovery of house rent and taxes etc.

5

Fifth Central Pay Commission

5.1 Fifth Pay Commission at a Glance

Fourth Pay Commission had recommended that there should be a permanent machinery to undertake periodical review of pay and allowances of Central Government employees. This was considered by the Government which did not find it possible to accept and implement this recommendation. Various employees' unions, associations and confederations were not satisfied with this decision of the Government. They were pressing over the years for the acceptance and implementation of this recommendation. The matter was discussed in a number of meetings of the National Council of the Joint Consultative Machinery. Finally, in September 1993 Government, without agreeing to implement the above recommendation, promised to appoint a new Pay Commission (Fifth) to review the pay structure of Central Government employees.

The Fifth Central Pay Commission was set up in April 1994 with Justice S. Ratnavel Pandian as chairman. The Commission submitted its report in January 1997. Government accepted most of the recommendations and announced the package in July 1997. The recommendations were implemented with effect from January 1, 1996.

Composition of the Fifth Pay Commission

Justice S. Ratnavel Pandian	Chairman
Professor Suresh Tendulkar	Member
Shri M.K. Kaw	Member-Secretary

The minimum starting pay was revised from ₹ 750 to ₹ 2,550. It recommended reduction in the number of pay scales from 51 to 34. Another recommendation was to slash Government workforce by about 30 percent. The Commission also suggested that the grant of salary hikes to employees be linked to issues of downsizing government, efficiency and administrative reforms.

The Commission recommended that pay revision should, in future, be entrusted to a Permanent Pay Commission—drawing its authority from a constitutional provision—the recommendations of which, made annually, should have a binding character. The Commission, as an alternative, suggested that dearness allowance (DA) should be converted into dearness pay every time the cost of living rises by 50 percent over the base level. In its opinion, DA would normally increase by 50 percent in a period of 5 years and that this relief could be combined with a decennial exercise of pay revision through a pay commission, meeting partially the demands of Central Government employees for a more frequent revision of salaries on the analogy of public sector employees.

The Commission recommended constitution of the next pay commission by 2003 so that its report was available by 2006. Although the Government did not appoint the next pay commission in 2003, it allowed merger of 50 percent of dearness allowance with pay with effect from April 1, 2004.

5.1.1 Terms of Reference: The terms of reference of the Commission were the following:

1. To evolve the principles which should govern the structure of emoluments and those conditions of service of Central Government employees which have a financial bearing.
2. To examine the present structure of emoluments and conditions of service of the following categories of Government employees, taking into account the total packet of benefits available to them and suggest changes therein which may be desirable and feasible:

- Central Government employees—industrial and non-industrial.
- Personnel belonging to the all-India services.
- Personnel belonging to the armed forces.
- Personnel of the Union Territories.
- Officers and employees of the Supreme Court of India and the High Court of Delhi.

3. To examine, with a view to having a proper pension structure for pensioners, the existing pension structure including death-cum-retirement benefits and make recommendations relating thereto which may be desirable and feasible.
4. To examine the work methods and work environment as also the variety of allowances and benefits in kind that are presently available to the aforementioned categories in addition to pay and to suggest rationalization and simplification thereof with a view to promoting efficiency in administration, reducing redundant paper work and optimizing the size of the Government machinery.
5. To make recommendations on each of the foregoing having regard, among other relevant factors, to the prevailing pay structure and retirement benefits available under the State Governments etc., economic conditions in the

country, the resources of the Central Government and the demands thereon such as those on account of economic and social development, defence and national security and requirements of sound fiscal management.

5.1.2 Interim Reports: Fifth Pay Commission submitted its First Report, which pertained to interim relief to pensioners, on October 21, 1994. It was recommended that all pensioners and family pensioners be sanctioned an interim relief at a uniform rate of ₹ 50 per month. This was to be treated as a distinct and separate element to be set off against the retirement benefits to be finally recommended.

The Second Report of the Commission was submitted to Government on May 2, 1995. It recommended the grant of interim relief equal to 10 percent of basic pay, subject to a minimum of ₹ 100 per month. A further instalment of interim relief equal to 10 percent of the basic pension/family pension, subject to a minimum of ₹ 50 per month, was also recommended. It was suggested that dearness allowance be treated as dearness pay for reckoning emoluments for the purpose of retirement and death gratuities, and the ceiling on gratuity be enhanced to ₹ 2.5 lakh. These recommendations were to be given effect to from April, 1, 1995.

It submitted its Third Report on interim relief on August 2, 1996. Interim relief equal to 10 percent of basic pay, subject to a minimum of ₹ 100 per month, was recommended. All pensioners and family pensioners were to be sanctioned a further instalment of interim relief equal to 10 percent of their basic pension/family pension, subject to a minimum of ₹ 100 per month. These recommendations were to be given effect from April 1, 1996. Recommendations contained in its interim reports were accepted by the Government.

The Final Report of the Commission was in nine parts.

Part I was a general introduction to the report. Part II dealt with public services management. Part III was devoted to principles of pay determination. Part IV focused on pay scales of civilian employees. Part V dealt with allowances and facilities. Part VI covered pensions and other retirement benefits for civilians. Part VII concerned itself with the pay scales and allowances of armed forces personnel. Part VIII dealt with their conditions of service and pensionary benefits. Part IX was the concluding part of the report.

5.1.3 Financial Impact of Fifth Pay Commission Recommendations: Implementation of the recommendations of the Fifth Pay Commission imposed a huge burden on the Central Government. It declared hike in salary of about 3.3 million of its employees. Further, it also insisted on pay revision at the level of State Governments. The whole exercise disturbed the financial position of both the Central and the State Governments and led to a public hue and cry against the extravagance of the Government. The Central Government's wage bill before the implementation of the Commission's recommendations was ₹ 21,885 crore in 1996-1997 which also included pension dues, and by 1999 it shot up by about 99 percent and the burden on the exchequer was about to ₹ 43,568 crore in 1999-2000. With regard to the State Governments, the wage bill went up by 74 percent. The State Governments which paid about ₹ 51,548 crore in 1997 as salaries, had to pay ₹ 89,813 crore in 1999 as salaries. About 90 percent of the revenue of the states went out as salaries. 13 states of India were not in a position to pay salaries to their employees due to the hike and hence the Central Government's help was sought.

It is notable that the Fifth Pay Commission did not suggest the steep hike that the Government of the day finally acceded to. It had broadly recommended a 20 percent rise in salary scale. However, the staff unions managed to push it up to a 40 percent rise from the existing levels. Some economists termed the implementation of the recommendations of the Fifth Pay Commission as *fiscal suicide.*

The World Bank criticized the Fifth Pay Commission as the *single largest adverse shock* to the public finances of India. It also said that the number of employees of the Government was *not unduly* large, but there was a *pronounced imbalance* in the skills.

It is noteworthy that the Commission had also recommended the slashing of Government workforce by about 30 percent. It also recommended not to recruit about 3,50,000 vacant positions in the Government. Following the usual *policy of least resistance*, none of these recommendations was implemented.

Fourth Pay Commission Scales versus Fifth Pay Commission Scales

(in ₹)

S. No.	Fourth Pay Commission Scales	Fifth Pay Commission Scales	Increase (X) Times
1.	750-12-870-14-940	2,550-55-2,660-60-3,200	3.4
2.	775-12-871-14-1,025	2,610-60-3,150-65-3,540	3.3
3.	800-15-1,010-20-1,150	2,650-65-3,300-70-4,000	3.3
4.	825-15-900-20-1,200	2,750-70-3,800-75-4,400	3.3
5.	950-20-1,150-25-1,400 950-20-1,150-25-1,500 1,150-25-1,500	3,050-75-3,950-80-4,590	3.2
6.	975-25-1,150-30-1,540 975-25-1,150-30-1,660	3,200-85-4,900	3.3
7.	1,200-30-1,440-30-1,800 1,200-30-1,560-40-2,040 1,320-30-1,560-40-2,040	4,000-100-6,000	3.3
8.	1,350-30-1,440-40-1,800-50-2,200 1,400-40-1,800-50-2,300	4,500-125-7,000	3.3

9.	1,400-40-1,600-50-2,300-60-2,600 1,600-50-2,300-60-2,660	5,000-150-8,000	3.5
10.	1,640-60-2,600-75-2,900	5,500-175-9,000	3.35
11.	2,000-60-2,120	6,500-200-6,900	3.25
12.	2,000-60-2,300-75-3,200 2,000-60-2,300-75-3,200-3,500	6,500-200-10,500	3.25
13.	2,375-75-3,200-100-3,500 2,375-75-3,200-100-3,500-125-3,750	7,450-225-11,500	3.13
14.	2,500-4,000 (proposed new pre-revised scale)	7,500-250-12,000	3.0
15.	2,200-75-2,800-100-4,000 2,300-100-2,800	8,000-275-13,500	3.5
16.	2,630 Fixed	9,000 Fixed	3.42
17.	2,630-75-2,780	9,000-275-9,550	3.42
18.	3,150-100-3,350	10,325-325-10,975	3.2
19.	3,000-125-3,625 3,000-100-3,500-125-4,500 3,000-100-3,500-125-5,000	10,000-325-15,200	3.3
20.	3,200-100-3,700-125-4,700	10,650-325-15,850	3.32
21.	3,700-150-4,450 3,700-125-4,700-150-5,000	12,000-375-16,500	3.24
22.	3,950-125-4,700-150-5,000	12,750-375-16,500	3.22
23.	3,700-125-4,950-150-5,700	12,000-375-18,000	3.24
24.	4,100-125-4,850-150-5,300 4,500-150-5,700	14,300-400-18,300	3.4
25.	4,800-150-5,700	15,100-400-18,300	3.1
26.	5,100-150-5,700 5,100-150-6,150 5,100-150-5,700-200-6,300	16,400-450-20,000	3.2
27.	5,100-150-6,300-200-6,700	16,400-450-20,900	3.2
28.	4,500-150-5,700-200-7,300	14,300-450-22,400	3.1
29.	5,900-200-6,700 5,900-200-7,300	18,400-500-22,400	3.1
30.	7,300-100-7,600	22,400-525-24,500	3.0
31.	7,300-200-7,500-250-8,000	22,400-600-26,000	3.0
32.	7,600 Fixed 7,600-100-8,000	24,050-650-26,000	3.1
33.	8,000 Fixed	26,000 Fixed	3.2
34.	9,000 Fixed	30,000 Fixed	3.3

5.2 Summary of the Recommendations of the Fifth Central Pay Commission

5.2.1 General Principles for Pay Determination:

A. Principles of Pay Determination: Coming to the principles of pay determination, the Commission has examined the concepts of inclusiveness, comprehensibility and adequacy, and the parameters of job evaluation, fair comparison, equal pay for equal work and model employer. The concepts have been applied. Among the parameters, that of job evaluation cannot be applied in such a short period; it can possibly be relevant if a permanent pay body is set up. Comparisons with the public and private sector have many limitations, but these have to be necessarily made not with a view to granting parities but in order to establish some broad relativities. The Central Government can no longer pretend to be a model or even a good employer in the context of other sectors of the economy having forged ahead of it in the matter of compensation packages to employees.

B. Commission's Strategy on Pay Determination: What this Commission has done is to apply a number of parameters simultaneously. One of the principles is the intrinsic value of a job, as shown by the skill, the drudgery, the work environment, the qualification required, the power, the prestige, the perquisites—all the quantifiable and non-quantifiable characteristics which make a job what it is. Then there is the delinking of pay from rank in the hierarchy, which has been introduced through the Assured Career Progression Scheme. A broad framework of qualification-based pay scales has also been hinted at, by trying to bring about a broad uniformity between jobs requiring a minimum qualification of middle, matric, 10+2, 10+2 with 2 years diploma, 10+2 with 3 years diploma, graduate in arts, agriculture, law, science, post-graduate degree in arts/science/commerce, degree in medicine, engineering, technology etc. An attempt has been made to link small entities to larger ones; isolated posts have been placed in cadres and disjointed cadres combined into services. Thus, for example, a subordinate economic service has been suggested to combine all the posts of junior and senior economic investigators in different Ministries and so has the Commission mooted the idea of new all-India services in the field of medicine and engineering and Central services for agriculture, veterinary science, informatics, libraries, archives, archaeology and the like.

C. Minimum and Maximum Salaries: In order to arrive at the new pay scales, the Commission has first tried to fix the two cardinal points of minimum and maximum salary. For minimum salary, the Commission had requested the National Productivity Council for advice. Based on one of the criteria, which adds dearness allowance to pay and then gives a weightage based on the percentage increase in the per capita net national product between January 1, 1986 and January 1, 1996, the Commission has arrived at a figure of ₹ 2,440 as the minimum salary. For the maximum salary, a study was entrusted to the Indian Institute of Public Administration (IIPA). This was conducted as an opinion survey to ascertain what the present consumption level of senior functionaries (joint secretaries and above) in Government was and what additionality they expected in order to meet their legitimate expenses. Although the IIPA had suggested a pre-tax amount of ₹ 36,000 for the secretaries to Government of India, the Commission has been more modest and has suggested a figure of ₹ 26,000. This incidentally keeps the minimum-maximum ratio stable at 1:10.7, which was the ratio determined by the Fourth Commission.

D. Classification of Employees: The services are currently classified into Groups A, B, C and D. The Commission had engaged Tata Consultancy Services for a study on the restructuring of the Government. One of the suggestions made in the study was to change the present status-based classification to a function-based one. Modifying the recommendations slightly, the Commission has suggested a classification into top executives (secretaries, special secretaries, additional secretaries and equivalent), senior executives (joint secretaries, DIGs and equivalent), executives (all others in Group A), supervisory personnel, supporting personnel and auxiliary personnel. The Commission has also recommended that the distinction between gazetted and non-gazetted officers in Government should be abolished. These two suggestions are intended to take bureaucracy out of its feudal past into a modern present.

5.2.2. Pay Scales of Civilian Employees:

A. Number of Pay Scales: The Commission has suggested a merger of some pay scales, with the result that the total of 51 pay scales which existed as on date were likely to be reduced to 34. Reduction of pay scales beyond this number was not found practicable.

B. Group D: Currently, group D scales had been reduced to two. The Commission has given a four-grade structure to auxiliary staff under the new dispensation. The new scales have a wider span in terms of years, so that they run for longer periods. The pejorative appellations of *khalasi* or unskilled worker have been done away with and replaced by the more graceful designation of *shramik*.

C. Group C: In the group C scales, a deliberate attempt has been made to give a better deal to the artisan category, by amalgamating the scales of pay of highly skilled I and II. Many of the categories have been upgraded, partly due to the higher educational qualifications prescribed as essential for them.

D. Group B: In group B scales, three patterns have emerged. In some services like the Central Secretariat service and its sister services in the railways and armed forces headquarters, an intermediate grade of ₹ 2,500-₹ 4,000 has been introduced with the rank of desk officer and 25 percent posts of section officer upgraded to this rank. In the technical services of the railways, ₹ 2,500-₹ 4,000 has emerged as the group B pay scale, in replacement of ₹ 2,375-₹ 3,750. Some group B Services like the Delhi, Andaman and Nicobar Islands Civil Services have been upgraded to ₹ 2,200-₹ 4,000, like State Civil Services elsewhere.

E. All India Services: Coming to all-India services (AIS), the Commission has suggested several steps to improve their all-India character. For direct recruits, the allotment of cadre has been recommended on the basis of merit-cum-option, while for promotees, it has been suggested that 50 percent of them should be allotted to contiguous States in the same region. The Commission has also recommended that each AIS officer should mandatorily have to do at least one stint in the Government of India.

In order to stiffen the backbone of the AIS officers, the Commission has made several suggestions. The State Governments should have only the power to recommend their suspension, giving full reasons, and the Central Government should decide the matter one way or the other within 5 days of the reference. The Central Government should have the power to change the cadre of an AIS officer if he is found to have developed too close a nexus with local elements. State Governments should also follow the procedure of posting officers on the recommendations of a Civil Services Board and through the appointments committee of the Cabinet. There should be prescribed minimum tenures for each post and no premature transfer should be allowed, except according to the prescribed procedure after a reference to the Civil Services Board.

With regard to the edge in pay scales that is currently enjoyed in respect of three scales of pay by the officers of the Indian Administrative Service and Indian Foreign Service, the Commission has not found any persuasive reason to disturb the same and as such the replacement pay scales have been suggested. In order to set the controversy of a single examination at rest, the restoration of the old system of examination which used to prevail before 1979 has been suggested.

F. Indian Administrative Service (IAS): For the IAS, it has been recommended that the Secretaries in-charge of Home and Forests in the States should be placed in the scale of ₹ 7,600-₹ 8,000 (pre-revised) in order to improve their interaction with their heads of departments. It has also been suggested that no IAS Officer should be posted as a district collector unless he has completed nine years of service.

G. Indian Police Service (IPS): In the IPS, the post of commissioner, Civil Aviation Security, which is currently in the scale of ₹ 7,300-₹ 7,600 has been recommended for upgradation as director general in the pre-revised scale of ₹ 8,000 (fixed). All posts of directors general of police in the States have been uniformly fixed in the pre-revised scale of ₹ 7,600-₹ 8,000. Currently, there is no cadre post of additional DGP in the States. In fact, the Ministry of Home Affairs had made an abortive attempt to abolish these posts but had to retrace its steps in view of the strong reaction from the State Governments. The Commission has recommended that the rank of additional DGP be recognized for creation of cadre posts in the pre-revised scale of ₹ 7,300-₹ 7,600. The demand of IPS Associations for abolition of the rank of DIG has not been accepted, as it is functionally required at the level of the range and there was no desire to disturb the established relativities with the armed forces. However, the condition that an officer should ordinarily put in four years of service in the grade of DIG for promotion to the scale of IG has been removed.

H. Indian Forest Service (IFS): There has been a long-standing demand that the Indian Forest Services should be at par with the IPS. This has been accepted. Accordingly, the pay scale of principal CCF has been raised to ₹ 7,600-₹ 8,000, posts of additional PCCF allowed in ₹ 7,300-₹ 7,600 and conservators of forests moved up to ₹ 5,100-₹ 6,150. The post of IG Forests in the Central Government has been re-designated as director general, while additional IGs have been upgraded to additional DGs in the scale of ₹ 7,600-₹ 8,000.

I. Central Services: The Commission has taken special steps to ameliorate the conditions of all Group A Central Services. Uniform career prospects in all services being a distant objective, the best option is to go for a model cadre structure. The distribution of posts at different levels has been laid down as under.

Scale	Percentage of Senior Duty Posts	Mandatory Eligibility Period
Senior time scale	30	5th Year
Junior administrative grade	30	9th Year
Selection grade	20	14th Year
Senior administrative grade	17	17th Year
Higher administrative grade	3	25th Year

5.2.3 Pay Scales for Officers and Employees of Supreme Court of India and High Court of Delhi: On a thorough consideration of the constitutional position and the historical background, the Commission has taken a conscious view that no recommendations be made on this subject. The matter should be decided in accordance with the provisions made in the Constitution and the various judgments pronounced by the highest court in the land.

5.2.4 Allowances and Facilities for Civilian Employees:

A. Dearness Allowance: As far as allowances are concerned, the Commission has noted that the existing formula of differential rates of neutralization of cost of living through the dearness allowance has operated unjustly against the middle and senior management in Government. While the peon's real wages increased by 53 percent between 1949 and 1996, the Secretary's real income has eroded to the extent of 72 percent during the same period. The Commission has, therefore, recommended that inflation neutralization be made uniform @ 100 percent at all levels. While the AICPI (IW) may continue to be used for calculating dearness allowance, the series using 1982 as the base should now be used. It has been further suggested that every time the CPI increases by 50 percent over the base index used by the last pay commission, the DA should be converted into dearness pay and be counted as pay for all purposes, including retirement benefit.

B. City Compensatory Allowance (CCA): With regard to CCA, the Commission has added one category of cities (called A-I cities). The existing and proposed rates of CCA are as under.

Existing CCA				Proposed CCA				
Pay Range (basic pay in ₹)	Class of City			Pay Range (unrevised) (basic pay in ₹)	Class of City			
	A	B-1	B-2		A-1	A	B-1	B-2
750-940	30	25	20	750-1000	90	65	45	25
950-1,500	45	35	20	1001-1500	125	95	65	35
1,500-2,000	75	50	20	1501-2000	200	150	100	65
2,000 and above	100	75	20	2001 and above	300	240	180	120

C. Special Compensatory Allowance (SCA): Special compensatory allowances are granted to employees for exceptionally difficult local conditions in different places. The Commission has suggested that the Government should appoint a committee to prepare a detailed scheme for the evolution of a composite index of difficulty/hardness of an area.

Meanwhile, the composite hill compensatory allowance, bad climate allowance and tribal area allowance should be subsumed under the head of special compensatory allowance.

D. Rates of SCA: The following rates of SCA have been recommended.

Rate Per Month (in ₹) for Pay + NPA + Stagnation Increment					
Areas Listed in	750-1,000	1,001-1,500	1,501-2,000	2,001-3,000	3,000 and above
Part A	300	500	700	1,000	1,300
Part B	250	400	550	800	1,050
Part C	150	300	450	600	750
Part D	40	80	120	160	200

E. Project Allowance: Project allowance is granted when employees work on major projects in undeveloped/underdeveloped areas to compensate them for lack of basic amenities and facilities. The Commission has doubled their rates as under:

Basic Pay Range	Rate of Project Allowance Per Month (₹)
Below ₹ 3,000	180
₹ 3,000-4,499	300
₹ 4,500-5,999	450
₹ 6,000-8,999	600
₹ 9,000 and above	750

F. Training Allowance: Training allowance is currently given @ 15 percent of basic pay. The Commission has recommended that the percentage should remain unchanged, and the allowance be made admissible to all faculty members, trainers on deputation from universities and other academic institutions.

G. Transport Allowance: A transport allowance ranging between ₹ 75 and ₹ 800 is being permitted to all employees to enable them to meet part of the expenditure on commutation between office and residence. However, staff cars are being restricted to top executives and field officers only, all others being served by a pool of hired taxis.

H. Leave Travel Concession (LTC): LTC is being allowed by air for some selected senior categories. Employees can opt for three home town LTCs instead of having one all-India and one home town LTC in a block of four years. An extra period of 60 days is being allowed for accumulation of earned leave. This can be encashed either at the time of superannuation or in batches up to ten days each along with the LTC.

I. Bonus: With regard to bonus, the Commission has shown its inability to devise individual departmental schemes within the short time at its disposal, especially in view of the reluctance of the major Federations to let the issue be decided by the Pay Commission. Broad parameters for working out bonus schemes have been enunciated. It has been stated that bonus should be linked to productivity and not to production. When changes in technology take place, norms should also undergo revision. An eligibility ceiling of ₹ 4,500 per month has been suggested and the calculation ceiling has been retained at ₹ 2,500 per month. The maximum bonus has been suggested as 30 days in case of ad hoc bonus and 55 days in case of productivity-linked bonus. It has been suggested that ad hoc bonus schemes should be converted into PLB schemes within a period of nine months.

J. Housing Facilities: The Commission has taken up housing as an important priority issue. A multi-pronged strategy has been suggested as under:

1. Government housing to have a target of 70 percent housing satisfaction in Delhi and 50 percent satisfaction in other cities within a period of 20 years.
2. Government to augment its resources by taking housing loans from Asian Development Bank (ADB), World Bank and housing finance companies. Employees to contribute to a compulsory housing fund.
3. Provision of leased accommodation and allowing self-lease of accommodation.
4. Government to evolve a suitable hire-purchase scheme to provide one dwelling unit to each employee at the time of his retirement.
5. House building advance raised from ₹ 2.5 lakh to ₹ 7.5 lakh. The cost ceiling range also increased from ₹ 2.5-6 lakh to ₹ 7.5-18 lakh. Rate of interest suggested at lower rates of 6-11 percent instead of 7.5-12 percent as at present.
6. House rent allowance has been recommended @ 30 percent of the maximum of the pay scales in A-1 cities and from 5 percent to 15 percent of the maximum in other cities.

K. Medical Facilities: The Commission has suggested that the network of CGHS dispensary should be expanded to cover more cities and at least one private hospital recognized for in-patient treatment in every town having a CGHS dispensary. All authorised medical attendants in a single station should be organized into CGHS agencies and identified for priority expansion of the scheme. Contribution of employees to the scheme has been recommended to be increased and it has been suggested that individual departments should also make contribution for expansion of the CGHS network. It has been suggested that timings of CGHS dispensaries be divided into two shifts either by paying a split-duty allowance or by dividing the existing staff into two shifts. For out-patient treatment in areas presently covered by medical reimbursement, a medical allowance of ₹ 100 per month has been recommended. There are also suggestions for compulsory medical check-up of employees at Government cost after they attain the age of 40 years, introduction of health credit cards on a pilot basis and for medical insurance to cover the hospitalization needs of employees.

L. Leave: No major changes have been suggested in the leave rules. Some of the minor changes are:

1. Accumulation of earned leave for encashment at the time of superannuation increased by 60 days to 300 days.
2. Rules for encashment of half-pay leave changed to the extent that commuted half-pay leave can be utilized to complete the period of 300 days in case there is a deficiency.

M. Hours of Work, Holidays and Overtime Allowance: Some quite drastic suggestions have been made under this head, in order to increase the time available for work in Government offices. These are:

1. Shift from 5-day to 6-day week, with second Saturday being an off-day. This would mean an increase of 40 working days in a year.
2. Gazetted holidays heave been reduced from 17 to 3, viz. Republic Day, Independence Day and Mahatma Gandhi's birthday. The reduction of 14 days here has been made up by increasing the number of restricted holidays.
3. No holidays to be declared on the demise of any leader, except the incumbent President and Prime Minister.
4. Overtime allowance has been abolished.

N. Women Employees in Government: The Commission has recommended a series of measures to benefit women employees in Government. Some of these are enumerated below:

1. The quantum of maternity leave has been enhanced from 90 days to 135 days.
2. Paternity leave of 15 days been recommended for male employees during the confinement of their wives.
3. Flexi-time and flex-place has been suggested for introduction on a pilot basis.
4. Age of initial recruitment for women has been enhanced to 35 days.
5. Part-time employment on optional basis has been introduced, with the proviso that they can work half-time for 6 years connected with two child-rearing periods at half the salaries, with the period of service counting for all purposes.

O. Advances: Amount of various advances currently available to Government employees have been raised and made more realistic. Car advance has been raised to ₹ 1.8 lakh; motor-cycle advance to ₹ 30,000; scooter advance to ₹ 20,000; bicycle advance to ₹ 1,500 and advance for purchase of personal computers fixed to ₹ 1 lakh. Eligibility criteria have also been suitably revised. Festival advance has been replaced by a general purpose advance equal to one month's basic pay + dearness allowance. In order to mitigate hardships to the families of Government employees dying in harness, the Commission has, for the first time, recommended a provision for waiving off outstanding loans in case of employees dying in harness whose next of kin has not been given a Government job on compassionate grounds, to the extent of ₹ 50,000 for auxiliary staff, ₹ 1 lakh for supporting and supervisory personnel and ₹ 2 lakh in the case of executives.

5.2.5 Pensions and other Retirement Benefits for Civilian Employees:

A. Age of Superannuation: The age of superannuation has been increased to 60 years for all employees, except for personnel of CPOs and armed forces. This will be applicable from a prospective date to be notified by the Government, and shall not apply to those who are on extension.

B. Voluntary Retirement: Voluntary retirement has been recommended under two different schemes. One is the normal scheme of voluntary retirement after a service of 20 years, which has been retained. A special scheme of VRS with golden handshake is being proposed for departments having identified surplus staff. Apart from the normal weightage of 5 years, this scheme envisages cent percent commutation of pension and a special ex-gratia payment @ 1.5 times pay plus dearness allowance for each year of service put in or year of service left, whichever is less.

C. Pensionary Benefits: The Commission visualizes a pension of 67 percent of last pay drawn as being sufficient to meet the post-retirement needs of an employee. This would be met to the extent of 50 percent through the normal scheme of pension to be funded by Government, with the balance 17 percent being made up by contributions from the employees to a pension fund. Additional pension has been recommended @ 1 percent for each additional year of service beyond 33 years. Ceilings on pensions and gratuities have been removed. Gratuity would now be paid on the basis of pay and dearness allowance on the date of retirement. Terminal gratuity would be admissible to those resigning from Government service also.

D. Family Pension: Family pension has been recommended at a uniform rate of 30 percent of pay. 100 percent neutralization of cost of living through dearness relief has been suggested. Such relief would now be available to employed family pensioners also.

E. Ex-gratia on Death: The Commission has rationalized the various schemes of ex-gratia award on the death and disability of a Government employee, with the result that uniform amounts of pension and ex-gratia awards would be available to civilian and military employees for death met in similar circumstances.

F. Commutation of Pension: The limit of commutation of pension for civilian employees has been raised from 33⅓ percent to 40 percent. The commuted portion would be restored after 12 years, instead of 15 years as at present.

5.2.6 Armed Forces Personnel:

A. Role and Operating Scenario: Looking at the role of the armed forces, the Commission has concluded that its participation in counter-insurgency operations should be minimized. Accordingly, Rashtriya Rifles should be disbanded and the Assam Rifles handed over to the Ministry of Home Affairs for being amalgamated with the Central Reserve Police Force (CRPF).

B. Optimisation of Force Levels: The Commission felt that a clear cut role for the armed forces should be delineated and a National Security Council formed in order to advise the Cabinet on security issues. A perspective manpower plan should be drawn up in order to optimize the manpower and increase investment in equipment and armaments.

C. Making Armed Forces Attractive: The Commission has surveyed the scenario of employment in the armed forces and concluded that the shortages are mainly in the short-service commissions. A number of steps to make a career in the armed forces more attractive have been initiated:

1. Cadets during training at Service Training Institutes will now be paid ₹ 8,000 per month as against ₹ 1,500 per month at present.
2. The rank of 2nd lieutenant has been abolished.
3. The starting basic salary for commissioned officers has been kept at ₹ 8,250 as against ₹ 8,000 p.m. for civilian officers.
4. The qualifying service for substantive promotion up to the rank of Lt. Colonel (TS) has been reduced by one year.
5. The ACP Scheme has been extended to the armed forces.
6. Integrated pay scales of the commissioned officers have been replaced by regular pay scales.

D. Pay Structure of Officers: The following revised pay scales have been recommended for service officers:

Lieutenant	₹ 8,250-300-10,050
Captain	₹ 9,600-300-11,400 + ₹ 400 rank pay
Major	₹ 11,600-325-14,850 + ₹ 1200 rank pay
Lt. Colonel	₹ 13,500-400-17,100 + ₹ 1600 rank pay
Colonel	₹ 15,100-450-17,350 + ₹ 2000 rank pay
Brigadier	₹ 15,350-450-17,600 + ₹ 2400 rank pay

The pay scales of higher ranks are equated to the corresponding civilian pay scales.

E. Pay Structure of Personnel below Officer Rank (PBOR): As regards the pay structure of PBOR, the following changes have been suggested.

1. Group D of PBOR has been brought at par with Group C.
2. ACP Scheme has been introduced on par with civilians.
3. Starting pay of infantry soldier has been increased to ₹ 3,000 per month.
4. Classification and appointment pay rates have been enhanced.

F. Allowances: Most of their specific allowances have been doubled.

However, keeping in mind the additional hazards involved in fighter flying and service in submarines, they have been granted a 2.5 times increase. Personal maintenance allowance has been rationalized. Travel entitlements have been brought at par with civilians. Gallantry awards have been substantially increased. In the case of Param Vir Chakra, there is a major increase to ₹ 1,500 per month.

G. Conditions of Service: The Commission has not changed the present scale of rations being granted to the armed forces personnel. However, in order to afford greater flexibility in purchase of items to officers posted in peace areas, they have been allowed a cash ration allowance in lieu of rations in kind.

H. House Building Advance: House building advance has been raised to ₹ 7.5 lakh as in the case of civilians. Rates of compensation in lieu of quarters have been enhanced.

I. Leave Entitlements: Leave encashment has been raised from 240 days to 300 days and proportionately for lower categorizations. Encashment of leave authorized at par with civilian employees.

J. Pension: The weightage in qualifying service for pension has been increased by two years. Family pension has been rationalized. Provisions on re-marriage of widows have been liberalized. Disability pensions have been thoroughly restructured as under:

1. Broad banding of degree of disability has been carried out, with those boarded out being treated as having 50 percent disability, those between 50 and 75 percent as having 75 percent disability and those between 75 and 100 percent treated as having 100 disability.
2. The attributability of disability to service is now to be judged by the officer higher in rank to the commanding officer.
3. The extent of disability once determined continues for life, unless review is demanded by the individual himself.

K. Past Pensioners: The scheme of granting near parity in pensions for past pensioners as is the case of civilians has been extended to armed forces personnel.

L. Ex-servicemen: Percentage of reservation of ex-servicemen has been proposed to be increased from 10 to 25 percent in CPOs. There is also a suggestion for recruitment of CPO personnel for short service commissions in the armed forces, followed by a lateral transfer to the CPOs after seven years of service. Two committees, one under the Raksha Rajya Mantri and the other under the additional secretary, Ministry of Defence have been recommended for monitoring resettlement of ex-servicemen.

M. Medical Allowance: Medical Allowance @ ₹ 100 per month has also been suggested for armed forces pensioners, living in remote areas where normal health facilities are not available.

5.2.7 Other Matters:

A. Tax on Income: The Commission has felt that the salaries and pensions recommended by it are not really adequate if they are to be fully taxed. Accordingly, it has recommended that all allowances and pensions should be paid net of taxes.

B. Fixation of Pay: With regard to fixation of pay in the revised scales, the Commission has suggested that one additional increment in the revised scale should be granted in case there is bunching of four batches of employees at the minimum of the scale. This is an improvement on the Fourth CPC where one increment for bunching of five batches was recommended.

C. Date of Effect: It has been suggested that the revised pay scales, dearness allowance and pension should be given in retrospective effect w.e.f. January 1, 1996. All other allowances, including CCA, HRA etc. should be made applicable prospectively.

D. Financial Implications: The Commission has estimated that the additional financial implications for one year would come to ₹ 8,800 crore. However, this figure would be reduced to ₹ 7,300 crore for the financial year 1997-98, if we deduct the savings expected from the postponement of retirement benefits. Arrears for fifteen months are to be paid only for some of the items listed above and the financial implication is estimated at ₹ 5,462.50 crore. As a third instalment of interim relief is to be deducted from this, the net additionality comes to ₹ 3,962.50 crore. The Commission has suggested that 50 percent of the arrears could be paid in cash and the rest deposited in the GPF accounts of the employees. Thus, the total financial implications of implementing the Pay Commission's Report for a period of 27 months from January 1, 1996 to March 31, 1998 is likely to be ₹ 11,262.50 crore.

E. Need for Continuing Machinery for Pay Revision: The Commission has recommended that pay revision should, in future, be entrusted to a permanent pay commission drawing its authority from a Constitutional provision, whose recommendations should have a binding character. Pay should be revised annually as in other countries. As an alternative, it has been suggested that dearness allowance should be converted into dearness pay every time the cost of living rises by 50 percent over the base level. This would imply a revision of pay every 4 to 5 years. The final option is to have a decennial exercise as at present, but with fixed dates. The Commission has suggested that the date of constitution of the next pay commission should not be later than January 1, 2003 and the date of implementation of its recommendations should be January 1, 2006, irrespective of when its report is submitted.

Proposed Scale of Pay

S. No.	Existing Standard Scales of Pay (₹)	Grades	Revised Standard Scales of Pay (₹)	Span in Years
1.	750-12-870-14-940	S-1	2,440-40-3,200	19
2.	775-12-871-14-1,025	S-2	2,550-45-3,540	22
3.	800-15-1,010-20-1,150	S-3	2,650-50-4,000	27
4.	825-15-900-20-1,200	S-4	2,750-55-4,400	30
5.	950-20-1,150-25-1,400 950-20-1,150-25-1,500 1,150-25-1,500	S-5	3,050-70-4,590	22
6.	975-25-1,150-30-1,540 975-25-1,150-30-1,660	S-6	3,200-85-4,900	20
7.	1,200-30-1,440-30-1,800 1,200-30-1,560-40-2,040 1,320-30-1,560-40-2,040	S-7	4,000-100-6,000	20
8.	1,350-30-1,440-40-1,800-50-2,200 1,400-40-1,800-50-2,300	S-8	4,500-125-7,000	20
9.	1,400-40-1,600-50-2,300-60-2,600 1,600-50-2,300-60-2,660	S-9	5,000-150-8,000	20
10.	1,640-60-2,600-75-2,900	S-10	5,500-175-9,000	20
11.	2,000-60-2,120	S-11	6,500-200-6,900	2
12.	2,000-60-2,300-75-3,200 2,000-60-2,300-75-3,200-100-3,500	S-12	6,500-200-10,500	20
13.	2,375-75-3,200-100-3,500 2,375-75-3,200-100-3,500-125-3,750	S-13	7,000-225-11,500	20
*	2,500-4,000 (proposed new pre-revised scale)	S-14	7,500-250-12,000	18
14.	2,200-75-2,800-100-4,000 2,300-100-2,800	S-15	8,000-275-13,500	20
15.	2630 Fixed	S-16	9,000 Fixed	
16.	2,630-75-2,780	S-17	9,000-275-9,550	2
17.	3,150-100-,3350	S-18	10,325-325-10,975	2
18.	3,000-125-3,625 3,000-100-3,500-125-4,500 3,000-100-3,500-125-5,000	S-19	10,000-325-15,200	16
19.	3,200-100-3,700-125-4,700	S-20	10,650-325-15,850	16
20.	3,700-150-4,450 3,700-125-4,700-150-5,000	S-21	12,000-375-16,500	12
21.	3,950-125-4,700-150-5,000	S-22	12,750-375-16,500	10

22.	3,700-125-4,950-150-5,700	S-23	12,000-375-18,000	16
23.	4,100-125-4,850-150-5,300 4,500-150-5,700	S-24	14,300-400-18,300	10
24.	4,800-150-5,700	S-25	15,100-400-18,300	8
25.	5,100-150-5,700 5,100-150-6,150 5,100-150-5,700-200-6,300	S-26	16,400-450-20,000	8
26.	5,100-150-6,300-200-6,700	S-27	16,400-450-20,900	10
27.	4,500-150-5,700-200-7,300	S-28	14,300-450-22,400	18
28.	5,900-200-6,700 5,900-200-7,300	S-29	18,400-500-22,400	8
29.	7,300-100-7,600	S-30	22,400-525-24,500	4
30.	7,300-200-7,500-250-8,000	S-31	22,400-600-26,000	6
31.	7,600 Fixed 7,600-100-8,000	S-32	24,050-650-26,000	3
32.	8,000 Fixed	S-33	26,000 Fixed	-
33.	9,000 Fixed	S-34	30,000 Fixed	-

6

Sixth Central Pay Commission

6.1 Sixth Pay Commission at a Glance

Initially, the Government refused to set up Sixth Pay Commission to review the pay and allowances of Central Government employees. The finance minister told that there was no need to constitute a pay commission since 50 percent of the dearness allowance was already merged with the basic pay. The employees had threatened to go on a nationwide strike if the government failed to set up a new pay commission. In July 2006, the Cabinet approved the setting up of the Sixth Pay Commission which was constituted on October 5, 2006 for revising the salaries of Central Government employees. The Commission was set up under the chairmanship of Justice B.N. Srikrishna with a timeframe of 18 months.

Composition of the Commission

Justice B. N. Srikrishna	Chairman
Professor Ravindra Dholakia	Member
Shri J.S. Mathur	Member
Shrimati Sushama Nath	Member Secretary

Report of the Commission was submitted to Finance Minister Mr. P. Chidambaram on March 24, 2008. The Cabinet approved the recommendations of the Commission with some modifications in August 2008. Revised pay scales were implemented with effect from January 1, 2006. The pay structure was so devised as to provide a decent entry grade and smooth career progression without any stagnation.

For fixing minimum salary, the Commission was mainly guided by various factors like ensuring fair wages keeping in view the capacity of the Government to pay, the inflationary impact of such increase on the economy in general and on the State Governments, various autonomous bodies and other organizations which followed the Central Government pattern of pay.

While formulating pay scales with upward revision and fixing the minimum salary at entry level at ₹ 6,660 (basic pay ₹ 4,860 and grade pay ₹ 1,800) and maximum at ₹ 80,000 at secretary level, the Commission mainly focused on removing ambiguity in respect of the existing pay scales and introducing the idea of *pay bands*, while reducing the number of pay scales. It recommended for removal of Group D cadre.

The Commission recommended introduction of contractual appointments for selected posts, particularly those requiring high professional skills. Under this, suitable persons from outside could be inducted in the Government. After the expiry of the tenure, the concerned employee may renegotiate the contract or leave.

A major departure from the earlier pay commissions was made in respect of pay scales. For the first time, the Commission recommended running pay bands for civilian employees as well as for the defence forces. It may be recalled that the Fourth Pay Commission had recommended running pay bands for defence forces that were implemented.

The Fifth Pay Commission, however, recommended specific pay scales for civilians as well as defence forces personnel. A conscious departure was made in recommending running pay bands because of the inherent advantages of such pay scales.

6.1.1 Terms of Reference: The terms of reference of the Commission were as under:

1. To examine the principles, the date of effect thereof that should govern the structure of pay, allowances and other facilities/benefits whether in cash or in kind to the following categories of employees:
   - Central Government employees—industrial and non-industrial.
   - Personnel belonging to the all-India services.
   - Personnel belonging to the defence forces.
   - Personnel of the Union Territories.
   - Officers and employees of the Indian audit and accounts department.
   - Members of the regulatory bodies (excluding the RBI) set up under Acts of Parliament.
2. To transform the Central Government organisations into modern, professional and citizen-friendly entities that are dedicated to the service of the people.
3. To work out a comprehensive pay package for the categories of Central Government employees that is suitably linked to promoting efficiency, productivity and economy through rationalization of structures, organizations, systems and processes within the Government, with a view to leveraging economy, accountability, responsibility, transparency, assimilation of technology and discipline.
4. To harmonize the functioning of the Central Government organisations with

the demands of the emerging global economic scenario. This would also take into account, among other relevant factors, the totality of benefits available to the employees, need of rationalization and simplification, thereof, the prevailing pay structure and retirement benefits available under the Central public sector undertakings, the economic conditions in the country, the need to observe fiscal prudence in the management of the economy, the resources of the Central Government and the demands thereon on account of economic and social development, defence, national security and the global economic scenario, and the impact upon the finances of the States if the recommendations are adopted by the States.

5. To examine the principles which should govern the structure of pension, death-cum-retirement gratuity, family pension and other terminal or recurring benefits having financial implications for the present and former Central Government employees appointed before January 1, 2004.
6. To make recommendations with respect to the general principles, financial parameters and conditions which should govern payment of bonus and the desirability and feasibility of introducing productivity linked incentive scheme in place of the existing ad hoc bonus scheme in various departments and to recommend specific formulae for determining the productivity index and other related parameters.
7. To examine desirability and the need to sanction any interim relief till the time the recommendations of the Commission are made and accepted by the Government.

Through a subsequent Resolution dated August 8, 2007, the terms of reference were enlarged to include the officers and employees of the Supreme Court.

Sixth Pay Commission was the first Central Pay Commission to be constituted after the coming into force of the Right to Information (RTI) and Fiscal Responsibility and Budget Management (FRBM) Acts. The Government machinery, therefore, had to gear up for better performance under stricter fiscal discipline and delivery mechanisms. These imperatives were reflected in the terms of reference of the Sixth Pay Commission which made it incumbent on the Commission to recommend systemic changes for: (a) transforming the Central Government organizations into modern, professional and citizen-friendly entities that are dedicated to the service of the people and (b) harmonizing functioning of the Central Government organizations with the demands of the emerging global economic scenario.

Term of reference at serial number 2 envisaged transforming the Central Government organizations into modern, professional and citizen-friendly entities that were dedicated to the service of the people. While the earlier Commissions were required to examine the work methods and work environment and to suggest rationalization and simplifications therein with a view to promoting efficiency and optimizing the size, it was for the first time that a Central Pay Commission was asked to look into the measures that would improve the delivery mechanisms which had a direct bearing on the services provided by various Government agencies to the common citizens.

Further, term of reference at serial number 4 made it incumbent upon the Commission to harmonize the functioning of the Central Government organizations with the demands of the emerging global economic scenario.

Sixth Pay Commission, therefore, had not only to evolve a proper pay package for the Government employees but also to make recommendations rationalizing the governmental structure with a view to improving the delivery mechanisms for providing better services to the common man. In addition, linking the pay packages with simplification of systems and processes within the Government, greater delegation with emphasis on accountability, responsibility and assimilation of technology etc. were the Commission's guiding philosophy.

The Commission achieved these objectives through reduction of layers within the Governmental structure so that decision-making and delivery was expedited. In the process, a number of superfluous levels were removed. This simplification was also reflected in the entire scheme of pay scales which was substituted by a system of running pay bands, where the existing 35 pay scales were replaced by 4 running pay bands, containing 20 grades. Additionally, the posts of cabinet secretary/equivalent and secretary to Government of India/equivalent were placed in distinct pay scales. A system that primarily laid emphasis on delivery and end results and which continuously rewarded performance was put in place by incorporating features like performance related incentive scheme (PRIS) and variable increments in the basic scheme of pay scales. This was not a new concept. Many of the earlier Central Pay Commissions, as well as various expert committees constituted in the past, had recommended performance related incentives in one form or the other. In its Report, however, the Commission tried to devise a workable and practical model by which the concept could be implemented in the Government. The PRIS recommended by the Commission envisaged a pecuniary component, over and above the salary, for higher performance that would be judged by improved delivery to the end user by an external independent agency. This scheme of PRIS was recommended to be implemented in all ministries/departments/organisations of the Central Government in a phased manner.

By incorporating systemic changes in the existing procedure of appointments, efforts were made to ensure a young and dynamic bureaucracy, with a result-oriented approach, where the best persons available were selected for holding specific posts. While proposing these changes, the Commission also kept in view the capacity of the Government to pay and the principle that every rupee spent on allowances, facilities and salaries of Government employees was translated into a specific measure for public good.

Sixth Pay Commission was given a period of 18 months to submit the Report. The Commission initiated its work immediately after the date of its notification on October 5, 2006. The Commission adopted a totally delayered approach where no hierarchical levels were allowed to exist and all functionaries could freely discuss the concerned issues with any one in the Commission irrespective of their hierarchy. This approach facilitated expeditious decision-making and the Commission was able to finish its task well within the stipulated timeframe with a very small complement of staff.

Government constituted the Sixth Pay Commission at a time of fast and accelerating economic development, emerging trade and commercial practices, increasing globalization of trade and industry with greater emphasis on increasing investment flows and transfer of technology. Indian economy was rapidly getting integrated with the rest of the world. In the economic and financial sectors, the earlier era of protectionism—where the Government largely played the role of a monopolistic supplier or of a restrictor or controller—had changed. The principal role of the Government was perceived to be that of a facilitator and regulator in the various economic activities. An imperative and urgent need existed to harmonize the functioning of the Central Government organisations with the demands of the emerging global economic scenario. In the social/developmental sectors—especially in the fields of food security, elementary education, primary health care, and rural/urban development—the functioning of government organizations had to be improved to make them more professional, cost-efficient, citizen-friendly and delivery-oriented.

Recommendations were also made to simplify the procedure for computation of pension. The Commission recommended delinking the payment of full pension on completing 33 years of qualifying service. Higher rates of pension were recommended for retirees on attaining the age of 80, 85, 90, 95 and 100 years. A revised commutation factor for commuting pension was also suggested taking into account the prevailing mortality rates, interest rates and the fact that the commuted portion is restorable after 15 years.

6.2 Summary of the Recommendations of the Sixth Central Pay Commission

6.2.1 Date of Implementation: Implementation of the revised pay scales to be done retrospectively from January 1, 2006. Recommendations relating to allowances to be implemented prospectively.

6.2.2 Running Pay Bands: Introduction of running pay bands for all posts in the Government presently existing in scales below that of ₹ 26,000 (fixed). Four distinct running pay bands being recommended—one running band each for all categories of employees in groups B and C (posts in the scale of ₹ 5,000-₹ 8,000 have, as a result of delayering and elongation of certain scales, been placed in Group B) with 2 running pay bands for Group A posts. All posts presently in Group D, after retraining and multi-skilling of the present incumbents, to be upgraded and placed in the lowest grade of pay band PB-1. The posts of secretary to Government of India/equivalent and cabinet secretary/equivalent to be kept in distinct pay scales. A separate running pay band, designated as 1S scale, is not to be counted for any purpose as no future recruitment is to be made in this grade and all the present Group D employees not possessing the prescribed qualifications are to be retrained and thereafter upgraded and placed in the Group C running pay band once they are suitably retrained.

6.2.3 Minimum and Maximum Salary: Minimum salary at the entry level of PB-1 pay band to be ₹ 6,660 (₹ 4,860 as pay in the pay band plus ₹ 1,800 as grade pay); maximum salary at the level of secretary/equivalent to be ₹ 80,000. The minimum:maximum ratio 1:12.

6.2.4 Grade Pay and Promotions in Running Pay Bands: All the employees belonging to Groups A, B, C and D to be placed in distinct running pay bands. Every post, barring that of secretary/equivalent and cabinet secretary/equivalent to have a distinct grade pay attached to it. Grade pay (being a fixed amount attached to each post in the hierarchy) to determine the status of a post with (apart from the two apex scales of Secretary/equivalent and Cabinet Secretary/equivalent that do not carry any grade pay) a senior post being given higher grade pay. The total number of grades reduced to 20 spread across four distinct running pay bands; one apex scale and another grade for the post of cabinet secretary/equivalent as against 35 standard pay scales existing earlier. At the time of promotion from one post to another in the same running pay band, the grade pay attached to posts in different levels within the same running pay band to change. Additionally, increase in form of one increment to be given at the time of promotion. A person stagnating at the maximum of any pay band for more than one year continuously to be placed in the immediate next higher pay band without any change in the grade pay.

6.2.5 Annual Increment: Annual increments to be paid in form of two and half percent of the total of pay in the pay band and the corresponding grade pay. The date of annual increments, in all cases, to be first of July. Employees completing 6 months and above in the scale as on July 1 to be eligible.

6.2.6 Variable Increments: Another form of differential increments for Group A Pay Band PB-3 introduced, where annual increments in the band will vary depending upon the performance. Eighty percent or more employees in the grade to be allowed normal increment at the rate of 2.5 percent with the high performers (not exceeding 20 percent) during the year being allowed increment at a higher rate of 3.5 percent. Government advised to extend the scheme of variable increments in running pay bands PB1 and PB2.

6.2.7 Pay Scales of Defence Forces: Introduction of running pay bands at par with those recommended for civilians in respect of the defence forces.

DG (AFMS) placed in the apex grade of ₹ 80,000 (fixed). Only two trade groups to be retained for personnel below officer ranks with the earlier trade groups Y and Z being merged. The personnel in trade group X to have a separate X group pay.

6.2.8 Performance Related Incentive Scheme (PRIS): Introduction of PRIS in the Government under which employees to be eligible for pecuniary remuneration over and above the pay. PRIS to replace ad hoc bonus scheme immediately and eventually replace PLB; PRIS to be budget neutral.

6.2.9 Dearness Allowance: Base year of the consumer price index (CPI) to be revised as frequently as feasible. Formulation of a separate index for Government employees suggested. National Statistical Commission to carry out this exercise.

6.2.10 Other Allowances: Existing rates of most of the allowances to be doubled both in case of defence forces as well as civilian employees.

Existing rates of HRA to be retained for A-1 cities with A, B-1 and B-2 cities being given this allowance at the rate of 20 percent and C/unclassified cities being given the allowance at the rate of 10 percent.

CCA to be subsumed in transport allowance and the rates of this allowance to be increased by 4 times.

Travel entitlements to be paid on actuals.

Rates of education allowance reimbursement to be raised from existing ₹ 50 to ₹ 1,000 per child per month, subject to the maximum of two children. Hostel subsidy to be raised from existing ₹ 300 per month to ₹ 3,000 per month.

Risk allowance to be replaced by risk insurance.

All the fixed allowances made inflation proof with provisions of automatic revision whenever dearness allowance payable on revised pay bands goes up by 50 percent. Transport allowance to be increased every year on the basis of the increase in the dearness allowance.

Encashment of earned leave in case of defence forces personnel delinked from the number of years of service. All defence forces personnel to be eligible for leave encashment of up to 300 days at the time of retirement/discharge.

6.2.11 Medical Facilities: A new medical insurance scheme recommended for Government employees. The scheme to be optional for existing Central Government employees and pensioners. New Government employees and pensioners to be compulsorily covered by the scheme.

6.2.12 Pension: Fitment formula recommended for serving employees to be extended in case of existing pensioners/family pensioners.

Rates of constant attendant allowance to be increased by five times to ₹ 3,000 per month.

Pension to be paid at 50 percent of the average emoluments/last pay drawn (whichever is more beneficial) without linking it to 33 years of qualifying service for grant of full pension.

A liberal severance package for employees, leaving service between 15 to 20 years of service.

Higher rates of pension for retirees and family pensioners on attaining the age of 80, 85, 90, 95 and 100 years.

Revision of the commutation table suggested for commutation of pension.

Framing of an appropriate insurance scheme suggested for meeting the OPD needs of pensioners in non-CGHS areas.

6.2.13 Other Recommendations:

1. **Advances:** A new mechanism for grant of advances under which an employee will take the advance from an approved bank and the Government will give an interest subsidy equal to two percentage points on the rate of interest being charged by the bank to the employee. Existing limits of various advances increased and provisions made for their automatic revision periodically.
2. **Public Holidays:** Continuation of five day week. Government offices to remain closed only on three national holidays. All other gazetted holidays to be abolished and compensated by increasing the number of restricted holidays from two to eight days in a year.
3. **Women Employees:** Benefits like staggered working hours, special leave for child care, enhanced maternity leave of 180 days, better accommodation facilities in the form of working women's hostels etc. specifically for women employees.
4. **Persons with Disabilities:** Government employees with disabilities recommended various benefits like enhanced number of casual leave, special aids and appliances for facilitating office work, higher interest subsidy for automobile loans, liberal flexi hours, higher rate of transport allowance, better prosthetic aids and proper grievance redressal machinery. Extra allowance for

disabled women employees to take care of young child till the time the child attains the age of two years.

6.2.14 Financial Implications: The recommendations contained in the Report to cost ₹ 12,561 crore in the year 2008-09. Savings of ₹ 4,586 crore likely to accrue on account of various measures suggested in the Report. The net financial implications of the recommendations contained in the Report estimated to be ₹ 7,975 crore for the year 2008-09. An additional, one-time burden of ₹ 18,060 crore on payment of arrears.

Part II:
Seventh Central Pay Commission

7

Seventh Central Pay Commission at a Glance

7.1 Appointment of the Commission

The Government of India, vide notification No.1/1/2013-E.III (A) of 28.02.2014, appointed the Seventh Central Pay Commission with specified terms of reference. The Commission was given 18 months from the date of its constitution to make its recommendations. To this end, the Commission was authorized to set up its team of officers, advisers, institutional consultants and experts and call for required information and documents from Ministries and Departments of the Government of India and various service associations.

The composition of the Commission was as under.

Composition of the Seventh Pay Commission

Justice Shri Ashok Kumar Mathur	Chairman
Shri Vivek Rae	Member
Dr. Rathin Roy	Member
Shrimati Meena Agarwal	Secretary

In May 2014, a group of retired government officials, challenged the inclusion of a senior IAS officer in the 3 member Seventh Pay Commission, in the Delhi High Court. They alleged that this would lead an inherent bias in the Commission's recommendations towards IAS officers.

While hailing the decision of the Government, the employees' unions demanded for the implementation of the Commission's recommendations to take effect from January 1, 2011 in the same pattern as with the conventional periodical wage revisions after every 5 years in public sector undertakings.

The Commission studied the structure of salaries of different cadres of the Central Government employees and pensioners and recommended for upward revision of scales and allied service matters. After due deliberations, it submitted its 900 pages report to the Government of India on November 19, 2015.

7.2 Terms of Reference

The terms of reference of the Commission were as follows:

1. To examine, review, evolve and recommend changes that are desirable and feasible regarding the principles that should govern the emoluments structure including pay, allowances and other facilities/benefits, in cash or kind, having regard to rationalization and simplification therein as well as the specialized needs of various Departments, agencies and services, in respect of the following categories of employees:

- Central Government employees—industrial and non-industrial.
- Personnel belonging to the all-India services.
- Personnel of the Union Territories.
- Officers and employees of the Indian audit and accounts department.
- Members of the regulatory bodies (excluding the RBI) set up under the Acts of Parliament.
- Officers and employees of the Supreme Court.

2. To examine, review, evolve and recommend changes that are desirable and feasible regarding the principles that should govern the emoluments structure, concessions and facilities/benefits, in cash or kind, as well as the retirement benefits of the personnel belonging to the defence forces, having regard to the historical and traditional parities, with due emphasis on the aspects unique to these personnel.
3. To work out the framework for an emoluments structure linked with the need to attract the most suitable talent to Government service, promote efficiency, accountability and responsibility in the work culture, and foster excellence in the public governance system to respond to the complex challenges of modern administration and the rapid political, social, economic and technological changes, with due regard to expectations of stakeholders, and to recommend appropriate training and capacity building through a competency based framework.
4. To examine the existing schemes of payment of bonus, keeping in view, inter alia, its bearing upon performance and productivity and make recommendations on the general principles, financial parameters and conditions for an appropriate incentive scheme to reward excellence in productivity, performance and integrity.
5. To review the variety of existing allowances presently available to employees in addition to pay and suggest their rationalization and simplification with a view to ensuring that the pay structure is so designed as to take these into account.
6. To examine the principles which should govern the structure of pension and other retirement benefits, including revision of pension in the case of

employees who have retired prior to the date of effect of these recommendations, keeping in view that retirement benefits of all Central Government employees appointed on and after 01.01.2004 are covered by the New Pension Scheme (NPS),

7. To make recommendations on the above, keeping in view:

- The economic conditions in the country and the need for fiscal prudence.
- The need to ensure that adequate resources are available for developmental expenditures and welfare measures.
- The likely impact of the recommendations on the finances of the State Governments, which usually adopt the recommendations with some modifications.
- The prevailing emolument structure and retirement benefits available to employees of Central public sector undertakings.
- The best global practices and their adaptability and relevance in Indian conditions.

8. To recommend the date of effect of its recommendations on all the above.
9. The Commission will devise its own procedure and may appoint such advisors, institutional consultants and experts, as it may consider necessary for any particular purpose. It may call for such information and take such evidence, as it may consider necessary. Ministries and Departments of Government of India shall furnish such information and documents and other assistance as may be required by the Commission. The Government of India trusts that State Governments, service associations and others concerned will extend to the Commission their fullest cooperation and assistance.
10. The Commission will have its headquarters in Delhi.
11. The Commission will make its recommendations within 18 months of the date of its constitution. It may consider, if necessary, sending interim reports on any of the matters as and when the recommendations are finalized.

7.3 Highlights of the Report

1. Implementation of the Report to take effect from January 1, 2016.
2. A minimum pay of ₹ 18,000 per month has been recommended. It was ₹ 6,600 under the Sixth Pay Commission.
3. A maximum pay of ₹ 2,50,000 has been recommended for cabinet secretary and officers of the same rank like chiefs of army, navy and air force and CAG. It was ₹ 90,000 under the Sixth Pay Commission.
4. Regulatory body chiefs (like SEBI and TRAI) to get ₹ 4.5 lakh per month.
5. Annual increment of 3 percent retained.

6. Grade pay, pay bands abolished.
7. 16 percent increase in the basic pay of Government employees.
8. 63 percent increase in allowances.
9. 23.5 percent overall increase (pay and allowances).
10. 24 percent increase in pension of Government employees.
11. Risk and hardship allowances raised sharply. Biggest hike in allowances for soldiers posted in Siachen—from ₹ 21,000 to ₹ 31,500.
12. Commission recommends abolition of 53 allowances. Another 36 allowances subsumed in existing allowances or in newly proposed allowances. Any allowance not mentioned in the report ceases to exist. **For an exhaustive list and status of various allowances, see section 8.8 of chapter 8 of this book.**
13. Recommendations to benefit 47 lakh Central Government employees and 52 lakh pensioners.
14. IAS versus non-IAS controversy divides the Commission. IAS loses 2-year edge. One member of the Commission disagrees.
15. One-rank-one pension (OROP) recommended for Central Government employees and para-military personnel.
16. Performance benchmarks made more stringent. Performance-linked pay recommended.
17. Introduction of a health insurance scheme for Central Government employees and pensioners to replace the current Central Government Health Scheme (CGHS).
18. Insured amounts in group insurance raised significantly up to ₹ 50 lakh. Premium deduction to rise correspondingly.
19. Introduction of performance-related pay (PRP) for all categories of Central Government employees, based on quality, results, framework documents, reformed annual performance appraisal reports and some other broad guidelines. PRP to subsume the existing bonus schemes.
20. Ceiling on gratuity doubled to ₹ 20 lakh. Ceiling to go up by 25 percent when DA rises by 50 percent.
21. Short Service Commission (SSC) in the armed forces has been made an attractive option by seeking easier norms for exiting service and increasing the payout of retiring personnel. SSC officers will be allowed to exit the armed forces at any point in time between 7 to 10 years of service.
22. Revised pension formula for civil employees as well as para-military and defence personnel who retired before January 1, 2006. This will bring parity between past pensioners and current retirees for same length of service.
23. Annual financial burden is estimated at ₹ 1.02 lakh crore.

After receipt of the Report, the Finance Minister said a secretariat will be set up to implement the pay panel recommendations. A separate empowered committee of various departments will examine the suggestions of the Commission. He assured that the recommendations would be examined expeditiously and a final decision taken in the matter.

Central Government usually accepts the broad proposals for pay revision and State Governments usually respond with their own hikes.

Unlike previous Pay Commissions, the Seventh Pay Commission has recommended salary increases which will not carry a major arrears burden because the recommendations will be implemented on a current basis (i.e. from January 1, 2016) and not retrospectively. It may be recalled that the Sixth Pay Commission's recommendations were notified in 2008-09 but were implemented retrospectively from January 1, 2006. The arrears were paid in two instalments: 40 percent in 2008-09 and 60 percent in 2009-10 to spread the fiscal impact.

8

Edited Extracts from the Report of the Seventh Central Pay Commission

Note: The Report of the Commission runs into 900 pages. Following extract (paragraphs) from the Report capture the essence of the lengthy document.

8.1 Foreword by the Chairman of the Commission

The Government of India has, from time to time, set up various Pay Commissions for improving the pay structure of its employees so that they can attract better talent to public service. In this 21st century, the global economy has undergone a vast change and it has seriously impacted the living conditions of the salaried class. The economic value of the salaries paid to them earlier has diminished. The economy has become more and more consumer economy. Therefore, to keep the salary structure of the employees viable, it has become necessary to improve the pay structure of their employees so that better, more competent and talented people could be attracted for governance.

In this background, the Seventh Central Pay Commission was constituted and the government framed certain terms of reference for this Commission. The salient features of the terms are to examine and review the existing pay structure and to recommend changes in the pay, allowances and other facilities as are desirable and feasible for civil employees as well as for the defence forces, having due regard to the historical and traditional parities. The framework should be linked with the need to attract the most suitable talented candidate to the government service and promote efficiency, accountability and responsibility in the work culture. In addition, it is to review the norms of bonus, keeping in view performance and productivity, as also examine the existing pension scheme and other retirement benefits. The terms of reference enjoin that the recommendations should be made keeping in view the economic conditions and available resources of the country and also the likely impact on the State Governments. The terms of reference also mandated the Commission to make the recommendations keeping the best global practices and their adaptability and relevance in Indian conditions. A closer look at the terms of reference reveals, thus, that there are many newer elements which have broadened the remit of this Commission.

The approach adopted by the Commission was to reach out to all stakeholders and seek their inputs in various forms. To start with, a website was set up giving all updated information about the working of the Commission. An exhaustive questionnaire was prepared, capturing, inter alia, all the important facets of the terms of reference, for seeking suggestions from the stakeholders. We wrote to ministries/departments seeking various data on pay and allowances, staff position, age profile, recruitment rules of cadres etc.

The Commission received a large number of representations from various recognised and unrecognised bodies. The Commission also permitted oral submissions through the representatives of these organisations.

The key expectation of employees at all levels is that there should be a significant increase in their pay and improvement in other facilities. Representatives of some of the recognised organisations have staked their claims for grant of a pay structure comparable to that of the private sector. At the core of this demand is the economic development the country has witnessed in recent times, resulting in the avenues for talented young persons having opened up; several of them are being hired by the private sector for emoluments much higher than in the government sector.

The Commission bestowed its best of consideration and has dealt with all the issues in appropriate chapters. It may be observed at the outset that government service is not merely a contract service, it provides a status in society which cannot be monetised in terms of money value. The focus for the Commission was that emoluments should be such which attract the right kind of talent by a transparent method, keeping in mind the financial limitations of the government. The attempt has been to provide wages commensurate with comfortable living. The pay structure should also need to address any significant deterioration in real value of emoluments as a consequence of inflation. One should get proper and adequate compensation for his merit. The increase in pay structure cannot keep pace with the market forces, at the same time it should not be so unattractive that talent is not attracted to government service. Therefore, we have attempted a pay structure which has as its basis the Aykroyd formula, which reflects the basic average cost of living in the country. The attempt has been to arrive at a proper pay package so that the essentials of life can be availed comfortably.

While finalizing the levels of salaries, allowances and other perquisites of compensation structure, we have tried to take a holistic approach. We also commissioned three studies by expert bodies towards this end:

1. Study by IIM, Ahmedabad to understand the nature and quantum of total compensation of select job profiles in the government sector vis-à-vis similarly placed profiles in the CPSUs and the private sector.
2. Study by Institute of Defence Studies and Analyses on nature, quantum and

components of defence expenditure and defence pension.

3. Study by IIM, Kolkata on fiscal implications of implementation of the V and VI CPC on the finances of the Union and State Governments.

The new pay structure has been laid out by and large broadly as an open ended, layered matrix, for civilians as well as for the armed forces personnel. It has been kept in view that a person should not stagnate but should have fair opportunity to progress by dint of merit and secure better emoluments so that frustration does not set in. The prevailing rate of increment is considered quite satisfactory and has been retained. The concept of separate grade pay has been done away with and the grade pay at all levels has been subsumed into the pay matrix.

The modified assured career progression (MACP) scheme has been further modified. It is expected that the present formulation will address the widespread dissatisfaction prevailing in the earlier system, in which the gain or progression through the MACP was considered inadequate. The remuneration package is such that employees would feel that they are valued and they are fairly paid and their remuneration is not less than a person who is similarly situated in another organisation. While addressing this aspirational need, we are also conscious of the fact that such employees who have outlived their utility, their services need not be continued, and the continuance of such persons in the system should be discouraged.

Separate pay matrices for civilian employees, defence forces personnel and those of the military nursing service (MNS) have been prepared, cell by cell, after due diligence and deliberations. The structure, which essentially is the same for all segments, has been simplified so that each employee can find his or her place in the proposed matrix. All the employees belonging to various services will proceed according to their respective service conditions by earning increment on the basis of merit. Any disturbance of the matrix structure will have a serious repercussion on the inter se positioning of various levels in the hierarchy, all of which have been extensively deliberated upon, along with the service conditions of all the employees serving in Government of India. Therefore, the importance of not altering any portion of the three matrices cannot be emphasised enough, as doing so will disturb the parity of the services and create anomalous situations.

Furthermore, the Commission's interaction with various unions/associations has revealed that there is a significant lack of standardization across cadres as far as their entry level qualifications (ELQ), pay scales, nomenclature and promotional avenues are concerned. The approach of this Commission is to bring about uniformity in the ELQs and pay scales while dealing with cadres with similar job content and responsibility across organisations.

It is also recommended that the matrix may be reviewed periodically without waiting for the long period of ten years. It can be reviewed and revised on the basis of the Aykroyd formula which takes into consideration the changing prices of the commodities that constitute a common man's basket, which the Labour Bureau at Shimla reviews periodically. It is suggested that this should be made the basis for revision of that matrix periodically without waiting for another pay commission.

We have also revised a large number of allowances and made them more relevant and rational. Those which have outlived their utility have been discontinued. We also recommend that each allowance should be placed in public domain as a step towards greater transparency in governance and ease of administration.

We have also kept in view the needs of the pensioners under the old pension system, (employees who joined before January 1, 2004) and suggested some measures to alleviate their plight. They should also not be left in straitened circumstances. We have suggested their proper fixation in the new pay matrix which will provide them a respectable living. Almost the whole lot of government employees appointed on after January 1, 2004 were unhappy with the new pension scheme. While the National Pension System does not form a part of our terms of reference, we have recorded the sentiments of the affected employees. The government should take a call and step in to look into their complaints.

Great dissatisfaction has been expressed with regard to medical facilities by in-service employees as well as retired personnel. We have suggested certain measures in the appropriate chapter, to take care of medical facilities to serving as well as retired government employees. The best answer appears to be medical insurance, which will not only reduce financial liability of the government, but, if well structured, provide quality medical services to all. We have been informed by the Health Ministry that this is being actively explored by them.

A serious grievance has been made by all services that cadre reviews have not taken place for years together, which has resulted in great anguish and frustration among the services. Though it is essentially an administrative matter, it has a serious impact on the status and emolument of employees. On account of delay in cadre reviews, many Central services lag behind and that gives rise to frustration and ultimately affects governance. We have tried to cover this issue in the appropriate chapter in this report. A great resentment and anguish has been expressed by Central civil service officers that they are not getting their legitimate due vis-à-vis all-India services. Therefore, the government should take a call and give them a proper representation in the government.

A number of grievances or so called anomalies have been placed before the Commission. Many have their roots not in the recommendations made by the VI CPC, but in the subsequent modifications made by the government and the resultant orders issued by it. Often these resulted in anomalies, many of which could not be rectified till date. Wherever possible we have tried to remove these anomalies. We also suggest that an appropriate body may be created to look into anomalies, if any arising out of the implementation of the recommendations of the Seventh CPC. The body so created may be in position for a period of six months at least so that if any anomaly arises in implementation of the recommendation of this Commission, it can be immediately attended to and the affected persons need not wait for another decade.

The terms of reference place emphasis on productivity, accountability and performance. This brings into focus the concept of performance related pay, which has emerged over the past three Central Pay Commissions. The VI CPC recommended a framework for performance pay. In furtherance of this, guidelines were drawn up based on the performance measurement methodology of the results framework document (RFD). However, at that time, the RFD system was still being put in place and many departments were in the process of adopting this system. As a result, the scheme on performance pay could not take off. RFD system has taken firm roots now.

We are recommending introduction of performance related pay for all categories of Central Government employees, based on RFD, annual performance appraisal reports and some broad guidelines. We are also of the view that there should not be automatic payment of bonus and all existing schemes of payment of bonuses should be linked to productivity. There is no blueprint for enhancing efficiency and productivity in the government. The organization systems in the government are generally large, multi-layered and complex. Improvement of efficiency and productivity in such a setting depends on a whole range of extrinsic and intrinsic factors. A large number of issues that were placed before this Commission by various cadres/associations related to cadre matters, issues of administrative nature, organizational structure etc. The broader issues of efficiency, productivity, excellence and service delivery should ideally be dealt with administratively by a body such as the Administrative Reforms Commission or Civil Service Reforms Commission.

Lastly, we must emphasize that the government should inspire confidence in mind of civil servants that they will not be hounded by unnecessary harassment by investigation agencies. The recent trend of hounding civil servants as criminals for the failure of bonafide decisions is not a happy one. This will discourage the bureaucracy to take bold decisions in fear of being hounded if such a decision misfires. Any misadventure should not be looked upon with suspicion unless it has definite criminal intent to benefit either himself or someone else. If this trend is not checked it will lead to disastrous consequences.

The sole consideration with the Commission was to ensure that employees do not suffer economic hardship so that they can deliver and render the best possible service to the country and make the governance vibrant and effective.

(*paras* 1.11-1.14; 1.16-1.28; 1.30-1.31)

8.2 Impact of Central Pay Commissions on State Finances

To address the question of implications of Seventh Central Pay Commission's recommendations on the States, it was necessary to ascertain the fiscal impact of the previous Commissions' awards on the states. To this end, Indian Institute of Management Calcutta (IIM, Kolkata) was asked to undertake a study on the subject for the Seventh CPC.

The broad conclusions of the study indicated that the states on the whole were able to manage their finances and absorb the fiscal shock caused by the VI CPC (relative to previous Pay Commissions) better, principally because of the implementation of the FRBM Act by the States.

The study finds that the macroeconomic impact on states depended on the speed and the extent to which individual states implemented their pay awards, which varied considerably. The empirical analysis conducted indicates that the macroeconomic impact on States' finances tends to taper off in two years in most cases. In this context, it is encouraging to note that States' finances continue to be reasonably sound at present.

(*paras* 2.2.1-2.2.3)

8.3 Principles of Pay Determination

The Seventh CPC has been set up at a time of many noticeable changes on the governance front. The principal role of the government as the prime facilitator has gained firm ground. E-Governance has made considerable progress, facilitating communication and improving coordination of authorities at different tiers of government. There is a specific emphasis on minimum government and maximum governance, harping on the concept of a leaner bureaucracy with more skilled people. There is also a definite need to harmonize the functioning of the Central Government with the demands of the emerging global economic scenario. This Commission had to keep all these factors while finalizing the compensation structure for the Central Government employees.

Employee compensation is an important element of government functioning. In general, the level and structure of compensation should aim to achieve four objectives: (i) pay should be sufficient to attract and retain high quality staff; (ii) pay should motivate staff to work hard; (iii) pay policy should induce other human resource management reforms; and (iv) pay should be set at a level to ensure long-term fiscal sustainability.

The real challenge before this Commission is to provide a pay structure which is competitive yet affordable, attractive yet acceptable, forward looking yet adaptable, simple yet rational, and one which matches with the current socio-economic and political conditions as well as the changing perception of the overall administrative machinery and the public governance system.

One of the peculiarities of the Indian civil structure and the pay structure that has been in vogue is the high degree of emphasis on uniformity and relativity. In interacting with various associations, federations, heads of institutions, what has clearly come across is the prevalence of historical equations across the various cadres in government. Disturbances caused in any of these have an immediate and very vocal effect by way of strident demands in restoring earlier parities. Extensive litigation has come to be the norm. The second issue relates to ease of administration. A simple structure with rules of fixation that are easy to understand and apply would take away the possibility of either inadvertent errors or any element of arbitrariness. This Commission has, therefore set simplicity and complete transparency as a basic guiding principle.

From the employees' perspective, the upper most aspect is naturally that the emoluments should appropriately reflect the qualifications and the skill sets that each individual brings to this system. Apart from being fair and adequate, what is crucial is that the pay structure should correctly reflect the relative positions in the hierarchy. In its deliberations, the Commission has found that the preponderance of grievances relates to the emoluments drawn by others as opposite to what is received by oneself. Due care, therefore, has been given to the aspect of equity.

Over the years, due to downsizing of bureaucracy, issues relating to diminishing or in some cases non-existent promotional avenues have impacted the employees' motivational levels. To address this problem, various schemes of assured career progression have been introduced by previous Pay Commissions. It is now one of the major aspirational challenges spurring work efficiency and which needs to be acknowledged by the Pay Commission. The emoluments structure is now expected to provide scope for career advancement by way of financial upgradation at reasonable intervals so as to keep the workforce motivated.

The efforts of the Commission have been to devise a pay structure to address all the above listed issues and concerns. Special emphasis has been laid on designing a pay matrix which is simple, transparent, predictable and easily comprehensible. During their interactions with the Commission, the stakeholders placed many demands, ranging from common entry pay, rationalization of the existing grade pay structure, common treatment of like cadres, transparent pay structure as also increasing the frequency of the MACP. The new pay matrix incorporates all these features: subsuming the grade pay, the rationalized matrix presents the whole universe of pay levels in one simple chart. The levels have been rationalized too, displaying a logical pay progression. Employees would be able to see their pay level, where they fit in and how they are likely to progress over their career span. The Commission has also recommended simplified procedures for computation of pension.

On the same pattern, the entire structure of allowances has been reviewed, rationalized and simplified. Inter-departmental and inter-Ministerial disparities regarding payment of various allowances have been sought to be removed as far as possible. An innovative risk and hardship matrix has been proposed. Also, the Commission recommends that each allowance should be put in the public domain as a step towards greater transparency in governance.

The pay matrix addresses the important issue of adequacy of the compensation structure. The Commission observes that the purpose of pay is to compensate the employees for work done, to motivate them to perform well. The purposes also include attracting talent to government service and also retaining them, thus avoiding the need for expensive recruitment and training for replacement.

Ideally speaking, the compensation package should be a well defined function of prescribed educational and other entry level qualifications, job content, roles and responsibilities attached to the position etc. However, this is a difficult task, especially in a government setting, which has hundreds of organizations and plethora of job roles. The Commission has, to the extent possible, while dealing with individual cadres, attempted to bring about uniformity in their qualification and pay structure. This should ameliorate grievances of many 'common' cadres across organizations.

The Commission has also analysed the important question of whether wages are sufficient to attract and retain qualified staff. One way to address this question is to compare wages in government sector positions with wages for comparable positions in the private sector. This presumes that if wages in the government sector are too far below private sector wages, the government sector will have difficulty attracting and retaining the sort of staff it requires. In their presentations before the Commission, many associations brought out this aspect highlighting, inter alia, that the compensation pattern in the private sector is more remunerative. Although private sector wage comparators are difficult to obtain, the Commission feels that this could be the case in respect of only a few specialized segments. The results of the IIM, Ahmedabad study on comparing job families between the government and private/public sector has brought out the fact that while at lower levels salaries are much lower in the private sector as compared to government jobs, at the highest echelons of governance, the compensation in government is nowhere comparable to their counterparts in the private/public sector.

But a mere comparison of the salaries should not form the benchmark for remuneration, it is to be viewed keeping in mind the uniqueness inherent in the government in terms of security of tenure, assured prospects of financial progression even when no promotional avenues exist, leave and pensionary privileges which are not available to their counterparts in the private/public sector.

Having said this, there is no denying that officers at higher level shoulder maximum responsibility and accountability and hence should be compensated accordingly. In light of this, the Commission has accorded slightly higher index of rationalisation at level of senior administrative grade and above.

The Commission notes that government employees are entitled to a host of tangible and non-tangible benefits—from job security, inflation indexed salary, assured prospects of financial progression—to name a few. It may be difficult to monetize some of these non-tangibles. That the government jobs retain their charm is evident from the increasing number of qualified candidates per advertised vacancy as well as from the low turnover rates among recent recruits.

The Commission has adopted an innovative design to make the remuneration structure attractive. It has adopted the need based minimum wage formula for designing the pay matrix. The rationalization of pay levels has been done keeping this minimum pay as the base for all calculations. It has been recommended that the minimum pay at each level will be the entry pay for direct recruits for those levels. Each level has been placed equidistantly. The various stages within a level moves upwards at the rate of 3 percent per annum. Owing to this rationalization, the quantum of increase in pay on promotion, either on regular basis or through the MACP, is likely to be substantial. This design will make the existing remuneration pattern in the government more attractive.

The basis for calculation of minimum and maximum pay, rate of pay progression across levels, basis for rationalisation and uniform approach towards fixation of pay have been clearly spelt out to leave no room for ambiguity or conjecture.

Historically, the qualification and skill set required as well as roles and responsibilities discharged at various levels in the overall hierarchy have been central to the basis for pay grading. The rationalisation index has been applied keeping this principle in mind.

There is uniformity in fixation of pay whether at entry level or on promotion or at the time of migrating from one pay regime to another. The new pay structure will bring out clearly what the total emoluments will be at a given point in time during one's career span. The rate of pay progression will also be stated upfront for existing as well as new entrants.

Since, substantial delayering had already been attempted by the previous Pay Commissions, this Commission is not removing any levels, but to simplify the pay structure, the grades pay have been subsumed in the pay band to form distinct levels. The new pay structure is a construct in the matrix format and provides open ended progression in pay at all levels.

One recurrent theme in the representations of various associations relates to 'equity' or 'equal pay for equal work'. Ideally, the remuneration package should establish horizontal equity: employees should feel that their pay is comparable with the remuneration structure of similarly placed positions outside their organization. The employees should also feel that the pay structure shows linear progression pattern and thus the notion of vertical equity is also maintained. The pay matrix addresses these issues as well. The Commission has designed the pay structure in such a manner that the pay progression recognises the importance of vertical relativities and also assigns a reasonable basis to such progression. This has been done by assigning a uniform fitment factor of 2.57.

The Commission feels that there is strong need to create a culture of performance in government—from establishing standards of performance, to measuring, and promoting people based on performance. To emphasize on the culture of performance, the Commission has recommended that all the non-performers in the system should be phased out after 20 years. The Commission has recommended that performance related pay should be introduced in the government and that all bonus payments should necessarily be linked with productivity.

(*paras* 4.1.1-1.1.2; 4.1.5-4.1.23)

8.4 Determination of Minimum Pay

The estimation of minimum pay in government is the first step towards building its pay structure. In doing so, the approach is to ascertain, by using the most logical and acceptable methodology, what the lowest ranked staff in government needs to be paid to enable him to meet the minimum expenditure needs for himself and his family in a dignified manner.

In its representation, the JCM-Staff Side has submitted that the Commission must determine a 'need-based minimum pay', estimated entirely from the ILC norms and factoring in the 1991 ruling of the Supreme Court to provide for education, medical, recreation, festivals and ceremonies. In addition, they have also sought the inclusion of a quantified skill factor on the lines of the VI CPC's approach for addressing the merger of the Group D staff into Group 'C'. They have further stated that unlike the previous CPCs, the Commission should not exclude any of the seven components (five ILS components + additional 25 percent provisioning + skill factor) on the apprehension that it would impose a heavy financial burden on the government.

Based on the various components of the ILC norms and the subsequent additions, the JCM-Staff Side has reported that the minimum pay should be ₹ 26,000 per month, as on January 1, 2014, the date from which it wants the Commission's recommendations to be implemented. The prices used for the calculation are stated to be the retail prices prevailing in New Delhi, Mumbai, Chennai, Kolkata, Hyderabad, Bhubaneswar, Trivandrum and Bangalore, as on January 1, 2014. The JCM-Staff Side has argued that this estimation of minimum pay is still on the lower side. This is on the basis of their argument that the 15th ILC norms need to be revised for including old and dependent parents as additional consumption units.

The 15th ILC norms were formulated in 1957. As such, the I CPC, which gave its recommendations in 1948, pre-dated the same. The II CPC did make an initial assessment using the ILC norms. However, it moderated the minimum pay so calculated in line with the then prevailing per capita income. The III CPC adopted a modified version of the norms to calculate the minimum pay. The IV CPC estimated the minimum pay by applying the growth of total emoluments index on the minimum pay estimated by the III CPC. As already discussed, the V CPC estimated the minimum pay through the 'constant relative income approach' whilst the VI CPC adopted the 15th ILC norms to arrive at a base figure, to which was added additional 25 percent for various additional items plus the skill factor. The Commission has thus noted that directly or indirectly, the ILC norms have always been at the core of the minimum pay calculations made by the previous Pay Commissions. The Commission is also of the view that the ILC norms, along with other supplements (the entire set of seven components), are the best approach to estimating the minimum pay as it is a need-based wage calculation that directly costs the requirements, normatively prescribed to ensure a healthy and a dignified standard of living.

The Commission has estimated the minimum pay (the calculations for which have been tabulated in the Annexure) through the following steps:

Step 1: The food, clothing and detergent products listed and their respective quantities specified by the 15th ILC have been adopted. These quantities indicate the monthly consumption of the listed products by a family comprising of three consumption units. [For e.g. for the product 'dal' the quantity specified for daily consumption is 80 grams per consumption unit per day. The monthly consumption of dal by a consumption unit thus works out to 2.4 kg. (80 x 30). Accordingly the monthly consumption of dal by a family comprising 3 units is 7.2 kgs. (2.4 x 3)].

Step 2: The quantities have been multiplied by their respective product prices to arrive at product-wise cost. The price adopted for each product is the average of prices of various items that are included in the product. The price of an item is the average of its prices prevailing in each month from July 2014 till June 2015. [At monthly family consumption of 7.2 kg., the Commission has estimated the monthly expenditure on dal at ₹ 704.44 after calculating the price of dal at ₹ 97.84 per kg. The price of dal has been calculated as the average of prices of toor, urad and moong dal items specified under the product Dal and whose prices have been determined at ₹ 87.86, ₹ 109.66 and ₹ 96.00 respectively. The prices of these three dal items are the twelve monthly average prices for the period July 2014-June 2015].

The prices of all items have been sourced from Labour Bureau, Shimla. These prices are used in the calculation of the CPI (IW) and subsequently the calculation of dearness allowance. In the current exercise, the prices of all items are for the period July 2014-June 2015 and have been used in the calculation of DA at 119 percent operative from July 1, 2015.

Step 3: The cost of food, clothing and detergent products obtained from Step 2 has been divided by 0.8 to arrive at a total, of which 20 percent provides for fuel and lighting expenses. This addresses the fifth component under para 4.2.3. The fourth component on housing under para 4.2.3 has not been addressed at this stage as its quantification at the final stage of pay estimation is considered more appropriate by the Commission.

Step 4: The cost estimated from Step 3 is divided by 0.85 to arrive at a total, of which 15 percent is towards recreation, ceremonies and festivities. The prescribed provision of 25 percent to cover education, recreation, ceremonies, festivals and medical expenses has been moderated to 15 percent because expenses on educational and medical necessities are being separately provided for through relevant allowances and facilities and thus need not be provided here. This partially addresses the first of the two components outside the 15th ILC norms.

Step 5: The cost estimated from Step 4 is increased by 25 percent to account for the skill factor, following the reasoning that there is no unskilled staff in the government after the merger of Group D staff in Group 'C'. This addresses the second of the two components outside the 15th ILC norms.

Step 6: The cost estimated from Step 5 is divided by 0.97 to arrive at a total, of which 3 percent provides for housing expenses. This is done in view of the observation that license fee for government accommodation is about 3 percent of the total pay. This addresses the fourth component stated under para 3 but partially so, as the 15th ILC norms had fixed the housing provision at 7.5 percent.

Step 7: The cost estimated from Step 6 is as on July 1, 2015 when the DA was 119 percent. The DA is assumed to be 125 percent as on January 1, 2016, the day from which the Commission expects its recommendations to be implemented by the government. Accordingly, the cost estimated from Step 6 has been increased by 3 percent (2.25/2.19 = 1.027 or nearly 3 percent).

The cost estimated from Step 7 is next rounded off to ₹ 18,000, which is the minimum pay being recommended by the Commission, operative from January 1, 2016. This is 2.57 times the minimum pay of ₹ 7,000 fixed by the government while implementing the VI CPC's recommendations from January 1, 2006. Accordingly, basic pay at any level on January 1, 2016 (pay in the pay band + grade pay) would need to be multiplied by 2.57 to fix the pay of an employee in the new pay structure. Of this multiple, 2.25 provides for merging of basic pay with DA, assumed at 125 percent on January 1, 2016, while the balance is the real increase being recommended by the Commission. The real increase works out to 14.2 percent (2.57÷2.25 = 1.1429).

The following table shows the real increase given by each CPC/Government over the previously set minimum pay:

(in percent)

Second Central Pay Commission (CPC)	14.2
Third CPC	20.6
Fourth CPC	27.6
Fifth CPC	31.0
Sixth CPC	54.0
Seventh CPC	14.3

The real pay in government is protected by providing dearness allowance (DA), which is that percentage of pay by which the CPI (IW)16 increases over a fixed base value. Consequently, the absolute amount of DA keeps on growing with every point increase in CPI (IW). On the other hand, the real value of the industrial minimum wage is protected by providing variable dearness allowance (VDA), which is a fixed amount of money given per point increase in CPI (IW) as notified by the Chief Labour Commissioner (central sphere) from time to time. Consequently, over a period of time, the minimum pay + DA in government becomes larger than the minimum wage + VDA in the private sector even though the basic minimum wage in both the sectors is calculated on the basis of the 15th

ILC norms. As on January 1, 2015 the minimum pay in government was ₹ 14,910 whereas minimum wage for a skilled worker was in the range of ₹ 9,000-₹ 11,000 per month.

Besides DA, government provides house rent, transport, location and function specific allowances besides leave travel allowance (LTA) which, along with the basic pay, constitute the gross pay of a government employee. If one were to only take HRA at 30 percent of the basic pay and transport allowance at ₹ 400+DA, as are admissible in A1/A class cities, together with educational allowances for two children at the rate of ₹ 1,500 per month, the gross pay further increases to ₹ 20,870 (20870 = 14910+2100+860+3000) as on January 1, 2015. In addition, government gives a host of other benefits that can be measured under the CTG (cost to Government of an employee) concept. From these numbers, it is clear that the benefits given to the lowest ranked government employees, whether monetized or not, are significantly higher than the minimum basic pay and also much higher than the emoluments of skilled industrial workers.

To obtain a comparative picture of the salaries paid in the government with that in the private sector enterprises, the Commission engaged the Indian Institute of Management, Ahmedabad to conduct a study. According to the study, the total emoluments of a general helper, who is the lowest ranked employee in the government is ₹ 22,579, more than two times the emoluments of a general helper in the private sector organizations surveyed at ₹ 8,000-₹ 9,500.

After considering all relevant factors, the Commission is of the view that the minimum pay in government recommended at ₹ 18,000 per month, w.e.f. January 1, 2016, is fair and reasonable and one which, along with other allowances and facilities, would ensure a decent standard of living for the lowest ranked employee in the Central Government.

(*paras* 4.2.1, 4.2.5-4.2.13)

8.5 Pay Structure (Civilian Employees)

The thrust of all the previous Pay Commissions has been to propose an improvement in the pay structure by way of 'simplification and rationalisation'. The most visible results of this exercise are evident in terms of reduction in number of pay scales as well as the compression ratio. Traditionally, compression ratio has been taken as a ratio of maximum salary drawn by the secretary to the Government of India to minimum salary drawn by the lowest functionary in the Government. Table on the next page brings out the trend in pay structure in the Government of India over the years.

It can be seen from the table that successive pay commissions have consciously tried to reduce the number of pay scales even though they tended to increase during the intervening period between any two pay commissions. There were, however, no significant changes in the pay structure per se until the IV CPC, when the concept of running pay scales was introduced in a limited way in respect of defence forces. For others, individual pay scales continued till the V CPC. It was the VI CPC which recommended running pay bands for both civilians as well as defence forces. This was coupled with the introduction of the concept of grade pay as a level differentiator.

Trends in Pay Structure

Central Pay Commission	Minimum Salary (₹)	Maximum Salary (₹)	Compression Ratio	Number of Pay Scales
First	55	2,000	1:36.4	150 → 30
Second	80	3,000	1:37.5	500 → 140
Third	196	3,500	1:17.9	500 → 80
Fourth	750	8,000	1:10.7	153 → 36
Fifth	2,550	26,000	1:10.2	51→ 34
Sixth	7,000	80,000	1:11.4	35 → 19

Another new feature was the calculation of the annual increment on percentage basis. Prior to VI CPC, the increment was a flat sum, depending on the pay scale. The effort at compression of levels was carried forward by the VI CPC, which reduced the existing 35 levels to 19. Another radical measure was the doing away with 'Group D' as a category and placement of 'Group-D' personnel in 'Group-C' after appropriate training whenever necessary. Hence, it can be seen that the simplification process set in motion by previous Pay Commissions acted as a precursor for progressive rationalisation by the subsequent Commissions.

Although the VI CPC had mentioned that grade pay would be equivalent to 40 percent of the maximum of the pre-revised scale and that the grade pay will constitute the actual fitment, yet the computation varied greatly. After the implementation of recommendations, the difference became more pronounced in pay band 4 as compared to the other three pay bands. This resulted in varying fitment factors for various levels and promotional benefits that were perceived to be rather differentiated. The same pattern was discernible in the pension fixation too.

After analysing the issues brought out by various stakeholders, this Commission is suggesting a new pay model that is expected to not only address the existing problems but will also establish a rationalised system which is transparent and simple to use.

To begin with, the system of pay bands and grade pay has been dispensed with and the new functional levels being proposed have been arrived at by merging the grade pay with the pay in the pay band. All of the existing levels have been subsumed in the new structure; no new level has been introduced nor has any existing level been dispensed with.

The pay structures in vogue, by way of pay scales or pay bands, indicate the definite boundaries within which the pay of an individual could lie. It is however difficult to ascertain the exact pay of an individual at any given point of time. Further, the way the pay progression would fan out over a period of time was also not evident. Since various cadres are designed differently, the relative pay progression also varies. The Commission believes that any new entrant to a service would wish to be able to make a reasonable and informed assessment of how his/her career path would traverse and how the emoluments will progress alongside. The new pay structure has been devised in the form of a pay matrix to provide complete transparency regarding pay progression.

The Commission has designed the new pay matrix keeping in view the vast opportunities that have opened up outside the government over the last three decades, generating greater competition for human resources and the need to attract and retain the best available talent in government services. The nomenclature being used in the new pay matrix assigns levels in place of erstwhile grade pay and the table below brings out the new dispensation for various grades pay pertaining to civil, defence and MNS.

Levels As Per the Pay Matrix

Existing Pay Bands	Existing Levels of Grade Pay	Available For*	New Levels
PB-1	1,800	C	1
	1,900	C	2
	2,000	C, D	3
	2,400	C	4
	2,800	C, D	5
PB-2	3,400	D	5A
	4,200	C, D	6
	4,600	C, D	7
	4,800	C, D	8
	5,400	C	9

PB-3	5,400	C, D, M	10
	5,700	M	10A
	6,100	D	10B
	6,100	M	10B
	6,600	C, D, M	11
	7,600	C	12
PB-4	7,600	M	12
	8,000	D	12A
	8,400	M	12B
	8,700	C	13
	8,700	D	13
	8,900	C	13A
	8,900	D	13A
	9,000	M	13B
	10,000		14
HAG			15
HAG+			16
Apex			17
Cabinet Secretary, Defence Chiefs			18
*C: Civil; D: Defence; M: Military Nursing Service (MNS)			

Prior to VI CPC, there were pay scales. The VI CPC had recommended running pay bands with grade pay as status determiner. The Seventh CPC is recommending a pay matrix with distinct pay levels. The level would henceforth be the status determiner.

(*paras* 5.1.1-5.1.2, 5.1.13-5.1.18)

8.6 Pay Structure (Defence Forces Personnel)

The Defence services in their joint services memorandum have contended that the emoluments in the defence services should stand a fair comparison with what is available in the civil services, otherwise the defence services will be denied their legitimate share of the available talent pool.

The Commission has devised pay matrices for civil and defence forces personnel, after wide ranging feedback from multiple stakeholders. The common aspects of the two matrices and the unique elements in the defence pay matrix are outlined in the succeeding paragraphs.

Pay levels have been set out in a pay matrix, separately for civilian and defence forces personnel. The Commission has evolved a fresh approach by merging the grade pay and pay bands into distinct pay levels. The approach regarding the pay levels and pay matrix has been explained in Chapter 5.1. Some of the major points in the pay matrix which have a common bearing on civilian and defence forces personnel, are highlighted below.

Pay Bands and Grade Pay: Pay bands and grade pays have been dispensed with and the new functional levels have been arrived at by merging the grade pay in the pay band. All the existing levels have been subsumed in the new structure.

Entry Pay: The entry pay for various ranks of defence forces personnel, other than MNS offices, has been arrived at on the same premise, as has been done in the case of civilians. As an illustration, entry pay for a captain has been arrived at as follows:

Entry pay in existing pay band + (residency period for promotion to captain from lieutenant x annual increment) + grade pay of the rank of captain

= ₹ 15,600 + (2 x ₹ 630) + ₹ 6,100 = ₹ 22,960.

An exception to this approach has been made in the case of brigadiers/equivalents where pay for the rank has been arrived at as per the fitment table notified by the Ministry of Defence through its Special Army Instructions of October 2008.

Fitment: The starting point of a sepoy (and equivalent), the entry level personnel in the defence forces, has been fixed in the defence pay matrix at ₹ 21,700. The starting point in the existing pay structure is ₹ 8,460 for a sepoy/equivalent. The fitment in the new matrix is essentially a multiple factor of 2.57. This multiple is the ratio of the new minimum pay arrived at by the Commission (₹ 18,000) and the existing minimum pay (₹ 7,000). The fitment factor is being applied uniformly to all employees.

It includes a factor of 2.25 to account for DA neutralisation, assuming that the rate of dearness allowance would be 125 percent at the time of implementation of the new pay as on 01.01.2016. The actual raise/fitment being recommended by the Commission is 14.29 percent. An identical fitment of 2.57 has also been applied to the existing rates of military service pay (MSP), applicable to defence forces personnel only.

Rationalisation: An 'index of rationalisation' has been applied while making enhancement of levels from pay band 1 to 2, 2 to 3 and 3 onwards on the premise that role, responsibility and accountability increases at each step in the hierarchy. At the existing PB-1, this index is 2.57, increasing to 2.62 for personnel in PB-2 and further to 2.67 from PB-3. Recognising the significantly higher degree of responsibility and accountability at levels corresponding to senior administrative grade, the entry pay is recommended for enhancement by a multiple of 2.72. The same multiple is also being applied at the HAG and HAG+ levels. At the apex level, the index applied is 2.81 and for the service chiefs/cabinet secretary the index has been fixed at 2.78.

As noted in Chapter 5.1, dealing with the civilian pay matrix, marked increase was accorded to directors in the GP 8700 at the stage of implementation of the VI CPC Report. Accordingly, in the matrix, the rationalisation index applied at this level has been fixed at 2.57, lower than the index of 2.67 applied to existing PB-3 officers. A similar formulation has necessarily to be applied to the defence pay matrix since the lieutenant colonels also received a marked increase in their pay level, post-VI CPC recommendations. Since the defence services have an additional level in the existing PB-4 and there is a common pay level for SAG level officers in defence and civil, the Commission has applied the rationalisation index of 2.57 also to the officers in the rank of colonel and brigadier and their equivalent.

MACP: The Commission is not recommending an increase in the number of MACPs. For defence forces personnel this will continue to be administered at 8, 16 and 24 years as before. In the new pay matrix, defence forces personnel will move to the immediate next pay level in the hierarchy. Fixation of pay will follow the same principle as that for a regular promotion in the pay matrix.

Equivalence in Pay Levels for Certain Levels: The starting pay level for officers at Group 'A' entry level is identical at ₹ 56,100 in the case of both civilian and defence service officers. Similarly, the pay of the major general and joint secretary and equivalent officers and those above [viz., lieutenant general (in HAG, HAG+ and Apex) and chief of each of the defence service] has been kept identical with their civilian counterparts. Identical pay levels have been devised for JCO/ORs and their civilian counterparts corresponding to the existing pay bands and grade pay.

For defence forces personnel, there are two separate matrices, one for the service officers and JCO/ORs and another for the military nursing officers. The existing ranks among officers and JCO/ORs in the defence forces personnel have been kept in view while devising the matrix. There are a number of common strands in the civil and defence pay matrices, indeed the principles and philosophy on which they are based are identical. In the case of the pay matrix for military nursing officers (MNS), the Commission has adopted an approach that blends elements of the principles and philosophy adopted in devising the pay matrices with the existing uniqueness in the pay structure of MNS officers. Some of the unique elements that merit mention in the defence pay matrix have been outlined below.

Commencement of Matrix: The commencement of the defence pay matrix for combatants corresponds to the existing GP 2000, which is the induction level for sepoys and equivalent.

More Compact: The pay matrix designed for the defence forces personnel is more compact than the civil pay matrix keeping in view the number of levels, age and retirement profile of the service personnel. For example, the term of engagement of various ranks of JCOs/ORs are fixed and of shorter duration. Service officers on the other hand are given time scale promotion up to the rank of colonel and equivalent and will therefore move, from one pay level to another, in accordance with the stipulated time frame.

Pay Levels Unique to Defence Forces Personnel: Pay levels corresponding to the existing GP 3400, GP 5700, GP 6100, GP 6600, GP 7600, GP 8000, GP 8400, GP 8700, GP 8900 and GP 9000 are unique to defence forces personnel. The minimum pay corresponding to each of these pay levels takes into account the normative residency period of the various ranks of officers.

The Commission emphasises that the pay structure designed by it for the defence forces personnel has been done keeping in view: (a) some of the aspects in their rank structure unique to them and (b) pay structure is not intended to determine the status of the personnel vis-à-vis their counterparts on the civil side.

(*paras* 5.2.1-5.2.16)

8.7 All India Services

The Indian Administrative Service (IAS), the Indian Police Service (IPS) and the Indian Forest Service (IFoS) constitute the all-India services (AIS). The IAS and IPS were initially constituted under provisions of Section 263 of the Government of India Act, 1935 and then were deemed to be services created by the Parliament of India in terms of Article 312 of the Constitution. The Indian Forest Service was constituted under the All India Services Act, 1951 by the Government of India. The All India Services Act, 1951 empowers the government to make rules for the regulation of recruitment, and the conditions of service of persons appointed to the all-India services common to the Union and the States.

A feature common to the all-India services is that the members of these services are recruited by the Centre, but their services are placed under various State cadres, and they have to serve both under the State as well as at the Centre.

Presently, recruitment to the IAS and IPS is carried out through the Civil Services Examination conducted annually by the Union Public Service Commission. Recruitment to the IFoS is through the Indian Forest Service Examination, also conducted by the UPSC annually. From the examination year 2013 onwards, a screening mechanism has been introduced for IFoS through Civil Services (Preliminary) Examination. Therefore, candidates applying for Indian Forest Service Examination are required to appear in the Civil Services (Preliminary) Examination and qualify the same for going to the second stage of

Indian Forest Service (Main) Examination, which consists of a written examination and interview, a pattern akin to the Civil Services Examination.

AIS officers are recruited and trained by the Central Government, and then allotted to different State cadres. There are now 25 State cadres including three joint cadres, namely: (i) Assam and Meghalaya, (ii) Manipur and Tripura, and (iii) Arunachal Pradesh, Goa, Mizoram and the Union Territories (AGMUT).

In their memorandum to the Commission, the Indian Civil and Administrative Service (Central) Association has raised six demands as follows:

1. Demand for retention of distinct 'edge in pay' in the IAS.
2. Demands related to 'two year edge'.
3. Demand for benchmarking pay of IAS with the private sector salaries.
4. Demand for separate exam/papers for recruitment of the IAS.
5. Demand for abolition of grade pay of 8900 and HAG+ available to IPS and IFoS as it is nullifying the initial edge given to the IAS.
6. Demand for special governance and enablement allowance, camp office allowance, research and professional development allowance and hard duty allowance.

The Commission deliberated on various aspects as to whether there is a case for retaining such an edge. If so, at which levels is it needed; and thirdly, who all should be the recipients. The Commission however was not able to arrive at a consensus view on the matter.

The Chairman is of the view that the fundamental principle for determining the remuneration for any position is that it should be based on the complexity and difficulty of the duties and responsibility of the job in question. The criticality of functions at the district administration level holds good equally for the IAS, IPS as well as the IFoS. Therefore, some additional remuneration, in the early stages of their career indeed is justified not only for the IAS but also for the IPS and IFoS.

Therefore, the edge presently accorded to the Indian Administrative Service at three grades mainly senior time scale, junior administrative grade and selection grade may continue in the form of two additional increments @ 3 percent each in the proposed pay matrix. The same is being recommended for Indian Police Service and Indian Forest Service as well. In so far as the Indian Foreign Service is concerned, the existing dispensation shall continue.

Shri Vivek Rae, Member, Seventh CPC is of the view that the financial edge for IAS and IFS is fully justified.

The matter regarding the edge for the IAS over the other AIS and Group 'A' services has been deliberated at length by CPCs over the last six decades and also by the Hon'ble Supreme Court, and there has been repeated endorsement about the IAS being the premier civil service in the country, flowing from its unique role and responsibilities. There cannot be an iota of doubt in this matter. No new factors have emerged for the Seventh CPC to conclude that the edge enjoyed by the IAS should be removed and the IPS and IFoS brought on par with the IAS. The objective reality in fact points in the opposite direction.

It may be noted that the financial edge enjoyed by the IAS over the IPS and IFoS is essentially at the State and field level and State chief ministers are key stakeholders who need to be consulted for taking a well-considered view in the matter. No such consultations have been held by the Seventh CPC with the political leadership at the State level.

Weak implementation and unsatisfactory delivery of public services is recognised as the bane of public administration in India. While there are many complex factors responsible for this outcome, fragmentation of authority and dilution of command and control are important proximate causes. The issue regarding the edge for the IAS needs to be considered in this larger context and not just in terms of service rivalries and inter-service equations. Removal of the financial edge for the IAS, will only further weaken command and control mechanisms at the field level, when the need of the hour is to move in the reverse direction.

IAS officers occupy the commanding heights of the civil service structure not through patronage, but through a highly competitive and transparent selection process. The outcome of this process cannot be questioned on grounds of denial of opportunity or unfair treatment. As the Hon'ble Supreme Court has observed, there cannot be any dispute that each service is a distinct and separate cadre, having its separate field of operation, with different status, prospects, pay scales, nature of duties, responsibilities of the post and conditions of service. In the considered view of the Hon'ble Supreme Court, the classification of civil services is not based on artificial inequalities but is truly founded on substantial differences. The Hon'ble Supreme Court has found it impossible to accept the proposition that the classification rests on an unreal and unreasonable basis and that it is arbitrary or absurd. The Hon'ble Supreme Court could not have stated its views in stronger and clearer language. To make a case for parity on grounds of fairness or legitimate expectations is, therefore, not tenable. The principle of equality of opportunity cannot be stretched to mean "equality of outcomes". The quest for equality of outcomes undermines basic incentive structures and rapidly degenerates into Utopian and Orwellian nightmares.

In view of the position explained above, no case is made out for placing the IPS and IFoS (or any other Civil Service) on par with the IAS in respect of career prospects and conditions of service. There is no doubt that the IPS, IFoS and other civil services are manned by highly competent, public spirited and well-motivated individuals. That, however, does not mean that they should be brought on par with the IAS in terms of the financial edge or anything else. The undersigned, therefore, does not agree with the proposal of Chairman, Seventh CPC in para 7.2.19 to provide two advance increments to IPS and IFoS on par with IAS till NFSG level, since the recommendation is based on untenable notions of parity. The financial edge for IFS should also continue for reasons elaborated in Para 7.2.20(n) above" (Vivek Rae).

Dr. Rathin Roy, Member, Seventh CPC is of the view that the financial edge accorded to the IAS should be removed and the 'edge' demonstrated in a different manner, as elaborated below.

With respect to Para 7.2.8, (the Edge), my view is that there exists no compelling reason to give an edge to any specific all-India service or Central service. I do believe that under the present administrative arrangements, the Indian Administrative Service has a multi-dimensional leadership role to play and that often means that in specific jobs, such as that of district magistrate/collector, officers occupying such positions must be able to exercise overall leadership and be primus inter pares vis-à-vis other district officers such as the district chief of police or the district forest officer. Such is desirably secured by showing leadership qualities backed by administrative affirmation. Simply granting two increments does not bestow such leadership or affirmation.

If the primus inter pares position of the IAS, IFS or any other service has to be reflected in superior financial remuneration, then their recruitment, too, must be conducted separately. These specific competencies should be specified and tested in the recruitment process, as indeed was the case historically. If the recruitment system is not to be altered then a purely financial edge cannot be justified for the IAS, IFS or any other service. Other administrative mechanisms must be found to establish the edge.

The argument for retaining the edge given by the VI CPC did not in fact cite leadership or postulate primus inter pares as one of the reasons. With respect to hardship and other reasons discussed in Para 7.2.16 of this Report, circumstances may impose identical hardships not just on officers of all-India services but also on officers of Central services. Therefore, all officers facing circumstances of hardship should be identically compensated for such, rather than generically compensating officers of any specific service. Such compensation should be addressed holistically when formulating recommendations on pay and allowances, as has been done in the Report. A case specific "edge" on these grounds is not warranted.

For these reasons, I feel that no edge should be granted to any service purely by virtue of belonging to such. If the edge given to the IAS is removed, then the historically iniquitous nature of this edge highlighted in the Paras 7.2.8 to 7.2.13 of the report does not arise" (Rathin Roy).

(*paras* 7.2.1-7.2.6, 7.2.17-7.2.21)

8.8 List and Status of Allowances

S. No.	Name of the Allowance	Recommendation
1.	Accident allowance	Not included in the report.
2.	Acting allowance	Abolished as a separate allowance. Eligible employees to be governed by the newly proposed "additional post allowance".
3.	Aeronautical allowance	Retained; enhanced by 50 percent.
4.	Air despatch pay	Abolished.
5.	Air steward allowance	Abolished.
6.	Air worthiness certificate allowance	Retained; enhanced by 50 percent.
7.	Allowance in lieu of kilometreage (ALK)	Not included in the report.
8.	Allowance in lieu of running room facilities	Not included in the report.
9.	Annual allowance	Retained; enhanced by 50 percent; extended to some more categories.
10.	Antarctica allowance	Retained; rationalised; to be paid as per Cell RH-Max of the newly proposed risk and hardship matrix.
11.	Assisting cashier allowance	Abolished.
12.	ASV allowance	Abolished.
13.	Bad climate allowance	Abolished as a separate allowance; subsumed in tough location allowance-III; to be paid as per Cell R3H3 of the newly proposed risk and hardship matrix.
14.	Bhutan compensatory allowance	Retained; status quo to be maintained.
15.	Boiler watch keeping allowance	Retained; rationalised; to be paid as per Cell R3H1 of the newly proposed risk and hardship matrix.

16.	Book allowance	Retained; status quo to be maintained.
17.	Breach of rest allowance	Not included in the report.
18.	Breakdown allowance	Abolished.
19.	Briefcase allowance	Retained; status quo to be maintained.
20.	Camp allowance	Abolished as a separate allowance; subsumed in the newly proposed territorial army allowance.
21.	Canteen allowance	Retained; enhanced by 50 percent.
22.	Caretaking allowance	Abolished as a separate allowance; eligible employees to be governed by the newly proposed "extra work allowance".
23.	Cash handling allowance	Abolished.
24.	Children education allowance (CEA)	Retained; procedure of payment simplified.
25.	CI ops allowance	Retained; rationalized.
26.	Classification allowance	Retained; enhanced by 50 percent.
27.	Clothing allowance	Abolished as a separate allowance; subsumed in the newly proposed dress allowance.
28.	Coal pilot allowance	Abolished.
29.	COBRA allowance	Retained; rationalised; to be paid as per Cell R1H1 of the newly proposed risk and hardship matrix.
30.	Command allowance	Abolished.
31.	Commando allowance	Abolished.
32.	Commercial allowance	Abolished.
33.	Compensation in lieu of quarters (CILQ)	Abolished as a separate allowance; eligible employees to be governed by the newly proposed provisions for housing for PBORs.
34.	Compensatory (construction or survey) allowance	Retained; rationalised; to be paid as per Cell R3H2 of the newly proposed risk and hardship matrix.
35.	Composite personal maintenance allowance (CPMA)	Retained; rationalised; enhanced by 50 percent; extended to some more categories.
36.	Condiment allowance	Abolished.

37.	Constant attendance allowance	Retained; enhanced by 50 percent.
38.	Conveyance allowance	Retained; status quo to be maintained.
39.	Cooking allowance	Retained; rationalised; to be paid as per Cell R3H3 of the newly proposed risk and hardship matrix.
40.	Cost of living allowance	Retained; status quo to be maintained.
41.	Court allowance	Abolished.
42.	Cycle allowance	Abolished.
43.	Daily allowance	Retained; rationalized.
44.	Daily allowance on foreign travel	Retained; status quo to be maintained.
45.	Dearness allowance (DA)	Retained; status quo to be maintained.
46.	Deputation (duty) allowance for civilians	Retained; ceilings enhanced by 50 percent.
47.	Deputation (duty) allowance for defence personnel	Retained; ceilings enhanced by 50 percent.
48.	Desk allowance	Abolished.
49.	Detachment allowance	Retained; rationalized; enhanced by 50 percent.
50.	Diet allowance	Abolished.
51.	Diving allowance, dip money and attendant allowance	Retained; enhanced by 50 percent.
52.	Dual charge allowance	Abolished as a separate allowance; eligible employees to be governed by the newly proposed "additional post allowance".
53.	Educational concession	Retained; rationalized; extended to some more categories.
54.	Electricity allowance	Abolished.
55.	Entertainment allowance for cabinet secretary	Abolished.
56.	Entertainment allowance in Indian railways	Abolished.
57.	Extra duty allowance	Abolished as a separate allowance; eligible employees to be governed by the newly proposed "extra work allowance".

58.	Family accommodation allowance (FAA)	Abolished as a separate allowance; eligible employees to be governed by the newly proposed provisions for housing for PBORs.
59.	Family HRA allowance	Retained; status quo to be maintained.
60.	Family planning allowance	Abolished.
61.	Field area allowance	Retained; rationalized.
62.	Fixed medical allowance (FMA)	Retained; status quo to be maintained.
63.	Fixed monetary compensation	Abolished as a separate allowance; eligible employees to be governed by the newly proposed "additional post allowance".
64.	Flag station allowance	Abolished as a separate allowance; eligible employees to be governed by the newly proposed "extra work allowance".
65.	Flight charge certificate allowance	Abolished as a separate allowance; eligible employees to be governed by the newly proposed "extra work allowance".
66.	Flying allowance	Retained; rationalised; to be paid as per Cell R1H1 of the newly proposed risk and hardship matrix.
67.	Flying squad allowance	Abolished.
68.	Free fall jump instructor allowance	Retained; rationalised; to be paid as per Cell R2H2 of the newly proposed risk and hardship matrix.
69.	Funeral allowance	Abolished.
70.	Ghat allowance	Not included in the report.
71.	Good service/good conduct/badge pay	Retained; enhanced by a factor of 2.25.
72.	Haircutting allowance	Abolished as a separate allowance; subsumed in composite personal maintenance allowance.
73.	Handicapped allowance	Abolished.
74.	Hard area allowance	Retained; rationalized by a factor of 0.8.

75.	Hardlying money	Retained; rationalised; full rate to be paid as per Cell R3H3 of the newly proposed risk and hardship matrix.
76.	Headquarters allowance	Abolished.
77.	Health and malaria allowance	Retained; rationalised; to be paid as per Cell R3H3 of the newly proposed risk and hardship matrix.
78.	High altitude allowance	Retained; rationalized.
79.	Higher proficiency allowance	Abolished as a separate allowance; eligible employees to be governed by language award or higher qualification incentive for civilians.
80.	Higher qualification incentive for civilians	Retained; rationalized.
81.	Holiday compensatory allowance	Abolished as a separate allowance; eligible employees to be governed by national holiday allowance.
82.	Holiday monetary compensation	Retained; rationalized.
83.	Hospital patient care allowance/patient care allowance	Retained; rationalised; to be paid as per Cell R1H3 of the newly proposed risk and hardship matrix.
84.	House rent allowance (HRA)	Retained; rationalized by a factor of 0.8.
85.	Hutting allowance	Abolished.
86.	Hydrographic survey allowance	Retained; rationalized.
87.	Initial equipment allowance	Abolished as a separate allowance; subsumed in the newly proposed dress allowance.
88.	Instructional allowance	Abolished as a separate allowance; eligible employees to be governed by training allowance.
89.	Internet allowance	Retained; rationalized.
90.	Investigation allowance	Abolished.
91.	Island special duty allowance	Retained; rationalized by a factor of 0.8.

92.	Judge advocate general department examination award	Abolished as a separate allowance; eligible employees to be governed by the newly proposed higher qualification incentive for defence personnel.
93.	Kilometreage allowance (KMA)	Not included in the report.
94.	Kit maintenance allowance	Abolished as a separate allowance; subsumed in the newly proposed dress allowance.
95.	Language allowance	Retained; enhanced by 50 percent.
96.	Language award	Retained; enhanced by 50 percent.
97.	Language reward and allowance	Abolished.
98.	Launch campaign allowance	Abolished.
99.	Leave travel concession (LTC)	Retained; rationalized.
100.	Library allowance	Abolished as a separate allowance; eligible employees to be governed by the newly proposed "extra work allowance".
101.	MARCOS and chariot allowance	Retained; rationalised; to be paid as per Cell R1H1 of the newly proposed risk and hardship matrix.
102.	Medal allowance	Retained.
103.	Messing allowance	Retained for "floating staff" under Fishery Survey of India, and enhanced by 50 percent; abolished for nursing staff.
104.	Metropolitan allowance	Abolished.
105.	Mileage allowance for journeys by road	Retained.
106.	Mobile phone allowance	Retained; rationalized.
107.	Monetary allowance attached to gallantry awards	Retained; status quo to be maintained.
108.	National holiday allowance	Retained; enhanced by 50 percent.
109.	Newspaper allowance	Retained; rationalized.
110.	Night duty allowance	Retained; rationalized.
111.	Night patrolling allowance	Abolished.

112.	Non-practicing allowance (NPA)	Retained; rationalized by a factor of 0.8.
113.	Nuclear research plant support allowance	Retained; enhanced by 50 percent.
114.	Nursing allowance	Retained; rationalized.
115.	Official hospitality grant in defence forces	Abolished.
116.	Officiating allowance	Not included in the report.
117.	Operation theatre allowance	Abolished.
118.	Orderly allowance	Retained; status Quo to be maintained.
119.	Organization special pay	Abolished.
120.	Out of pocket allowance	Abolished as a separate allowance; eligible employees to be governed by daily allowance on foreign travel.
121.	Outfit allowance	Abolished as a separate allowance; subsumed in the newly proposed dress allowance.
122.	Outstation (detention) allowance	Not included in the report.
123.	Outstation (relieving) allowance	Not included in the report.
124.	Out-turn allowance	Abolished.
125.	Overtime allowance (OTA)	Abolished.
126.	Para allowances	Retained; rationalised; to be paid as per Cell R2H2 of the newly proposed risk and hardship matrix.
127.	Para jump instructor allowance	Retained; rationalised; to be paid as per Cell R2H2 of the newly proposed risk and hardship matrix.
128.	Parliament assistant allowance	Retained; enhanced by 50 percent.
129.	PCO allowance	Retained; rationalized.
130.	Post-graduate allowance	Retained; enhanced by 50 percent.
131.	Professional update allowance	Retained; enhanced by 50 percent; extended to some more categories.
132.	Project allowance	Retained; rationalised; to be paid as per Cell R3H2 of the newly proposed risk and hardship matrix.

133.	Qualification allowance	Retained; enhanced by 50 percent; extended to some more categories.
134.	Qualification grant	Abolished as a separate allowance; eligible employees to be governed by the newly proposed higher qualification incentive for defence personnel.
135.	Qualification pay	Retained; enhanced by a factor of 2.25.
136.	Rajbhasha allowance	Abolished as a separate allowance; eligible employees to be governed by the newly proposed "extra work allowance".
137.	Rajdhani allowance	Abolished.
138.	Ration money allowance	Retained; rationalized.
139.	Refreshment allowance	Retained; enhanced by a factor of 2.25.
140.	Rent free accommodation	Abolished.
141.	Reward for meritorious service	Retained; enhanced by a factor of 2.25.
142.	Risk allowance	Abolished.
143.	Robe allowance	Abolished as a separate allowance. Subsumed in the newly proposed dress allowance.
144.	Robe maintenance allowance	Abolished as a separate allowance; subsumed in the newly proposed dress allowance.
145.	Savings bank allowance	Abolished.
146.	Sea going allowance	Retained; rationalised; to be paid as per Cell R2H2 of the newly proposed risk and hardship matrix.
147.	Secret allowance	Abolished.
148.	Shoe allowance	Abolished as a separate allowance; subsumed in the newly proposed dress allowance.
149.	Shorthand allowance	Abolished.
150.	Shunting allowance	Not included in the report.
151.	Siachen allowance	Retained; rationalised; to be paid as per Cell RH-Max of the newly proposed risk and hardship matrix.

152.	Single in lieu of quarters (SNLQ)	Abolished as a separate allowance; eligible employees to be governed by the newly proposed provisions for housing for PBORs.
153.	Soap toilet allowance	Abolished as a separate allowance; subsumed in composite personal maintenance allowance.
154.	Space technology allowance	Abolished.
155.	Special allowance for child care for women with disabilities	Retained; enhanced by 100 percent.
156.	Special allowance to chief safety officers/safety officers	Retained; rationalized by a factor of 0.8.
157.	Special appointment allowance	Abolished as a separate allowance; eligible employees to be governed by the newly proposed "extra work allowance".
158.	Special compensatory (hill area) allowance	Abolished.
159.	Special compensatory (remote locality) allowance	Abolished as a separate allowance; eligible employees to be governed by the newly proposed tough location allowance-I, II or III.
160.	Special DOT pay	Abolished.
161.	Special duty allowance	Retained; rationalized by a factor of 0.8.
162.	Special forces allowance	Retained; rationalised; to be paid as per Cell R1H1 of the newly proposed risk and hardship matrix.
163.	Special incident/investigation/ security allowance	Retained; rationalized.
164.	Special LC gate allowance	Retained; rationalised; to be paid as per Cell R3H3 of the newly proposed risk and hardship matrix.
165.	Special NCRB pay	Abolished.
166.	Special running staff allowance	Retained; extended to some more categories.
167.	Special scientists' pay	Abolished.

168.	Specialist allowance	Retained; enhanced by 50 percent.
169.	Spectacle allowance	Abolished.
170.	Split duty allowance	Retained; enhanced by 50 percent.
171.	Study allowance	Abolished.
172.	Submarine allowance	Retained; rationalised; to be paid as per Cell R1H1 of the newly proposed risk and hardship matrix.
173.	Submarine duty allowance	Retained; rationalised; to be paid as per Cell R3H1 of the newly proposed risk and hardship matrix, on a pro-rata basis.
174.	Submarine technical allowance	Retained; rationalised; to be paid as per Cell R3H3 of the newly proposed risk and hardship matrix; extended to some more categories.
175.	Subsistence allowance	Retained; status quo to be maintained.
176.	Sumptuary allowance in training establishments	Abolished.
177.	Sumptuary allowance to judicial officers in Supreme Court registry	Abolished.
178.	Sunderban allowance	Abolished as a separate allowance; subsumed in tough location allowance-III; to be paid as per Cell R3H3 of the newly proposed risk and hardship matrix.
179.	TA bounty	Abolished as a separate allowance; subsumed in the newly proposed territorial army allowance.
180.	180 TA for retiring employees	Retained; rationalized.
181.	TA on transfer	Retained; rationalized.
182.	Technical allowance	Abolished as a separate allowance; eligible employees to be governed by the newly proposed higher qualification incentive for defence personnel.
183.	Tenure allowance	Retained; ceilings enhanced by 50 percent.

184.	Test pilot and flight test engineer allowance	Retained; rationalised; to be paid as per Cell R1H3 of the newly proposed risk and hardship matrix.
185.	Training allowance	Retained; rationalized by a factor of 0.8; extended to some more categories.
186.	Training stipend	Abolished.
187.	Transport allowance (TPTA)	Retained; rationalized.
188.	Travelling allowance	Retained; rationalized.
189.	Treasury allowance	Abolished.
190.	Tribal area allowance	Abolished as a separate allowance; subsumed in tough location allowance-III; to be paid as per Cell R3H3 of the newly proposed risk and hardship matrix.
191.	Trip allowance	Not included in the report.
192.	Uniform allowance	Abolished as a separate allowance; subsumed in the newly proposed dress allowance.
193.	Unit certificate and charge certificate allowance	Retained; enhanced by 50 percent.
194.	Vigilance allowance	Abolished.
195.	Waiting duty allowance	Not included in the report.
196.	Washing allowance	Abolished as a separate allowance; subsumed in the newly proposed dress allowance.

(Chapter 8.1 of the Report)

8.9 Leave Travel Concession (LTC)

LTC is granted to Central Government employees to facilitate home travel as well as travel to different parts of the country. Presently, two hometown visits are allowed in a block of four years with one hometown visit substitutable with "all-India" visit. However, for the first two 4-year blocks, three hometown visits and one "all-India" visit are permissible. LTC is not granted to an employee whose spouse is working in Indian Railways.

There are demands to increase the frequency of LTC, especially of the "all-India" visit, and extend LTC to foreign countries also. Personnel posted on islands have requested the Commission that splitting of hometown LTC may be permitted so that their families can visit them from the mainland once a year and they (the employees) can also travel to the mainland once a year to visit the family. Personnel of Sashastra Seema Bal (SSB) have sought parity with other CAPFs for facility of additional LTC. Railway employees have strongly represented that there are many places that are not connected by rail and in absence of LTC, they are not able to visit these places. Hence, they should be allowed the facility of LTC in lieu of certain number of their free passes. Similar sentiments have also been expressed by employees whose spouses are railway employees.

Extension of LTC to foreign countries is not in the ambit of this Commission.

The proposal to split hometown LTC has merit and can be considered. Hence, it is recommended that splitting of hometown LTC should be allowed in case of employees posted in North East, Ladakh and Island territories of Andaman, Nicobar and Lakshadweep. This will enable these employee and their families to meet more often.

Presently, personnel of defence forces serving in field/high altitude/CI Ops areas are granted one additional free railway warrant. This should be extended to all personnel of CAPFs and the Indian Coast Guard mutatis mutandis.

The facility of additional LTC should be extended to SSB personnel, at par with other CAPFs.

Regarding bringing railway employees (and employees whose spouses are railway servants) into the fold of LTC, the following is recommended:

1. No hometown LTC will be admissible to railway employees, only "all-India" LTC will be granted once in four years.
2. For the grant of LTC, all passes for the current year will have to be surrendered.
3. If the employee has already availed of a pass in any year, then LTC will not be allowed in that year.
4. If both spouses are railway servants, then surrender of passes of any one of them will suffice.
5. For the purposes of this allowance, year means a calendar year.

(*paras* 8.15.28-8.15.34)

8.10 Holidays and Leave

Presently, Central Government offices observe a five-day week which results in 104 holidays every year on account of weekends. In addition, there are three national holidays, fourteen gazetted holidays and two restricted holidays. Further, civilian government employees are entitled to 8 days' casual leave, 20 days' half pay leave (commutable to medical leave) and 30 days' earned leave. Besides the above, quite a few other types of leave are admissible.

The following paragraphs bring out, in alphabetical order, the different kinds of holidays and leave admissible, demands received (if any) and views of the

Commission on each one of them. Unless otherwise stated, the existing terms and conditions regulating these holidays and leave shall remain unchanged.

8.10.1 Casual Leave (CL): Casual leave is granted to enable a government servant to attend to sudden/unforeseen needs/tasks. Presently, 8 days CL is normally granted to a Central Government employee per calendar year. The number goes up to 10 days for industrial workers, 20 days for defence officers and 30 days for defence PBORs.

Certain other categories of staff, particularly in the railways, are granted CL ranging from 11 to 13 days in a year. Demands have been made to increase the number of CL to 15 days for industrial workers and 12 days for other employees. CAPFs have also sought parity with defence forces in matters of casual leave.

Regarding the number of casual leaves, the Commission is of the view that the present system is working well and need not be altered. As far as the case of CAPFs for parity with defence forces is concerned, the Commission notes that CAPFs are essentially civilian forces and their service conditions are different from defence forces. Hence, parity in terms of number of casual leaves cannot be considered. To sum up, status quo is recommended.

8.10.2 Child Adoption Leave: This leave is granted to female employees, with fewer than two surviving children on valid adoption of a child below the age of one year, for a period of 135 days immediately after the date of valid adoption. No demands have been received regarding this leave. Accordingly, status quo may be maintained.

8.10.3 Child Care Leave (CCL): CCL is granted to women employees for a maximum period of two years (i.e. 730 days) during their entire service for taking care of their minor children (up to eighteen years of age). There are several demands relating to CCL which include converting the same into "family care" leave, extending the facility to male parents and many representations stressing that it should be extended at least to single male parents.

Suggestions have also been received that in cases where the child is differently-abled, the clause stipulating that the child should be minor, should be done away with. Single mothers have highlighted their unique problems and requested the Commission for liberalising the grant of CCL. Interestingly, representations have also been made for discontinuance of the CCL, primarily on the grounds that it disrupts office working and also because it promotes gender discrimination.

When CCL was first introduced by the VI CPC, it generated considerable interest as it represented a positive measure benefiting women employees. It also took a while to stabilise and it is seen that as many as five amendments/clarifications were issued within a short period of time. As it stands, it is meant for women employees "for taking care of up to two children whether for rearing the children or looking after their needs like examination, sickness etc.". It is treated akin to earned leave and is sanctioned as such. It may not, however, be granted in more than three spells in a calendar year.

In the first two years of its implementation, the experience was that women employees tended to treat this as casual leave or an extension of the same, and the resultant frequent absences caused disruptions at work. To address this, in September 2010, a clarification was issued stipulating that CCL may not be granted in more than three spells in a calendar year and also that it may not be granted for less than 15 days at a time. However, the latter stipulation was subsequently withdrawn and as per the latest clarification issued on June 5, 2014, the government has decided to remove the requirement of minimum period of 15 days CCL. It has been brought to the notice of the Commission that the capping of maximum three spells in a calendar year has, to some extent, addressed the problems relating to disruption of work. Notwithstanding that, in the course of discussions with various stakeholders, the sense that has come across is that what was introduced as a welfare measure to help employees in times of need, is seen as a benefit that has to be availed simply because it exists. There is, therefore, a palpable need to bring in some inhibiting feature so as to ensure that only genuinely affected employees avail of this scheme.

Towards this end, the Commission recommends that CCL should be granted at 100 percent of the salary for the first 365 days, but at 80 percent of the salary for the next 365 days. In making this recommendation, the Commission has also kept in mind the fact the concept of a paid (whether 100 percent or 80 percent) leave solely for child care for a period of two years, is a liberal measure unmatched anywhere else.

The Commission notes that in the event a male employee is single, the onus of rearing and nurturing the children falls squarely on his shoulders. Hence, extension of CCL to single male parents is recommended. Moreover, the Commission recognizes the additional responsibility on the shoulders of employees who are single mothers. Accordingly, it is recommended that for such employees, the conditionality of three spells in a calendar year should be relaxed to six spells in a calendar year.

8.10.4 Commuted Leave: Presently, commuted leave not exceeding half the amount of half-pay leave due can be taken on medical certificate. Demands have been made to do away with the need for medical certificate.

The Commission does not find merit in the demand. Status quo is recommended.

8.10.5 Earned Leave (EL) or Leave on Average Pay (LAP): Presently, 30 days EL per annum is granted to civilian employees and 60 days to defence personnel. EL can be accumulated up to 300 days in addition to the number of days for which encashment has been allowed along with LTC. Suggestions have been made to increase the accumulation to 450 days, allow encashment of 50 percent of the accumulated EL after 20 years of service and delink encashment of leave from LTC. A novel concept of "gifting" has been put forward, wherein employee should be allowed to 'gift' certain number of days of leave to one's spouse or one's colleague. "Vacational" staff like teachers, principals, etc. have demanded restoration of 10 days EL, which was changed to 20 days half pay leave by the VI CPC.

In many organizations, employees are encouraged to take leave on the premise that it revitalizes them and is beneficial for the organization in the long run. Such a system is not prevalent in the government sector in India, but substituting leave with cash is also not desirable. Hence, no change in encashment guidelines is recommended.

The Commission recognizes that earned leave is, as the name suggests, earned by an employee through the services rendered. Hence, it is personal to the employee and the concept of "gifting" cannot be considered.

The demand of "vacational" staff can, however, be agreed to. Hence, it is recommended that "vacational" staff be granted 10 days EL in place of 20 days half pay leave. Other than this no other change is recommended.

8.10.6 Extra Ordinary Leave (EOL): EOL is granted to a government servant when no other leave is admissible or when other leave is admissible, but the government servant applies in writing for extraordinary leave. This leave is neither debited to leave account nor is any leave salary paid. No demands have been received regarding this leave. Accordingly, status quo may be maintained.

8.10.7 Furlough Leave: This leave is admissible only to defence officers for up to 60 days. It can be availed at half pay, once in a cycle of three calendar years. No demands have been received regarding this leave. However, the Commission is of the view that furlough leave is a legacy of the pre-Independence era. Since defence officers are already entitled to double the earned leave and more than double the casual leave available to civilian employees, there is no justification for continuation of furlough leave. Hence, it is recommended that furlough leave be abolished.

8.10.8 Gazetted and Restricted Holidays: Besides the three national holidays, employees are presently entitled to 14 gazetted and 2 restricted holidays every year. Out of the 14 gazetted holidays, 11 are observed throughout India, while 3 are decided locally. For restricted holidays, a list is drawn up at the local level taking local factors into consideration; an employee is entitled to choose any two in a year out of that list. There are demands to include May Day and 14th April as compulsory holidays throughout India. Suggestions have also been received to increase the number of locally decided gazetted holidays from 3 to 6.

The Commission is of the view that the present system is working well. Accordingly, status quo is recommended.

8.10.9 Half Pay Leave (HPL) or Leave on Half Average Pay (LHAP): Presently, government employees are entitled to 20 days of half pay leave for each completed year of service, credited @10 days on the 1st of January and 1st of July every year. There are representations that encashment of HPL should be allowed at the time of superannuation.

The demands lack merit. Elsewhere in the report it has been recommended that 20 days HPL granted to "vacational" staff be converted into 10 days EL. Hence, HPL will henceforth not be available to them. No change other than this is recommended.

8.10.10 Hospital Leave: This leave is granted to Group 'C' railway employees if they are suffering from illness or injuries directly due to risks incurred in the course of official duties, on production of medical certificate. Full pay is admissible for first 120 days and half pay thereafter.

The leave may be combined with any other kind of leave due and admissible, provided total period of leave does not exceed 28 months. Demands have been received to increase this leave to an unlimited period of time as applicable to PBORs of defence forces.

This has been discussed under special disability leave.

8.10.11 Leave Not Due (LND): LND is granted when the employee has no half-pay leave at credit and he/she requests for the grant of leave not due. It is granted only on medical certification, if the leave sanctioning authority is satisfied that there is a reasonable prospect of the employee returning to duty on its expiry. LND during the entire service is limited to a maximum of 360 days and will be debited against the half-pay leave that the employee may earn subsequently. No demands have been received regarding this leave. Accordingly, status quo may be maintained.

8.10.12 Maternity Leave: Maternity leave is granted to women government employees—up to 180 days for pregnancy and 45 days in the entire service for miscarriage/abortion. Maternity leave can be combined with any other leave up to two years without medical certificate. The Commission has received representations for enhancement of maternity leave to 240 days with full pay and further 120 days with half pay.

It is noted that maternity leave was raised from 135 days to 180 days and 'period in continuation' raised from 1 year to 2 years by the VI CPC. No further increase is warranted. Status quo is recommended.

8.10.13 Paternity Leave: Presently, a male employee with less than two surviving children may be granted paternity leave for a period of 15 days during the confinement of his wife, up to 15 days before or six months from the date of delivery of child. Paternity leave may also be granted to a government servant with less than two surviving children on valid adoption of a child below the age of one year, within a period of 6 months from the date of valid adoption. There are demands to increase the period to 30 days.

Present dispensation of 15 days is adequate. Status quo may be maintained.

8.10.14 Sick Leave: This leave is admissible to defence personnel only on account of sickness attributable/aggravated due to service conditions. Full pay is granted for the entire duration of hospitalization. Beyond that, defence officers are allowed sick leave with full pay and allowances for first six months and fully pay only for next 18-24 months, while there is no such limit for PBORs. There are demands from CAPFs for complete parity with defence forces in respect of provisions of sick leave.

It is discussed under Special Disability Leave.

8.10.15 Special Casual Leave (SCL): SCL is granted to employees to cover their absence from duty for various occasions like sports events, cultural activities, participation in Republic Day Parade, voluntary blood donation, trade union meetings, etc. Full pay is granted during SCL and it can be sanctioned with retrospective effect also. There are demands to extend SCL to organ donors till the time they are fit to resume duty.

The Commission would like to express its concern at the widespread use of SCL as a means of getting away from duty. However, because of the extensive scope and case specific nature of this leave, no concrete recommendations can be made. The government may, however, consider the following suggestions:

1. Review the purposes for which SCL is presently granted.
2. Limit the number of purposes for which an employee can be granted SCL in a year.
3. Limit the total number of days that an employee can be granted SCL in a year.

8.10.16 Special Disability Leave: It is admissible to civilian employees when disabled by injury intentionally or accidentally inflicted or caused by or in consequence of the due performance of official duties or in consequence of official position held. Full pay is admissible for the first 120 days and half pay thereafter. The leave may be combined with any other kind of leave due and admissible, provided the total period of leave does not exceed 24 months.

There are demands to remove the ceiling limit of 24 months—the duration of leave may be left to the discretion of doctor and full pay paid for the entire period.

There are three different kinds of leave admissible to civilian/defence employees which are granted for work related illness/injuries—hospital leave, special disability leave and sick leave. It is an established worldwide practice that employees who suffer illness/injuries that are attributable to/aggravated in the course of their duty need to be adequately compensated. However, due to the inherent difference between the nature of duties of civilians and uniformed forces, a distinction needs be made in the level of compensation provided. Having said that, there is some similarity in the risks faced by different uniformed forces, and consequently parity amongst them may be considered as far as this leave is concerned.

The following is, therefore, recommended:

1. Hospital leave, special disability leave and sick leave should be subsumed in a new leave named work related illness and injury leave (WRIIL).
2. Full pay and allowances will be granted to all employees during the entire period of hospitalization on account of WRIIL.
3. Beyond hospitalization, WRIIL will be governed as follows:

- For civilian employees, RPF employees and personnel of police forces of Union Territories: Full pay and allowances for the 6 months immediately following hospitalization and half pay only for 12 months beyond that. The half pay period may be commuted to full pay with corresponding number of days of half pay leave debited from the employee's leave account.
- For officers of defence, CAPFs, Indian Coast Guard: Full pay and allowances for the 6 months immediately following hospitalization, for the next 24 months, full pay only.
- For PBORs of defence, CAPFs, Indian Coast Guard: Full pay and allowances, with no limit regarding period.

4. In the case of persons to whom the Workmen's Compensation Act, 1923 applies, the amount of leave salary payable under WRIIL shall be reduced by the amount of compensation payable under the Act.
5. No earned leave or half pay leave will be credited during the period that employee is on WRIIL.

8.10.17 Study Leave: Presently, study leave may be granted to all government employees with not less than five years' service for undergoing a special course consisting of higher studies or specialized training in a professional or technical subject having a direct and close connection with the sphere of his duties as a civil servant. It is limited to 24 months, except for CHS officers who are allowed 36 months.

No demands have been received regarding this leave. Accordingly, status quo may be maintained

(*paras* 9.2.1-9.2.39)

8.11 Medical Facilities for Serving Employees and Pensioners

The Central Government provides health care facilities for both serving and retired employees. Employees of some Central Government organisations, like railways and defence, are covered by captive medical facilities provided by the concerned administrative ministries. Certain other organisations have limited medical facilities covering out-patient treatment and limited hospitalisation. The general coverage of Central Government employees is under the Central Government Health Scheme (CGHS) and the Central Service (Medical Attendance) Rules, 1944 [CS(MA) Rules].

CGHS, under the aegis of Department of Health and Family Welfare, provides out-patient (OPD)/in-patient (IPD) treatment to its beneficiaries—both serving and retired employees— within its area of operation. Serving employees of the Central Government, outside CGHS area and thus not under its coverage, avail medical facilities under CS (MA).

CS (MA) Rules, 1944 are statutory provisions for medical relief to the serving Central Government employees and their family members who are not residing in CGHS covered cities. There is a provision for appointment of authorized medical attendants (AMA) by the concerned department for their employees either from the medical officers working under the State/Central Government or from private practitioners depending upon the situation.

Pensioners are not covered under the CS (MA) Rules. Pensioners residing outside CGHS areas are entitled to fixed medical allowance (FMA) @ ₹ 500 per month for their OPD/IPD needs. Such pensioners can also avail IPD/OPD under CGHS subject to some conditions, details of which have been explained in a subsequent paragraph.

During its interactions with various stakeholders, the Commission has received numerous demands relating to medical facilities. Broadly, these demands are as follows:

1. CGHS should be expanded and improved: It has been demanded that facilities offered by CGHS should be strengthened and more private hospitals should be empanelled in such a way that they are nearer to the residence cluster of the beneficiaries.
2. Pensioners be treated at par with serving employees: It has been represented that CS (MA) be extended to pensioners residing outside CGHS Area. It has

been demanded that smart cards be issued to all pensioners for availing cashless medical facilities across the country in all government hospitals, all accredited multi super speciality hospitals which have been allotted land at concessional rates, all CGHS, (ex-servicemen contributory health scheme (ECHS) empanelled hospitals.

3. It has been demanded that the amount of FMA be raised to □2,000 with DA thereon.
4. It has been pointed out that P&T pensioners who did not subscribe to CGHS while in service are not covered under CGHS post-retirement. It has also been demanded that all P&T dispensaries should be merged with CGHS so that these pensioners can avail IPD/OPD benefits.

CGHS has benefited a significant number of government employees and pensioners. The Commission notes that the pressure on CGHS has been increasing over the years. This has affected its efficient functioning at times. However, the Commission is aware that services provided by CGHS are valued by a number of employees and most of the pensioners.

The demands of the various stakeholders, listed above, have been analysed keeping these facts in the backdrop. Broadly, these demands can be classified into three segments:

1. Expansion of CGHS to more areas.
2. Strengthening of the existing facilities under CGHS.
3. Provision of medical facilities for pensioners living outside CGHS areas.

8.11.1 Expansion of CGHS to More Areas: CGHS is presently operational in 25 cities. The government is opening at least one CGHS wellness centre in 12 more cities. The Commission notes that with this addition, almost all the state capitals will be covered under CGHS.

The VI CPC had recommended that all postal dispensaries should be merged with CGHS and all postal employees including retired postal employees be covered under CGHS wherever available. It is noted that out of 52 postal dispensaries, 19 have been merged with existing CGHS centres. During his presentation, DG, CGHS highlighted scarcity of resources, particularly that of manpower, due to which government is not in a position to extend CGHS to more areas. The Commission feels that modalities should be worked out to utilise the existing manpower of the postal dispensaries and steps should be taken to merge the remaining 33 postal dispensaries with CGHS. This will benefit a large number of postal employees and pensioners. This will also benefit those Central Government employees/pensioners who are otherwise eligible for coverage under CGHS but are being denied this facility because of absence of CGHS centres in their cities. The Commission feels that Ministry of Health and Family Welfare's order dated August 1, 1996 which states that P&T pensioners who were not participating in CGHS while in service may not be extended medical facility under CGHS is discriminatory and should therefore be revoked. This would enable all P&T pensioners, irrespective of their participation in CGHS while in service, to avail medical facilities under CGHS after making requisite subscription.

8.11.2 Strengthening of the Existing Facilities under CGHS: At present, CGHS is providing facilities to about 36 lakh beneficiaries (card holders and their dependents). This includes about 26 lakh serving employees and their dependants and about 10 lakh pensioners and their dependants. CGHS has a network of 273 allopathic and 85 AYUSH wellness centres, 73 labs, 19 poly-clinics, 19 dental clinics, 4 hospitals and 2 geriatric clinics (Delhi only). CGHS has also empanelled about 750 private hospitals and diagnostic centres.

CGHS, thus, has indeed been catering to a sizeable population of government employees. However, there are many limitations on this count. The Commission notes that financial constraints, non-availability of sufficient health care professionals and other administrative limitations impede rapid expansion of CGHS to more areas or strengthening of its services. Even with the limited expansion, possibly a large number of employees/pensioners will still remain uncovered given their spatial distribution.

8.11.3 Provision of Medical Facilities for Pensioners Living Outside CGHS Areas: Pensioners residing in non-CGHS areas have three options. First, they may draw FMA. In this case, pensioners will have to make their own arrangements for both IPD and OPD treatment. Second, pensioners may draw FMA for OPD and avail CGHS benefits for IPD from the nearest CGHS city after making the required subscription to CGHS card. Third, pensioners may avail CGHS facility both for OPD and IPD from the nearest CGHS city after making the required subscription to CGHS.

In case of emergency, pensioners, under the second and the third options, can take treatment in a private hospital empanelled under CS (MA)/ex-servicemen contributory health scheme (ECHS) or any private hospital in the domicile city. However, such pensioners will have to make payment upfront for their treatment and thereafter seek reimbursement from CGHS. This reimbursement is capped at CGHS rates.

Various pensioners' associations have demanded that CS (MA) Rules should be extended to cover Central Government pensioners residing outside CGHS areas. As referred to earlier, CS (MA) Rules do not cover the pensioners. The Commission notes that the VI CPC was not in favour of extending CS (MA) to the pensioners on the grounds of huge financial implications and administrative difficulties relating to submission and reimbursement of bills.

8.11.4 Health Insurance Scheme: In this backdrop, the Commission opines that health insurance for the government employees and pensioners remains the most optimal route for ensuring complete coverage for all employees, pensioners and their dependants in the long run. The IV CPC had suggested that feasibility and modalities of an insurance scheme for government employees in lieu of medical reimbursement may be considered by the government. The VI CPC had recommended introduction of a health insurance scheme for Central Government employees and pensioners. It had recommended that for existing employees and pensioners, the scheme should be available on a voluntary basis, subject to their paying the prescribed contribution. It had also been recommended that the health insurance scheme should be compulsory for new government employees who would be joining service after the introduction of the Scheme.

Similarly, it had recommended that those retiring after the introduction of the insurance scheme would be covered under the Scheme.

The Commission observes that in view of the recommendations of the earlier pay commissions and various high power committees, the government has been contemplating the introduction of a health insurance scheme on pan-India basis. The Commission notes that although the Committee of Secretaries had given its 'in principle' approval way back in 2011, and an amount of ₹ 2,061 crore had been earmarked under the XII Five Year Plan, the Scheme has still not been implemented.

The Commission notes that given the tardiness in the introduction of the long awaited insurance scheme, as already mentioned earlier, the pensioners residing outside CGHS area will continue to be at a disadvantage, in terms of medical facilities, compared to their counterparts residing in CGHS areas. As stated earlier, according to existing provisions, pensioner residing outside CGHS area but subscribing to CGHS for OPD/IPD can avail medical facility from any hospital—private or public or empanelled under CS (MA)/ECHS—in his/her own city. However, in such cases, the pensioners have to make upfront payment to the hospital and claim reimbursement later. The Commission feels that this could be a limiting factor for many pensioners who may not have the resources to pay hospital expenses upfront. The Commission notes that under CS (MA) Rules/ECHS, there are empanelled hospitals in every part of the country, at least in all major locations. In this backdrop, after identification of some major centres/cities based on minimum population threshold of pensioners, these hospitals could be empanelled by CGHS as well, for extending medical facilities on a cashless basis.

Considering all the issues, the Commission makes the following recommendations:

1. The Commission strongly recommends the introduction of health insurance scheme for Central Government employees and pensioners. In the interregnum, for the benefit of pensioners residing outside the CGHS areas, the Commission recommends that CGHS should empanel those hospitals which are already empanelled under CS (MA)/ECHS for catering to the medical requirement of these pensioners on a cashless basis. This would involve strengthening of administrative capacity of nearest CGHS centres. However, this step will go a long way in ameliorating the pending grievances of these pensioners.
2. The Commission recommends that the remaining 33 postal dispensaries should be merged with CGHS. The Commission further recommends that all postal pensioners, irrespective of their participation in CGHS while in service, should be covered under CGHS after making requisite subscription.
3. Currently, there are various health care schemes in the Central Government catering to specific sets of employees. For example, apart from CGHS, there are ex-servicemen contributory health scheme (ECHS) and railways employees liberalized health scheme (RELHS) which cover ex-servicemen and railway employees/pensioners, respectively. Although the patterns in these schemes vary, a combined entity of CGHSECHS-RELHS would result in a very strong network of health facilities for the Central Government employees across the length and breadth of the country. The Commission recommends that possibility of such a combined network of various medical schemes should be explored through proper examination.

(*paras* 9.5.1-9.5.18)

8.12 Pension and Related Benefits of Civilian Employees

Article 366(17) of the Constitution defines pension as, "Pension means a pension, whether contributory or not, of any kind whatsoever payable to or in respect of any person, and includes retired pay so payable, a gratuity so payable and any sum or sums so payable by way of the return, with or without interest thereon or any other addition thereto, of subscriptions to a provident fund".

Pension has been the subject matter of a number of landmark judgements by the Supreme Court of India in which its nature, obligations of the government thereon and the recognition of distinctiveness in categories of pensions and pensioners has been settled.

In its judgment in *D.S. Nakara and others vs. Union of India* [AIR 1983 SC 130] the Supreme Court held that a pension scheme consistent with available resources must provide that a pensioner would be able to live free from want, with decency, independence and self-respect and standard equivalent at pre-retirement level. It held that pension is not an ex-gratia payment but payment for past services rendered. At the same time in *Indian Ex-Services League and Others vs. Union of India and Others* [(1991) 2 SSC 104], the Supreme Court held that the decision in the Nakara case has to be read as one of a limited application and its ambit cannot be enlarged to cover all claims made by the pension retirees or a demand for an identical amount of pension to every retiree from the same rank irrespective of the date of retirement, even though the reckonable emoluments for computation of their pension be different. In the judgement in *Vasant Gangaramsachandan vs. State of Maharashtra and Others* [(1996) 10 SSC 148], the Supreme Court reiterated that pension is not a bounty of the State. It is earned by the employee for service rendered to fall back upon after retirement. It is attached to the office and it cannot be arbitrarily denied.

In the case of petitioners who were retired railway employees, covered by or who opted for the Railway Contribution Fund Pension Scheme, the Supreme Court in *Krishna Kumar vs. Union of India and Others* [(1990) 4 SSC 207] averred that it was never held that both the pension retirees and PF retirees formed a homogenous class and that any further classification among them (viz., pension retirees and PF retirees) would be violative of Article 14. Under the pension scheme, the government's obligation does not begin until the employee retires but it begins on his/her retirement and then continues till the death of the employee. Thus, on the retirement of an employee, government's legal obligation under the PF account ends while under the pension scheme it begins. The rules governing the PF and its contribution are entirely different from the rules governing pension. An imaginary definition of obligation to include all the government retirees in a class was not decided and could not form the basis for any classification for this case.

8.12.1 Demands Made with Regard to Pension: The principal demands made before the Seventh Central CPC in respect of pensions for civil personnel and those common to both civil and defence personnel are:

1. Raising the existing rates of pension and family pension
2. The quantum of minimum pension should equal the minimum wage.
3. Increase in the rate of additional pension and family pension to the older pensioners as also reducing the age the eligibility for its receipt from the existing 80 years.
4. Increasing the existing time period of seven years for enhanced family pension.
5. Enhancement in the gratuity ceiling of ₹ 10 lakh and its indexation.
6. Rationalisation of death gratuity.

7. Reduction in the time period for restoration of basic pension, reduced on account of commutation.
8. Ex-gratia lump sum compensation.
9. Enhancement of ceiling of earned leave for purposes of leave encashment.
10. Enhancement in the existing rates of fixed medical allowance.
11. Enhancement in the rates of constant attendance allowance.
12. Parity in pension between pre- and post-Seventh CPC retirees.

8.12.2 Raising the Existing Rates of Pension and Family Pension: In representations to and in meetings with the Commission, a number of entities have, while seeking a raise in pension from the existing level of 50 percent of last pay drawn, questioned the basis for determination of pension at 50 percent of last pay drawn. Similarly, representations for increasing family pension from existing 30 percent to 50 percent of the last pay drawn have been received by the Commission.

The Commission sought the views of the government in this regard. The Department of Pension and Pensioners Welfare stated that the VI CPC had recommended calculation of pension @ 50 percent of last pay or the average emoluments (for last 10 months) whichever is more beneficial. The Commission also recommended delinking of pension from qualifying service of 33 years. Effectively the dispensation on pension has already been liberalised by the VI CPC. Further, the recommendations of this Commission in relation to pay of both the civilian and defence forces personnel will lead to a significant increase in the pay drawn and therefore in the 'last pay drawn'/'reckonable emoluments'. Therefore, the Commission does not recommend any further increase in the rate of pension and family pension from the existing levels.

8.12.3 Quantum of Minimum Pension Should Equal the Minimum Wage: In representations/depositions before the Commission, it has been stated that the existing minimum pension fixed at ₹ 3,500 is low and it has been argued that minimum pension be fixed equal to minimum pay for sustenance.

The Commission sought the views of the government in this regard. The Department of Pension and Pensioners Welfare stated that as per the orders issued after the V CPC, the minimum pension in the government was ₹ 1,275. The normal revised consolidated pension of a pre-2006 pensioner is 2.26 of the pre-revised basic pension. The revised minimum pension of ₹ 3,500 is much more than 2.26 time of the pre-revised pension of ₹ 1,275. Further the recommendations of this Commission in relation to pay of personnel will lead to a significant increase in the minimum pay from the existing ₹ 7,000 per month to ₹ 18,000 per month. This, based on the computation of pension, will raise minimum pension from the existing ₹ 3,500 to ₹ 9,000. The minimum pension based on the recommendations of this Commission will increase by 2.57 times over the existing level.

8.12.4 Increase in the Rate of Additional Pension and Family Pension to the Older Pensioners: In representations/depositions before the Commission, a case has been made by a number of pensioners bodies/associations for lowering the existing age slabs of old pensioners for payment of additional quantum of pension and family pension from the existing 80 years of age. Enhancing the rates for payment of additional quantum of pension and family pension with advancing age have also been made.

The Commission sought the views of the government in this regard. Department of Pension and Pensioners Welfare stated that the additional pension for old pensioners of the age of 80 years and above has been allowed as per the recommendations of VI CPC. However, it is felt that the same should be allowed from 75 years onwards. The Ministry of Defence has not supported the proposal. The Commission is of the view that the existing rates of additional pension and additional family pension are appropriate.

8.12.5 Increasing the Existing Time Period of Seven Years for Enhanced Family Pension: The Commission has received representations seeking enhancement in the period of enhanced family pension from the existing seven years or 67 years, whichever is less, to ten years in case of death of retirees.

The current rates of enhanced family pension are:

1. In the case of death in service: Payable to the family of a government servant for a period of ten years from the date of death of a government servant, without any upper age limit.
2. In the case of death after retirement: Payable for a period of seven years or up to the date on which he would have attained 67 years had he survived, whichever is less.

The Commission notes that the revision with regard to period of eligibility for the enhanced family pension of ten years was made based on recommendations of the VI CPC Report. No further change is being recommended by this Commission.

8.12.6 Enhancement in the Gratuity Ceiling and its Indexation: A number of representations have been received by the Commission stating that there is a need to revise the existing ceiling of ₹ 10 lakh with regard to payment of service gratuity.

Rules 49 and 50 of the CCS (Pension) Rules provides that a government servant is entitled to get retirement gratuity equal to one-fourth of his emoluments for each completed six monthly period of qualifying service subject to a maximum of 16.5 times of the last emoluments subject to a maximum of ₹ 10 lakh.

The Commission sought the views of the government in this regard. The Department of Pension and Pensioners Welfare stated that the VI CPC has increased the amount of gratuity from ₹ 3.5 lakh to ₹ 10 lakh w.e.f. 01.01.2006. This amount, in the view of the department, is not commensurate with emoluments that are available to senior officers at the time of retirement. The department has suggested to the Commission that a view could be taken to index gratuity with amount of DA admissible at the time of retirement.

The Commission notes that there is merit in the argument advanced to index the ceiling on gratuity so that the benefits of the enhanced ceiling are available to personnel in a manner which is more even over a time frame. The Commission recommends enhancement in the ceiling of gratuity from the existing ₹ 10 lakh to ₹ 20 lakh from January 1, 2016. The Commission further recommends, as has been done in the case of allowances that are partially indexed to dearness allowance, the ceiling on gratuity may increase by 25 percent whenever DA rises by 50 percent.

8.12.7 Rationalisation of Death Gratuity: The Commission has received representations pointing to a need for rationalization of current slabs for death gratuity, especially for the slab of 5 to 20 years of qualifying service in which family pensioners are stated to be placed at a disadvantageous position.

As per Rule 50 of the Pension Rules, the death gratuity admissible will be as follows, subject to the maximum limit prescribed for the gratuity:

Length of Service	Rate of Death Gratuity
Less than 1 year	2 times of monthly emoluments
1 year or more but less than 5 years	6 times of monthly emoluments
5 years or more but less than 20 years	12 times of monthly emoluments
20 years or more	Half month of emoluments for every complete six monthly period of qualifying service subject to a maximum of 33 times of monthly emoluments

The Commission sought the views of the government in this regard. Department of Pension and Pensioners Welfare stated that it had received similar demands from pensioners' association and it feels a need for a review of the existing slabs for death gratuity.

The Commission, after examination of the matter, recommends the following revised rates for payment of death gratuity:

Length of Service	Rate of Death Gratuity
Less than 1 year	2 times of monthly emoluments
1 year or more but less than 5 years	6 times of monthly emoluments
5 years or more but less than 11 years	12 times of monthly emoluments
11 years or more but less than 20 years	20 times of monthly emoluments
20 years or more	Half month of emoluments for every complete six monthly period of qualifying service subject to a maximum of 33 times of monthly emoluments

8.12.8 Reduction in the Time Period for Restoration of Basic Pension: The Commission has received a number of representations requesting reduction of restoration period of commuted portion of pension from the existing 15 years.

The Commission notes that prior to V CPC, the commutation allowed was one-third. However, there was no restoration. The Supreme Court, vide their judgement dated December 9, 1986, allowed restoration of pension after 15 years. The Supreme Court in its judgement specifically stated that though the amount is recovered in 12 years, yet since there is a risk factor and some of the states are restoring pension after 15 years, the period of restoration is fixed at 15 years. The V CPC in its recommendation increased the percentage of commutation to 40 percent and recommended restoration period at 12 years. But the reduction of restoration period was not accepted by the government. The VI CPC did not recommend any change in the maximum percentage of commutation allowed or in the period of restoration. This Commission also does not recommend any change either in the maximum percentage of commutation or in the period of restoration.

8.12.9 Enhancement of Ceiling of Earned Leave for Purposes of Leave Encashment: The Commission has received representations seeking raising the ceiling limit of 300 days to 450 days for purposes of leave encashment.

Commission notes that based on the recommendations of the VI CPC, serving employees are entitled for encashment of earned leave up to 60 days while in service. This is not to be deducted from the maximum number of earned leave of 300 days encashable at the time of retirement. The VI CPC, therefore, has further liberalised the regime of leave encashment.

The recommendations in relation to pay of both the civilian and defence forces personnel will also lead to a significant increase in the pay drawn and therefore in the total amount of leave encashment available for an employee. Therefore, raising the present ceiling of 300 days is not recommended by the Commission.

8.12.10 Ex-gratia Lump Sum Compensation: The Commission has received representations seeking enhancement in ex-gratia lump sum compensation for next-of-kin (NoK) of CAPF, Assam Rifles and defence forces personnel who die in harness in performance of their bonafide official duties.

The issue has been dealt with in Chapter 10.2.

8.12.11 Fixed Medical Allowance: The Commission has received representations seeking enhancement in fixed medical allowance, currently payable at the rate of ₹ 500 per month for pensioners not covered under Central Government Health Service (CGHS).

The Commission has examined the matter in Chapter 8.17.

8.12.12 Constant Attendance Allowance: The Commission has received representations seeking enhancement in constant attendance allowance from the present rate of ₹ 4,500 per month.

The Commission has examined the matter in Chapter 8.17.

8.12.13 Parity in Pension between Pre- and Post-Seventh CPC Retirees: This Commission has received a number of representations on the issue of disparities in pensions between past pensioners and existing pensioners. The JCM-Staff Side, has in its memorandum, stated that the pay of every pre-Seventh CPC retiree should be notionally re-determined (corresponding to the post from which he or she retired and not corresponding to the scale from which he or she retired) as if he or she is not retired and then the pension be computed under the revised liberalised rules which are to be applicable to the post-Seventh CPC retirees. A similar view has been expressed by a number of other associations/bodies representing Central Government pensioners. Further, certain groups of pensioners have contended that based on the recommendations of the VI CPC, the new pay structure consisting of pay bands and grade pays has led to bunching of a number of pre-revised pay scales into a particular pay band. This, in their view, has placed pre-January 1, 2006 pensioners in certain pay scales/pay bands at a disadvantage not only compared to the post-January 1, 2006 pensioners in the corresponding pay scales but also in comparison to post-January 1, 2006 retirees of lower pay scales.

The Commission is of the view that the issue of parity in pensions is extremely important from the viewpoint of inter-temporal equity and merits a careful examination.

8.12.14 Recommendations of the Commission: For employees joining on or after January 1, 2004, the concept of pension, so far as civilian employees including CAPFs are concerned, has undergone a complete change. After the enactment of the Pension Fund Regulatory and Development Act, 2013, it is not the exclusive liability of the government to pay the pension. As per the new dispensation the employee and the government are to make equal matching contribution towards their pension. This dispensation is not applicable to the defence forces personnel. They continue to get the defined benefit pension as before. In this section, the Commission is dealing with civilian pensioners under the old pension scheme, i.e., those who joined before January 1, 2004.

The Commission recommends the following pension formulation for civil employees including CAPF personnel, who have retired before January 1, 2016:

(i) All the civilian personnel including CAPF who retired prior to 01.01.2016 (expected date of implementation of the Seventh CPC recommendations) shall first be fixed in the pay matrix being recommended by this Commission, on the basis of the pay band and grade pay at which they retired, at the minimum of the corresponding level in the matrix. This amount shall be raised, to arrive at the notional pay of the retiree, by adding the number of increments he/she had earned in that level while in service, at the rate of three percent. Fifty percent of the total amount so arrived at shall be the revised pension.

(ii) The second calculation to be carried out is as follows. The pension, as had been fixed at the time of implementation of the VI CPC recommendations, shall be multiplied by 2.57 to arrive at an alternate value for the revised pension.

(iii) Pensioners may be given the option of choosing whichever formulation is beneficial to them.

It is recognised that the fixation of pension as per formulation in (i) above may take a little time since the records of each pensioner will have to be checked to ascertain the number of increments earned in the retiring level. It is therefore recommended that in the first instance the revised pension may be calculated as at (ii) above and the same may be paid as an interim measure. In the event, calculation as per (i) above yields a higher amount, the difference may be paid subsequently.

Illustration on fixation of pension based on recommendations of the Seventh CPC.

Case I: Pensioner 'A' retired at last pay drawn of ₹ 79,000 on 30 May, 2015 under the VI CPC regime, having drawn three increments in the scale ₹ 67,000 to ₹ 79,000:

S. No.		Amount (in ₹)
1.	Basic Pension fixed in VI CPC	39,500
2.	Initial Pension fixed under Seventh CPC (using a multiple of 2.57)	1,01,515-option 1
3.	Minimum of the corresponding pay level in 7 CPC	1,82,200
4.	Notional pay fixation based on 3 increments	1,99,100
5.	50 percent of the notional pay so arrived	99,550-option 2
6.	Pension amount admissible (higher of option 1 and 2)	1,01,515

Case II: Pensioner 'B' retired at last pay drawn of ₹ 4,000 on January 31, 1989 under the IV CPC regime, having drawn 9 increments in the pay scale of ₹ 3000-100-3500-125-4500:

S. No.		Amount (in ₹)
1.	Basic Pension fixed in IV CPC	1,940
2.	Basic pension as revised in VI CPC	12,543
3.	Initial pension fixed under Seventh CPC (using a multiple of 2.57)	32,236-option 1
4.	Minimum of the corresponding pay level in Seventh CPC	67,700
5.	Notional pay fixation based on 9 increments	88,400
6.	50 percent of the notional pay so arrived	44,200-option 2
7.	Pension amount admissible (higher of Option 1 and 2)	44,200

(*paras* 10.1.2-10.1.5, 10.1.23-10.1.28, 10.1.30-10.1.54, 10.1.66-10.1.71)

8.13 Pension and Related Benefits of Defence Forces Personnel

8.13.1 Demands Relating to Defence Pensioners: The Commission has received a number of demands relating to pensions for defence forces personnel through the joint services memorandum (JSM) from the services, pensioners associations and bodies including those dealing with the needs of special categories like war veterans, disability etc. The demands/representations received in the Commission have been examined under the broad categories of retiring pension, family pension, disability pension and ex-gratia lump sum compensation.

8.13.2 Demand Relating to Retiring Pension: The principal demands made before the Seventh CPC in respect of retiring pensions as applicable to the defence personnel were:

1. Minimum pension should be fixed at 75 percent of reckonable emoluments for JCOs/other ranks or a compulsory early retirement compensation package or lump sum amount.
2. Additional quantum of pension with advancing age should commence at the age of 70 years for JCOs/other ranks instead of 80 years as prevails today.
3. Pre-2006 honorary *naib subedar* may be given pension of *naib subedar*.
4. Defence security corps (DSC) personnel may be granted second pension on completion of 10 years of service at par with civilians.
5. The depression in pension for qualifying service between 15 and 20 years may be removed and complete earned pension may be made admissible to territorial army personnel.

8.13.3 Minimum Pension for JCOs/ORs: The Services, in the JSM, have sought enhancement of the service pension to 75 percent of last drawn reckonable emoluments for JCOs and ORs. In case enhancement of pension to 75 percent of last drawn reckonable emoluments is not granted for JCOs/OR, the services have sought a compulsory early retirement compensation package or compulsory lateral absorption in government or PSU as an alternative.

Service pension for all categories of employees has been fixed at 50 percent of the last pay drawn. The recommendations in relation to pay of both the civilian and defence forces personnel will lead to a significant increase in the pay drawn and therefore in the 'last pay drawn'/'reckonable emoluments'. It is also to be noted that in the case of defence forces personnel, in particular all JCOs/ORs, the last pay drawn includes the element of military service pay, which is also taken into account while reckoning pension. The Commission has also recommended an increase in military service pay. The increase in pay and MSP will automatically and significantly raise the level of pension of JCOs/ORs, since pension is related to the last pay drawn/reckonable emoluments. Therefore, the Commission does not recommend any further increase in the rate of pension for JCOs/ORs.

8.13.4 Additional Quantum of Pension with Advancing Age: The Services have sought a modification in the existing old age pension scheme for JCOs/ORs whereby the additional quantum of pension should commence at the age of 70 rather than the existing age of 80. The quantum of increase has also been sought to be raised upwards for various categories of old age pensioners.

The scheme of additional pension and additional family pension with advancing age was introduced subsequent to recommendations of the VI CPC. The amount of pension for existing pensioners will be revised upwards in accordance with the fitment formula that has been prescribed by the Commission. No further increase in the existing rate of additional pension and additional family pension with advancing age is therefore recommended by the Commission.

8.13.5 Pre-2006 Honorary Naib Subedar: The Services have sought that the provision of grant of pension of *naib subedar* to Havildars and equivalent who are given honorary rank of *naib subedar* after retirement, currently applicable to post-January 1, 2006 retirees only, should also be extended to pre-January 1, 2006, retirees. The services have contended that the current policy has resulted in creation of two classes of pensioner's viz., pre- and post-January 1, 2006, which is undesirable.

The Commission has examined the matter. It notes that the VI CPC had recommended that the pension of all honorary rank *naib subedar* will be payable by taking this placement as a regular promotion to the higher grade and this would applicable "henceforth". The VI CPC has been unambiguous as far as the date of effect of the benefit. This Commission does not find any merit in re-opening an issue that has been clearly settled. Therefore no change is being recommended in this regard.

8.13.6 Defence Security Corps (DSC) Personnel: The Services have sought reduction in the qualifying service for entitlement of second pension to defence security corps (DSC) personnel from 15 to 10 years. To support their demand, it has been contended that all employees taking up second employment in Central Government establishments earn their second pension after completing 10 years of service whereas for DSC personnel 15 years of service is mandatory.

The Commission notes that personnel in the defence security corps are tasked to protect defence units/installations and defence civil establishments and they are subject to the Army Act. The personnel in the Corps are drawn from amongst JCOs and ORs retiring from active service from the three Services. The present demand is made on the premise that all employees taking up second employment in Central Government establishments earn their second pension after completing 10 years of service. This does not however hold true post- January 1, 2004. Civilian personnel joining after January 1, 2004 are covered only by the National Pension System, therefore those taking up second employment in Central Government establishments will also not be entitled to any pension, other than through the defined contribution regime. The Commission therefore does not recommend reduction in the qualifying service for entitlement of second pension to defence security corps (DSC) personnel from 15 to 10 years.

8.13.7 Depression in Pension for Qualifying Service: Territorial army personnel qualify for pension after 20 years of service. Those with qualifying service between 15 and 20 get a 'depressed' pension. The Services have asked for this depression to be removed and for the complete earned pension be made admissible to territorial army (TA) personnel. To advance their case they have contended that TA personnel are governed by the same conditions and guidelines as are applicable to all other defence service personnel while calculating the pension. Therefore reducing their pension would create a lower category of personnel and an implied class system. The demand for this is to be done away with.

The Commission, on perusal of the statutes governing the territorial army, notes that the qualifying 'embodied' service for a territorial army personnel may be continuous or rendered in broken spells. For calculating the total 'embodied' service, the break in service due to dis-embodiment is condoned but the period of break itself is not treated as qualifying service for pension. The five percent cut is only imposed on the pension of those JCO/ORs, whose qualifying, embodied service has been rendered in broken spells.

The Commission observes that pension formulation is appropriate and finds no justification for a review of the existing arrangements with regard to pension of territorial army personnel.

8.13.8 Demand Relating to Family Pension: The principal demands made before the Seventh CPC in respect of family pension in respect of defence forces personnel are as follows:

1. Enhanced ordinary family pension to be made admissible for a duration of 10 years after death of the individual, both in harness as well as after retirement.
2. Special family pension at the rate of 80 percent of the last reckonable emoluments as against the existing level of 60 percent.
3. Additional quantum of family pension with advancing age should commence at the age of 70 for JCOs/other ranks instead of 80 as it prevails today.
4. Inclusion of war injury element/disability element in computation of family pension for widows of ex-servicemen who were in receipt of war injury pension/disability pension and commutation of the war injury element/disability element, if already not done by the individual prior to his demise.

8.13.9 Enhanced Ordinary Family Pension: The Services have sought that the enhanced rate of ordinary family pension should be continued to be paid at a rate equal to service/retiring pension and made admissible for a duration of 10 years after death of the individual, both in harness as well as after retirement. In addition, the existing cap of minimum service of seven years for being eligible for this pension be removed.

The Commission has considered the issue. It notes that the regime of enhanced rate of ordinary family pension applies to both civil and defence pensioners. No change is being recommended by the Commission for either civilian or defence pensioners.

8.13.10 Special Family Pension: The Services have sought that the special family pension be enhanced and be paid at the rate of 80 percent of last drawn reckonable emoluments from the existing rate of 60 percent.

Increase in rate, it is contended, is justified as the widow is not in extended government employment unlike widow of civilian Central Government servant, when the spouse dies in service.

The recommendations of the Commission in relation to pay of defence forces personnel will lead to a significant increase in the pay drawn and therefore in the 'last pay drawn'. No further increase in the existing rate of special family pension is therefore recommended by the Commission.

8.13.11 Additional Quantum of Family Pension with Advancing Age: The Services have sought a modification in the existing old age pension scheme for JCOs/ORs whereby the additional quantum of pension should commence at the age of 70 rather than the existing age of 80. The quantum of increase has also been sought to be raised upwards for various categories of old age pensioners.

The scheme of additional pension and additional family pension with advancing age was introduced subsequent to recommendations of the VI CPC. The amount of pension for existing pensioners will be revised upwards in accordance with the fitment formula that has been prescribed by the Commission. No further increase in the existing rate of additional pension and additional family pension with advancing age is therefore recommended by the Commission.

8.13.12 Inclusion of War Injury Element/Disability Element in Computation of Family Pension: War injury pension/disability pension for defence personnel on invalidment/retirement/superannuation has two elements: (i) service and (ii) war injury/disability. As per the existing orders on the death of the said personnel the widow is entitled to a family pension on account of the service element only. The demand is for continuance of the war injury pension/disability pension received by the personnel upon invalidment/retirement/superannuation to the widow of the defence service personnel, in addition to the family pension fixed at 30 percent of reckonable emoluments. Commutation of the war injury element/disability element, if already not done by the individual prior to his demise has also been sought.

The recommendations of the Commission in relation to pay of defence forces personnel will lead to a significant increase in the pay table and therefore in the 'last pay drawn'/'reckonable emoluments'. In view of the enhancement in pay, the Commission is not recommending any further change in the existing provisions with regard to inclusion of war injury element/disability element in the computation of family pension. The demand made with the regard to commutation of war injury element/disability element is also not being recommended.

8.13.13 Demands Relating to Disability and War Injury Pension: The orders regulating grant of disability pension in the case of defence forces personnel are detailed in view of the circumstances in which they operate. Disability pension is granted in two broad categories: (a) non-battle cases and (b) war injury cases.

Armed forces personnel retired with disability attributable to or aggravated by such service and assessed at 20 percent or more are awarded disability pension. Those invalided out with any disability attributable to or aggravated by such service are also awarded disability pension.

The regime of disability element for non-battle cases has, over time, moved from fixed slab rates to one based on percentage of reckonable emoluments. This shift was recommended by the VI CPC.

Non-battle Cases: In non-battle cases, there are two categories: (i) cases attributable/aggravated to service and (ii) cases neither attributable/nor aggravatable to service.

War Injury Cases: Currently, in war injury cases, there are two distinct categories: (i) those invalided out and (ii) those retained in service. In case of those invalided out, the pension paid is 50 percent of reckonable emoluments, subject to a minimum of ₹ 7,020. This is in addition to 100 percent of reckonable emoluments for those with 100 percent disability and on pro rata basis for those with lesser disability. For personnel suffering war injury but who are retained in service, the pension paid out is 50 percent of reckonable emoluments in addition to 60 percent of reckonable emoluments for those with 100 percent disability and on pro rata basis for those with lesser disability.

The principal demands made before the Seventh CPC in respect of disability pensions as applicable for defence forces personnel were:

1. In the case of disability pension, an upward revision from the existing rate of 30 percent to 50 percent of last pay drawn, in cases of 100 percent disability.
2. Enhancing the cover of disability.
3. Additional old age pension should be applicable for disability/war injury pension.
4. All cases of invalidment due to disability neither attributable nor aggravated (NANA) to service, be awarded disability pension.
5. Enhancement in the rate of war injury pension where individual is retained in service.
6. Ex-gratia lump sum compensation to invalided out defence personnel.
7. Ex-gratia award for 100 percent disability be made equal to the stipend being paid to cadets.
8. The need to empanel well established civil prosthetic centres so as to make facilities for good quality repairs and replacement of artificial limbs easily accessible.
9. Ex-gratia lump sum compensation.

8.13.14 Enhancement of the Rate of Disability Pension: The Services have sought enhancement of the rate of disability pension for 100 percent disability from the existing level of 30 percent of the last drawn reckonable emoluments to 50 percent. For lower percentages of disability, the amount of disability element is sought to be pro-rated.

The feature that stands out when the historical evolution of the regime relating to disability pension is studied is the shift from slab based system to a percentage based disability pension regime consequent to the implementation of the VI CPC's recommendations. This move has been contrary to the tenets of equity insofar as treatment of disability element between officers and JCOs/ORs is concerned borne out by the fact that the ratio of maximum to minimum quantum of compensation for disability across the ranks is now disproportionately high at 8.6. The Commission is therefore of the considered view that the regime implemented post-VI CPC needs to be discontinued, and recommends a return to the slab based system. The slab rates for disability element for 100 percent disability would be as follows.

Rank	Levels	Rates (in ₹ per month)
Service Officers	10 and above	27,000
Honorary Commissioned Officers		
Subedar Major/Equivalent	6 to 9	17,000
Subedar/Equivalent		
Naib Subedar/Equivalents		
Havildar/Equivalents	5 and below	12,000
Naik/Equivalents		
Sepoy/Equivalents		

8.13.15 Enhancing the Cover of Disability: The Services have sought that disability element should be made admissible to personnel on retirement as well as invalidment in the event of his/her acquiring any amount of disability (presently nil in case of disability less than 20 percent) that is attributable to/ aggravated by military service or otherwise.

The issue of how disability element should be determined for personnel retiring with disability, as distinct from those being invalided out, has been the subject matter of judicial pronouncements in the recent past. In *Ram Avatar vs. Union of India*, the Supreme Court has held that personnel retiring on attaining the age of superannuation or on completion of tenure of engagement, if found to be suffering from some disability which is attributable to/aggravated by military service, would be entitled to the benefit of 'rounding' of disability pension for disability greater than 20 percent. The Commission has also noted that the government has decided to implement the benefit of broad banding of disability ('rounding' of disability pension) w.e.f. January 1, 2015 for all eligible cases except premature cases/voluntary retirement cases. The Commission, keeping in view the above, recommends broad banding of disability for all personnel retiring with disability, including premature cases/voluntary retirement cases for disability greater than 20 percent. This will ensure uniformity in treatment of disability cases as far as determination of disability element is concerned and bring the regime at par with those invalided out for disability greater than 20 percent.

8.13.16 Additional Old Age Pension should be Applicable for Disability/War Injury Pension: The Services have sought that the clauses of additional old age pension be made applicable to both the elements of disability/war injury pension.

The scheme of additional pension and additional family pension with advancing age was introduced subsequent to recommendations of the VI CPC. The amount of pension for existing pensioners will be revised upwards in accordance with the fitment formula that has been prescribed by the Commission. No further enhancement by inclusion of elements of disability/war injury pension is therefore recommended by the Commission.

8.13.17 Neither Attributable Nor Aggravated (NANA) Cases, be Awarded Disability Pension: The Services have sought the discontinuation of invalid pension and gratuity in all cases of invalidment due to disability neither attributable nor aggravated (NANA) by service; instead, they have sought award of disability pension for all such cases.

As per the existing regulations, in cases of disability neither attributable nor aggravated (NANA) by service for personnel with less than ten years' service, the individual is entitled to invalid gratuity only, payable at half a month's last drawn reckonable emoluments plus dearness allowance for every six months of service. Those having more than ten years of service are entitled to invalid pension payable at fifty percent of last reckonable emoluments. The Commission, taking note of the legal position settled by the Supreme Court, is of the view that a member of the armed forces is presumed to be in a sound physical and mental condition at the time of his entry into the service if there is no note or record to the contrary made at the time of such entry. Therefore, in the event of his subsequent discharge from service on medical grounds, any deterioration in his health is presumed to be attributable to military service. The Commission therefore recommends that while the existing regulations involving disability neither attributable nor aggravated (NANA) by service may continue, it is for the authorities to establish, in each case, through a reasoned order that disability was neither attributable nor aggravated (NANA) by military service.

8.13.18 War Injury Pension Where Individual is Retained in Service: For cases of war injury where the individual is retained in service, the Services have sought that the war injury element should be enhanced and awarded at the rate of 80 percent of last drawn reckonable emoluments for 100 percent disability. For lesser percentage of disability, the amount of disability element be reduced prorata.

The Commission notes that the war injury element as per existing regime is calculated at 60 percent of the last drawn reckonable emoluments for cases of 100 percent disability. For lower percentages of disability, the amount of disability element is reduced pro rata. The pay of all defence forces personnel as per the recommendations of the Commission are being enhanced. This will itself translate into enhancement of payout to those retiring with war injury and retained in service. In view of the foregoing, the Commission does not recommend any change in the existing regime of payouts for those with war injury and retained in service.

8.13.19 Ex-gratia Lump Sum Compensation to Invalided out Defence Personnel: The Services have sought application of broad banding principle for determining the extent of disability for payment of ex-gratia award to service personnel boarded out on account of disability/war injury attributable to or aggravated by military service.

The existing orders involve payment of ex-gratia lump sum compensation of ₹ 9 lakh for 100 percent disability. For disability/war injury lower than 100 percent but not less than 20 percent, the amount of ex-gratia compensation is proportionately reduced. No ex-gratia compensation is payable for disability/war injury less than 20 percent. The Commission is recommending an increase in the existing lump sum compensation of ₹ 9 lakh for 100 percent disability to ₹ 20 lakh. However, it finds no justification to recommend broad banding for payment of ex-gratia award to service personnel boarded out on account of disability/war injury attributable to or aggravated by military service.

The Services have sought enhancement of ex-gratia disability award equal to stipend paid to cadets from the existing ₹ 6,300 per month for 100 percent disability. In support of their demand it has been contended that training of cadets is extremely demanding and a cadet is susceptible to injuries. Therefore there is a need to indemnify a cadet against any disability which may occur during the period of training.

The Commission notes that cadets are not considered on duty during training and therefore cannot be treated at par with serving defence forces personnel. The Commission, however, keeping in views the facts relating to cadets recommends an increase in ex-gratia disability award from the existing ₹ 6,300 per month to ₹ 16,200 per month for 100 percent disability.

8.13.20 Empanelment of Well-established Civil Prosthetic Centres: In the case of pensioners with disabilities, one of the submissions made before the Commission was that all disabled ex-servicemen have to travel to Artificial Limb Centre (ALC), Pune for repair and replacement of their prosthetic fittings. In addition to ALC there are only five sub-centres in the entire country and they are ill-equipped and unable to carry out even minor repairs. A case has therefore been made for empanelment of well-established civil prosthetic centres to make facilities for good quality repair and replacement of artificial limbs easily accessible to disabled ex-servicemen. In view of the hardships faced by disabled ex-servicemen, the Commission recommends that the government may empanel well established civil prosthetic centres where retired pensioners can avail the facility.

8.13.21 Ex-gratia Lump Sum Compensation: The Commission has received representations seeking enhancement in ex-gratia lump sum compensation for next-of-kin (NoK) of CAPF, Assam Rifles and defence forces personnel who die in harness in performance of their bonafide official duties.

The Commission has considered the existing regime regulating the ex-gratia lump sum compensation and the demands made before the Commission and observes that while the set of circumstances in which defence forces personnel and those in CAPFs and Assam Rifles are accorded ex-gratia payment are broadly similar, some variations do exist. In this regard, the Commission is of the view that as far as possible these should apply identically to all the personnel covered.

As regards the new categories sought to be added by the defence services to the existing circumstances, the Commission recommends the following.

Addition Asked For	Recommendation
Death occurring while on duty in fire/ blasts/explosions on board ships/submarines/ aircrafts	Not recommended for inclusion as a separate category. It may be included in the existing circumstance 'death occurring due to accidents in course of performance of duties'.
Death occurring in action against sea pirates	May be included in the existing circumstance 'death occurring in border skirmishes and action against militants, terrorists, extremists'.
Death while handling the indigenised weapons/machinery	Not recommended for inclusion as a separate category. It may be included in the existing circumstance 'death occurring due to accidents in course of performance of duties'.
Death on account of natural disasters, extreme weather/sea conditions	Not recommended for inclusion as a separate category. It may be included in the existing circumstance 'death occurring due to accidents in course of performance of duties'.
Death during evacuation of Indian nationals from a war-torn zone in foreign country etc.	May be included in the existing circumstance 'death occurring during enemy action in international war or such war like engagements, which are specifically notified by Ministry of Defence'.

The Commission recommends a common regime for payment of ex-gratia lump sum compensation for civil and defence forces personnel, payable to the next-of-kin at the following rates.

(₹ lakh)

Circumstances	Existing	Proposed
Death occurring due to accidents in course of performance of duties.	10	25
Death in the course of performance of duties attribute to acts of violence by terrorists, anti-social elements etc.	10	25
Death occurring in border skirmishes and action against militants, terrorists, extremists, sea pirates.	15	35
Death occurring while on duty in the specified high altitude, inaccessible border posts, on account of natural disasters, extreme weather conditions.	15	35
Death occurring during enemy action in war or such war like engagements, which are specifically notified by Ministry of Defence and death occurring during evacuation of Indian Nationals from a war-torn zone in foreign country.	20	45

8.13.22 Parity in Pension between Pre- and Post-Seventh CPC Defence Forces Retirees: The differential in pension between past and new retirees from the defence forces has been an issue that has engaged the attention of the government and various Parliamentary Committees. A number of committees and bodies have been appointed to examine the issue. This differential arises on account of the fact that computation of pension depends upon the pay scale of the person at the time of retirement. With the passage of time and revision of pay scales by successive Pay Commissions, the pay and therefore the pension, of those retiring in later years undergoes a change.

The Estimates Committee (1980-81), in its report on Resettlement of Ex-Servicemen, noted that the disparity in pension between past and present pensioners of equal rank was inequitable and recommended that the matter should be examined and a just solution found.

The IV CPC, on the other hand, observed that the amount of pension undergoes changes as and when the pay scales are revised. Any attempt to equalise pension with reference to revised scale of pay would, in fact, amount to the retrospective application of these scales of pay.

In 1991, the government set up a High Level Empowered Committee which recommended a one-time increase (OTI) in pension from January 1, 1992. All pre-1973 pensioners (JCOs/ORs/commissioned officers) were brought to the level of post-1973 retirees. Graded addition with reference to post-1973 rates of pension was also made to determine OTI in rates to bridge the gap to some extent up to post-1986 level.

The V CPC, after taking into account the historical background including the recommendations of High Level Committees, recommended that total parity may be brought between pre-January 1, 1986 and post-January 1, 1986 retirees. Thereafter, for all pre-January 1, 1996 retirees, their pension was consolidated as per the specified fitment formula. If the resultant figure fell short of the pension applicable to the post-January 1, 1996 retirees for the same rank, it was to be stepped up to the minimum pension prescribed for the same rank. It went on to state that every Pay Commission gives certain benefits in pay which are over and above the impact of inflation, either due to upgradation of recruitment qualifications or change in job contents. The benefits accorded on this account need not necessarily be passed on to the pensioners. Thus, the additional benefits suggested by them for future pensioners would not be fully available to the pre-January 1, 1996 retirees. It, however, recommended partial parity known as modified parity in respect of pre- and post-January 1, 1996 pensioners. This provided that in case the revised consolidated pension of a person was less than 50 percent of the minimum of the revised pay scale, it would be stepped up to that level.

The Commission notes that a number of improvements have been brought about, aimed at narrowing the gap between past and current pensioners. These include:

1. All pre-1997 PBOR pensioners have been brought at par with post-1997 pensioners.
2. Pension of all pre-2006 PBOR pensioners has been reckoned with reference to notional maximum pay in post-January 1, 2006 revised pay structure corresponding to the maximum pre-VI CPC pay scales as per fitment table of each rank with enhanced weightage awarded by the group of Ministers.
3. A separate pay scale of ₹ 67,000-₹ 79,000 was created to address the issue of disparity in pension of pre- and post-January 1, 2006 pensioners at the level of lieutenant general and equivalent in the other two services to enable them to get pension at the rate of ₹ 36,500
4. Linkage of full pension with 33 years of qualifying service has been removed w.e.f. January 1, 2006 instead of September 1, 2008 in case of commissioned officers.

The concept of pension, so far as civilian employees including CAPFs are concerned, has undergone a complete change. Entrants on or after January 1, 2004 on the civilian side are covered under the National Pension System. In the case of defence forces personnel however, the government has continued with the defined benefits pension regime. This regime, as far as past pensioners is concerned, has also witnessed significant improvements with a view to establishing parity between old and new pensioners. The Commission has dwelt on the judicial pronouncements regulating the regime of pensions in detail in Chapter 10.1.

The Commission recommends the following with regard to fixation of pension for past defence forces personnel retirees:

(i) All the defence forces personnel who retired prior to January 1, 2016 (expected date of implementation of the Seventh CPC recommendations) shall first be fixed in the pay matrix being recommended by this Commission, on the basis of the pay band and grade pay at which they retired, at the minimum of the corresponding level in the matrix. This amount shall be raised to arrive at the notional pay of the retiree by adding the number of increments he/she had earned in that level while in service, at the rate of three percent. Military service pay shall be added to the amount which is arrived at after notionally fitting him in the Seventh CPC matrix. Fifty percent of the total amount so arrived at shall be the revised pension.

(ii) The second calculation to be carried out is as follows. The pension, as had been fixed at the time of implementation of the VI CPC recommendations, shall be multiplied by 2.57 to arrive at an alternate value for the revised pension.

(iii) Pensioners shall be entitled to the higher of the two.

It is recognised that the fixation of the pension as per the above formulation (i) above may take a little time since the records of each pensioner will have to be checked to ascertain the number of increments earned in the retiring level. It is, therefore, recommended that in the first instance the pension, may be fixed in terms of formulation (ii) above, till final fixation of the pension under the Seventh CPC matrix is undertaken.

Illustration on fixation of pension for defence forces personnel based on recommendations of the Seventh CPC.

Case I: Pensioner 'A' retired at last pay ₹ 46,310 in PB-4 with GP 8700 on March 31, 2006 under the VI CPC regime, having drawn one increment in the V CPC pay scale ₹ 15,100-450-17,350.

S. No.		Amount (in ₹)
1.	Basic pension fixed in VI CPC	30,505
2.	Initial pension fixed under Seventh CPC (using a multiple of 2.57)	78,398-option 1
3.	Minimum of the corresponding pay level in 7 CPC	1,25,500
4.	Notional pay fixation based on 1 increment	1,29,300

5.	Notional pay after adding Military Service Pay of ₹ 15,500	1,44,800
6.	50 percent of the notional pay in pay level so arrived and Military Service Pay	72,400-option 2
7.	Pension amount admissible (higher of option 1 and 2)	78,398

Case II: Pensioner 'B' retired at last pay ₹ 13,100 in GP 2800 on 31 May, 2015 under the VI CPC regime, having drawn two increments in PB-1.

S. No.		Amount (in ₹)
1.	Basic pension fixed in VI CPC	8,950
2.	Initial pension fixed under Seventh CPC (using a multiple of 2.57)	23,002-option 1
3.	Minimum of the corresponding pay level in 7 CPC	35,400
4.	Notional pay fixation based on 2 increment	37,600
5.	Notional pay after adding Military Service Pay of ₹ 5,200	42,800
6.	50 percent of the notional pay in pay level so arrived and Military Service Pay	21,400-option 2
7.	Pension amount admissible (higher of option 1 and 2)	23,002

(*paras* 10.2.19-10.2.46, 10.2.55-10.2.70, 10.2.75-10.2.83, 10.2.86-10.2.90)

8.14 National Pension System (NPS)

The Commission notes that the NPS is the culmination of a series of social security and pension related reform initiatives in India. As in many other countries, pension reforms in India were driven by the fiscal constraints of supporting a public pension system and the long-term problem of an ageing population. Government of India, in 1998, set up the Committee for Old Age Social and Income Security (OASIS). The OASIS committee concluded, among other things, that the defined benefit scheme (DBS), serving the Central Government retirees, is unaffordable for government and it should be replaced by a defined contribution scheme (DCS).

The Commission notes that the total pension liability on account of Central Government employees had risen from 0.6 percent of GDP (at constant prices) in 1993-94 to 1.66 percent of GDP (at constant prices) in 2002-03. Pension expenditure of the Central Government grew at a compounded annual growth rate (CAGR) of 21 percent during the period 1990 to 2001. This was also reflected in the increasing fiscal deficits. Further, in the DBS, pensions were wage indexed, and thus the outgo on this account would have increased manifold. The stressed fiscal situation, thus, set the stage for introduction of the NPS in India. The

Bhattacharya Committee Report (HLE Group on NPS) (February 2002) recommended that an unfunded defined benefit (DB), pay-as-you-go (PAYG) scheme or a pure defined contribution (DC) scheme would not be suitable and therefore recommended a hybrid DB/DC scheme to meet the requirements of central civil servants.

8.14.1 International Experience on Pension Reforms: Pension reforms, in recent times, have been initiated in many countries across the world. The Commission notes that an ageing population, changing social structures, uncertain and inadequate social security benefits and rising fiscal liabilities have been the major causes behind pension reforms, especially for a transition from DBS to DCS.

8.14.2 Introduction of NPS: On the basis of various reports, the Central Government made the decision to place all new recruits into Central Government from January 1, 2004 onwards (excluding defence forces) under NPS. NPS is managed by the Pension Fund Regulatory and Development Authority (PFRDA), which was initially set up as an interim authority. The PFRDA Act was passed by Parliament and notified w.e.f. February 1, 2014, bestowing statutory status on the authority.

8.14.3 NPS Features: Under the NPS, employees contribute 10 percent of their monthly salary (basic plus DA) towards their pension with matching contribution from Central Government. In respect of the AIS officers working under them, the matching contribution is made by the State Governments. The professional pension fund managers invest the funds under NPS following an asset allocation framework mandated by the government. The Central Record Keeping Agency (CRA) maintains a separate pension account for each individual employee identified by a unique permanent retirement account number (PRAN). Individual employees have been given online access through the CRA website to view the status of their pension wealth.

Under the NPS, upon superannuation, the individual is required to invest at least 40 percent of pension wealth for purchase of annuity and the remaining up to 60 percent is paid to him as lump sum. The annuity provides for pension for the lifetime of the employee. Individual subscribers to the NPS are not covered under the general provident fund. Regulations issued by the PFRDA now provide for partial withdrawals up to 25 percent of the contribution made by the subscriber to his individual account after at least ten years from the date of joining, up to a maximum of three times during the tenure of the subscription for certain specified purposes, before superannuation. The regulations issued by PFRDA also provide that if the employee dies in service, then at least 80 percent of the accumulated pension wealth shall be mandatorily utilized for purchase of annuity and the balance amount would be paid to the nominee(s)/legal heirs.

8.14.4 Grievances against the NPS: The NPS has now been in effect for over 10 years. During this period, there has been perceptible progress in putting together the architecture and providing information to subscribers. Major concerns, however, remain. Broadly, these are as under:

1. The larger federations and staff associations advocated scrapping the NPS on the ground that it discriminates between two sets of government employees.
2. Individuals covered under NPS have pleaded for reverting to the OPS on the grounds of uncertainty regarding the actual value of their future pension in the face of market related risks.
3. Individuals have pointed out that under NPS, the effective salary becomes less since the employee has to mandatorily contribute 10 percent of pay towards the pension fund.
4. Individuals have stated that grievance redressal facility is not effective and consultation with stakeholders has been non-existent. This communication gap has generated insecurity in the minds of stakeholders including staff and group 'A' officers of Central Government as well as all-India service officers.
5. Associations have complained that family pension after the death of the employee is not ensured in the NPS. Moreover, if an employee dies at an early age, the family would suffer since annuity from the contribution would be grossly inadequate.
6. Individuals have complained that NPS subscribers have no recourse to GPF for their savings. Their personal savings (10 percent of salary) are considered part of a larger corpus. It has been pointed out that the right approach would be to consider only government's contribution and the returns earned on it as the effective amount available for purchase of annuities.
7. Associations have pointed out that unlike the facility under GPF, it is not possible to take refundable advances under NPS, even to meet obligatory social expenditure. This forces employees towards increased indebtedness as they have to borrow from elsewhere.
8. Grievances also relate to tax treatment under NPS. While contributions and accumulations in NPS are exempt, lump sum withdrawals from NPS at any time are taxable at par with any other income. In addition, there is a service tax liability on any amount utilised for purchase of annuity.
9. It has been pointed out that though NPS became effective from 2004, detailed instructions were issued only in late 2009 and in many cases the credit of contributions began from 2012. In the case of AIS officers in some States, contributions by the concerned State Government are yet to be fully made and

deployed. The net result of this has been that contributions for the period 2004-2012 have not been made in full or have earned simple interest and did not get any market linked returns. Because of the prevailing confusion, contributions made by some AIS officer have been returned to them without interest. This will have a huge impact on the eventual corpus as the benefits of compounding were not available for the first 8-9 years.

10. Individuals, in their presentation before the Commission, stated that annuities under NPS have no compensation for inflation unlike dearness relief under OPS. Further, in the case of OPS there is a revision in basic pension itself after every Pay Commission. This too is not available in respect of annuity of NPS subscribers.
11. It has been pointed out that government employees are not given freedom of choice in choosing their fund manager based on performance and track record as the contributions are divided in a pre-specified ratio among selected pension fund managers. It has been stated that government employees have no say in asset allocation of their money.
12. Concerns were raised that the contribution of 10 percent + 10 percent will not be sufficient to create a corpus which provides reasonable assurance that pension will be 50 percent of the last pay drawn.

8.14.5 Analysis of the Issues by the Commission: The Commission has examined these concerns raised by the stakeholders. The Commission also interacted with Chairman, PFRDA, and representatives of the Department of Pensions and Pensioners Welfare (DPPW), Department of Personnel and Training (DoPT), Department of Expenditure (DoE) and the Department of Financial Services (DFS).

In so far as the future value of pension under NPS is concerned, the Commission notes that this would depend upon a combination of factors: (i) performance of the invested fund, which in turn would depend on the asset mix of the investment and general economic situation of the country, (ii) cost of financial intermediation, (iii) contribution rates, (iv) period of contribution, (v) performance of the fund manager and (vi) development of the annuity market.

8.14.6 Analysis of the Asset Mix of Investments: On asset mix of the investment, the pension funds, the world over, are invested in different assets including government and corporate bonds, equities, foreign securities etc. Government bonds generally have the lowest risk and lowest yield. Corporate bonds and equities have higher risk and higher yields. Typically, systems use a mix of at least two types of assets—government bonds and corporate bonds/equities.

As per the investment guidelines stipulated by the government for Central Government employees under NPS, up to 55 percent can be invested in government bonds, up to 40 percent in corporate debt securities, up to 15 percent in equities and up to 5 percent in money market instruments. International experiences on asset mix vary across countries which have adopted the DCS.

The Commission notes that an innovative approach to investment under the DCS is the *life cycle approach*. Under this, the asset mix of each individual changes based on his/her age. The underlying assumption under this approach is that younger workers are better able to absorb year on year volatility and therefore can undertake risk while older workers should reduce risk as they approach retirement.

A carefully selected asset mix is the sine qua non to higher returns. The Commission recommends that the investment choices under NPS be calibrated on a life cycle approach and the choices be offered in a simple manner so that any lay person can understand and act accordingly. The Commission also recommends that government, in consultation with PFRDA, come up with different options for investment mix and provide subscribers a range of options.

8.14.7 Contribution Rates: In DCS, typically, the employees as well as the employers contribute towards a pension fund. As discussed earlier, the quantum of pension payouts would also depend upon the contribution rates. Higher the contribution rate, better would be the pension payouts. The contribution rates for both the employees and the employers vary across the globe. The Commission has received suggestions that the government's contribution should be enhanced from the present 10 percent in aid of a higher payout under the NPS. Associations and individuals have made presentations before the Commission highlighting that forecasts suggest that a 10 percent contribution from government will not be adequate to provide reasonable post-retirement financial security in all cases. The Commission, therefore, recommends that this important aspect should be re-examined in detail by an expert body for making course corrections if required.

8.14.8 Period of Contribution: The Commission notes that time is of the essence in building up a reasonable corpus and ensuring that effects of compounding are significant. It is, therefore, essential that contributions by individuals and corresponding contributions by government are made in time, and more importantly, are deployed without any loss of time. Any delays in this respect, particularly in the initial years can have a large impact on the eventual corpus.

8.14.9 2004-2011 Entrants: Government employees who have joined service between 2004 and 2011 have suffered due to delay in finalizing the structure of the NPS and the issue of detailed instructions. Although they have made regular contributions, in many cases, this money and/or counterpart contributions were not deployed in the market. In the case of AIS officers, some states are yet to release counterpart contributions or pay interest on delayed contributions. This has led to a situation where the accumulated corpus even after 11 years of service could be meagre. It is necessary that this situation which arose during the transition from OPS to NPS be addressed. The Commission therefore recommends that Central Government and State Governments should, in a time bound manner, ensure that all the due contribution along with compounded interest, where contributions have been delayed, be deposited in the accounts of the beneficiaries. Advisories should be issued to the State Governments to deposit amounts, if not already done, in respect of NPS beneficiaries belonging to all-India services.

Many associations have pointed out that unlike the facility under GPF, it is not possible to make withdrawals under NPS, even to meet obligatory social expenditure. This forces employees towards increased indebtedness as they have to borrow from elsewhere.

The Commission notes that under the NPS Tier-I account, a subscriber is permitted to make partial withdrawal of twenty five percent of the contribution made to his/her individual pension account for certain specified purposes. Such withdrawals are permitted a maximum of three times during the entire tenure of subscription and a period of at least five years should have elapsed between two such withdrawals.

The Commission further notes that there exists a voluntary Tier-II account. Under this account, a subscriber can, at any time, withdraw the accumulated wealth either in full or part and there is no limit on such withdrawals provided the account has sufficient balance of accumulated pension wealth to cover the amount being withdrawn. However, the Tier-II account is yet to be made operational. The Commission therefore recommends that PFRDA should take steps to make the Tier-II accounts operational as early as possible to enable the NPS subscribers the facility of withdrawals from their accounts in case of requirement.

8.14.10 Transparency under NPS: Many associations and individuals have complained that the information relating to the NPS is inadequate, resulting in high degree of uncertainty in the minds of contributors about post-retirement benefits. The Commission noted that PFRDA sends a communication to every participant each month with the current pension wealth and the latest contribution that has been credited. The Commission recommends that focused efforts be made to capture email addresses and mobile numbers of subscribers so that seamless communication is ensured for all subscribers. The Commission recommends that consultation with stakeholders should also be held periodically in different parts of the country.

The Commission notes that no department of Government of India is taking ownership of the NPS. The Commission recommends that a Committee consisting of Secretary, Department of Financial Services; Secretary, Department of Pensions and Pensioners Welfare and Secretary, Department of Administrative Reforms and Public Grievances may be constituted to review the progress of implementation of NPS. The Commission also recommends that steps should be taken for establishment of an ombudsman for redressing individual grievances relating to NPS.

8.14.11 Tax Treatment under the NPS: NPS is under the exempt-exempt-tax (EET) regime while the general provident fund under the OPS is under exempt-exempt-exempt (EEE) dispensation. Under the NPS, while the contributions and the accumulations are tax exempt, withdrawals are taxable. As such, this is an inferior tax treatment when compared to other pension programmes such as general provident fund, contributory provident fund, employees' provident fund and public provident fund wherein contributions, accumulations and withdrawals are tax exempt. The Commission feels that tax neutrality should be ensured across various avenues for long-term savings for post-retirement incomes so that the employees covered by NPS are not at a disadvantage. The Commission therefore recommends that withdrawals under the NPS should be tax exempt to place NPS at par with other pension schemes. The Commission also recommends that the service tax levied at the time of annuity purchase by NPS subscribers should be exempted.

8.14.12 Issue of Family Pension in Case of Death of the Subscriber: Another complaint received by the Commission from staff associations and individuals is that family pension after the death of the employee is not ensured in the NPS. The Commission notes that the government had provisionally extended benefits under the Central Civil Service (Extraordinary Pension) Rules, Family Pension/Extraordinary Family Pension/Liberalised Pensionary Award to government servants appointed on or after January 1, 2004.

Rules regulating these benefits have now been notified by the PFRDA. PFRDA regulations provide for an exit option from NPS in case of premature death of the subscriber by availing of additional relief from government, in which case the entire accumulated pension wealth inclusive of subscriber's contribution would be transferred to the government. The Commission recommends notification of a scheme by government for provision of additional relief in such cases consequent to exit from NPS.

8.14.13 Framing of Rules and Regulations: The Commission notes that rules and regulatiions relating to NPS are being framed and notified by PFRDA from time to time. Associations and individual officers have raised the issue of the need for greater involvement of stakeholders in finalizing these regulations. The Commission recommends that government encourage the PFRDA to set up a strong consultative mechanism involving the DPPW, DoPT, DFS and some associations of employees for a review of regulations and for finalizing future regulations to bring clarity and remove uncertainty relating to NPS. The Commission also recommends that draft regulations should be widely publicized to enable subscribers to respond to any proposed changes, as normally done by other regulatory authorities.

(*paras* 10.3.3-10.3.8, 10.3.11-10.3.29)

8.15 Bonus Schemes and Performance Related Pay

Apart from DAE/DoS, there are bonus payments to Group `B' (non-gazetted) and Group``C' Central Government employees. The bulk of these employees are covered under the productivity linked bonus (PLB) scheme, which is implemented in railways, posts and telecommunications, production units under the Ministry of Defence and other establishments.

The functioning of the PLB Scheme was reviewed in 1982-83 by a Group of officers. The Group of officers also considered the demands for grant of bonus made by those Central Government employees who were not covered by the PLB Scheme. The Group suggested evolution of a productivity linked bonus scheme for Central Government employees as a whole. Based on the recommendations of the Group and pending evolution of a single scheme of bonus for employees, an ad hoc bonus scheme was evolved and the remaining employees, who were not covered by the PLB Scheme, were allowed ex-gratia payment. The Commission notes that the financial outgo on these two bonus schemes stood at ₹ 1847.08 crore for the year 2013-14.

These bonus schemes have no clear, quantifiable targets and performance evaluation of any individual, therefore, is not possible in an objective fashion. The Commission notes that Ministry of Finance has been insisting on revision of the PLB Scheme. It has been suggested, inter alia, that the PLB scheme should be on the basis of an input-output ratio, should be based on productivity and profitability and that productivity should be assessed on financial parameters based on profitability of the organisation.

The VI CPC too had recommended that all departments should ultimately replace the existing PLB Schemes with PRIS. The VI CPC further opined that in places where PLB is applicable and it is not found feasible to implement PRIS immediately, the existing PLB schemes may be continued in a modified manner where the formula for computing the bonus has a direct nexus with the increased profitability/productivity under well-defined financial parameters.

The Commission notes that since PRIS could not be implemented, it could not supplant the existing system of performance linked and ad hoc bonus schemes.

Pay flexibility reforms are not a silver bullet, and involve trade-offs and risks. A study of the literature on the subject reveals that employee motivation and performance are not exclusively linked to performance related pay (PRP) which may only enforce temporary compliance.

The Commission notes that it may be relatively easier to implement PRP in private sector organizations which are, generally speaking, guided by profit motives. Targets, thus, are often based on quantitative criteria making the assessment of performances easier. In the governmental context, on the other hand, the targets are more in the nature of social and public goods. These may not necessarily be tangible and discernible within a stipulated period. Proportioning credit for such a larger public good amongst various departments may not be possible so as to reward some and leave out others. There may be genuine difficulties in separating individuals from the collective, in terms of contribution made towards achieving results. The problem of PRP degenerating into routine entitlements also needs to be reckoned with.

Despite the potential difficulties with PRP, recognition for good effort and achievement through an incentive can, over time, energize the bureaucratic culture of the civil service into one that is focused on meeting citizens' and the government's expectations for speedy and efficient delivery of services.

Any attempt to implement PRP in a governmental framework has to be preceded by proper understanding of the system, adequate planning and capacity building at various levels. The Commission feels that given the enormous size of the government and the wide diversity in the basic structures, sizes and patterns that are observed across Ministries/Departments/Divisions, it would be erroneous to recommend a one-size-fits-all model for PRP. The Commission is of the view that prescribing any particular model for PRP may not be sustainable. Ministries and departments should be given enough flexibility to design individual models suiting to their requirements.

The Commission would prescribe some broad guidelines:

1. **Simple Design:** Performance related pay system must be simple, transparent and easy to implement.
2. **Smart and Effective:** Performance related pay must be smart and should be effective in rewarding excellence and in managing poor performers in a targeted manner.
3. **Consistent across Departments:** PRP framework should be consistent across departments with enough autonomy to design context specific criteria, targets and indicators.

4. **Non-additive Cash Increment:** The award for high performers may be a non-additive cash component of their current pay, given at the end of the financial year as one time incentive for the particular period.
5. **No Linkage with Saving:** The monetary incentive should not be linked to savings.
6. **Training:** Proper training and capacity building of the stakeholders is a must before launching PRP.

In addition to the guidelines suggested above, the Commission notes that introduction of performance related pay should be done keeping in mind two important aspects. First, need to evolve proper criteria to measure performance along with setting a context where individual and organizational goals are clearly aligned, and second, need to devise a performance appraisal system in which the objectives of the appraisal system match with that of the reward system.

The Commission opines that the results framework document (RFD) can be used as the primary assessment tool for linking the targets of the organization with that of the individuals. Suitable changes in the existing annual performance appraisal report (APAR) can provide the necessary linkage between the targets of the appraisal system with those of the RFD document.

The Commission suggests the following modifications in the existing APAR system so that it can used as another anchor for determining performance related pay.

A. Alignment of Objectives: At present, the linkage between individual and organizational performance is not clearly aligned in the APAR. The current APAR focuses more on the individual's performance compared to organizational performance. This results in a situation where individual officer can be rated excellent while the rating of the department could be lower. This is an anomaly which needs to be corrected. Conceptually, the Ministry's vision/mission needs to be translated into a set of strategic objectives for each department and these objectives need to be cascaded by the department head to his subordinates and subsequently down the chain.

B. Prioritizing Objectives, Assigning Success Indicators and their Weights: Objectives reflected in the APAR should be prioritized and assigned weights along with success indicators or key performance indicators (KPIs). This is required for evaluation of the KPIs in the end. The current PAR system assigns 60 percent weight on personal attributes and functional competencies and only 40 percent weight to work output. It would be useful to devise the performance framework in such a way that it captures all the KPIs in a holistic manner: on work output, effectiveness of process adherence, management of tasks, other competencies—behavioural/leadership/functional. The Commission recommends

60 percent weight on work output and 40 percent weight on personal attributes.

C. No Ex-ante Agreement: The indicators in the APAR of an officer/staff will need to be discussed and set with the supervisor at the beginning of the year. This will set the agenda for performance assessment on scientific lines, obviate the possibility of gaming during target setting exercise and facilitate midcourse correction, in case of requirement, in a transparent manner.

D. Timelines: The Commission notes that timelines have been prescribed for drafting, reviewing and finalizing RFDs. The Commission recommends that these timelines may be synchronized with the preparation of the APAR so that the targets set under RFD get reflected in individual APARs in a seamless manner.

E. Online APAR System: The Commission notes that 'Smart Performance Appraisal Report Recording Online Window' has been introduced for IAS officers. Such a system ensures adherence to the prescribed timelines in filling up the APARs. The Commission recommends introduction of such online APARs systems for all Central Government officers/employees.

The Commission feels that any performance related pay (PRP) for Central Government employees should provide a credible framework to drive performance across ministries/departments. Rather than a new system design, the favoured approach should be an incremental adaptation which can operate within the existing framework of rules with minor changes that can enable smooth implementation and operationalization of PRP.

In this backdrop, the Commission recommends introduction of the performance related pay for all categories of Central Government employees, based on quality RFDs, reformed APARs and broad guidelines, as enumerated above.

The Commission also recommends that the PRP should subsume the existing bonus schemes. The Commission notes that there could be a time lag in implementing the performance related pay by different departments. Till such time, the existing bonus schemes should be reviewed and linked with increased profitability/productivity under well-defined financial parameters

(*paras* 15.8-15.15, 15.18-15.19, 15.26-15-29)

8.16 Financial Implications

The financial impact of the recommendations of this Commission will be reflected through increases in expenditure on pay, allowances and on pension. The likely quantum of increase on account of each of these is summarised below:

The total financial impact in the financial year 2016-17 is likely to be ₹ 1,02,100 crore, an increase of nearly 23.55 percent over the business-as-usual scenario.

(₹ crore)

	2016-17 (without VII CPC)	2016-17 (with VII CPC)	Financial Impact	Percentage Increase
Pay	2,44,300	2,83,400	39,100	16.00
Allowances				
HRA	12,400	29,600	17,200	138.71
TPTA	9,900	9,900	0	0.00
Other allowances	24,300	36,400	12,100	49.79
Pensions	1,42,600	1,76,300	33,700	23.63
Total	4,33,500	5,35,600	1,02,100	23.55

(*para* 16.1)

9

Summary of Recommendations of the Seventh Central Pay Commission

(Chapter 17 of the Report)

Note: Chapters and paragraphs at the end of each recommendation refer to the chapters and paragraphs of the Report of the Commission.

Minimum Pay: After considering all relevant factors and based on the Aykroyd formula, the minimum pay in government is recommended to be set at ₹ 18,000 per month. (chapter 4.2)

New Pay Structure: The present system of pay bands and grade pay has been dispensed with and a new pay matrix has been designed. The status of the employee, hitherto determined by grade pay, will now be determined by the level in the pay matrix. Separate pay matrices have been drawn up for civilians, defence personnel and for military nursing service. All existing levels have been subsumed in the new structure; no new levels have been introduced nor has any level been dispensed with. (paras 5.1.13 to 5.1.17)

The "horizontal range" of the pay matrix level corresponds to a 'functional role in the hierarchy' and as the employee's level rises he or she moves from level to level. The "vertical range" for each level denotes 'pay progression' within that level and an employee would move vertically within each level as per the annual financial progression of three percent. The starting point of the matrix is the minimum pay which has been arrived based on 15th ILC norms or the Aykroyd formula. (para 5.1.21)

Fitment: The starting point for the first level of the matrix has been set at ₹ 18,000. This corresponds to the present starting pay of ₹ 7,000, which is the beginning of PB-1 viz., ₹ 5200 + GP 1800, on the date of implementation of the VI CPC recommendations. Hence, the starting point now proposed is 2.57 times of what was prevailing on January 1, 2006. This fitment factor of 2.57 is being proposed to be applied uniformly for all employees. (para 5.1.27)

Annual Increment: The rate of annual increment is being retained at 3 percent. (para 5.1.38)

Entry Pay: The differential of entry pay between new recruits and promoted employees at various levels has been done away with. (para 5.1.32 and 5.1.33)

Modified Assured Career Progression (MACP):
1. This will continue to be administered at 10, 20 and 30 years as before.
2. In the new pay matrix, the employees will move to the immediate next level in the hierarchy.
3. In the interest of improving performance level, the benchmark for MACP has been recommended to be enhanced from 'good' to 'very good.'
4. The Commission has proposed withholding of annual increments in the case of those employees who are not able to meet the benchmark either for MACP or a regular promotion within the first 20 years of their service. (paras 5.1.44-5.1.46)

Defence Pay Matrix: A pay matrix similar to that for civilian employees has been drawn up for defence personnel. The commencement of the defence pay matrix for combatants corresponds to the existing GP 2000, which is the induction level for sepoys and equivalent. The pay matrix designed for the defence forces personnel is more compact than the civil pay matrix keeping in view the number of levels, age and retirement profile of the service personnel. (paras 5.2.13 and 5.2.14)

Military Nursing Officers (MNS): Similarly, in the case of the pay matrix for (MNS), the existing uniqueness in the pay structure of MNS officers has been captured in the pay matrix designed for the MNS. (para 5.2.12)

Military Service Pay (MSP): The defence forces personnel will continue to be entitled to payment of military service pay for all ranks up to and inclusive of brigadiers and their equivalents. The MSP per month recommended is as follows:
- Service officers: ₹ 15,500
- Nursing officers: ₹ 10,800
- JCO/Ors: ₹ 5,200
- Non-combatants enrolled in the air force: ₹ 3,600

MSP will continue to be reckoned as basic pay for purposes of dearness allowance, as also in the computation of pension. Military service pay will however not be counted for purposes of house rent allowance, composite transfer grant and annual increment. (para 5.2.22)

The military service pay, which is a compensation for the various aspects e.g., intangibles linked to special conditions of service, conducting full spectrum operation including force projection outside India's boundaries, superannuation at a younger age and for the edge historically enjoyed by the defence forces over the civilian scales, will be admissible to the defence forces personnel only. (para 6.1.31)

MACP: MACP for defence forces personnel will continue to be administered at 8, 16 and 24 years of service. (para 6.2.85)

Rationalisation of Trades: All X trades should mandatorily obtain a qualification which is equivalent of a diploma in engineering (recognised by AICTE). The incentive structure will henceforth be linked with the qualifications as follows:

1. X pay for JCOs/ORs in Group X at ₹ 3,600 per month for those currently in X pay, but not having a technical qualification recognised by AICTE.
2. X pay for JCOs/ORs in Group X at ₹ 6,200 per month for all X trades which involves obtaining a qualification which is equivalent of a diploma recognised by AICTE. (para 6.2.79 and para 6.2.88)

Defence Security Corps (DSC): The benefit of MACP be permitted to DSC personnel also. However, this benefit should be limited to a total of three upgrades in the entire service career, taking the combined length of the regular employment and the course of reemployment as defence service corps personnel. The first benefit of MACP may be extended to them after a period of eight years from their date of re-employment, in case they do not get a promotion during this period. (para 6.2.98)

Grant of Annual Increment to Recruits: The benefit of grant of first annual increment to recruits will be reckoned from the date of enrolment. (para 6.2.94)

Short Service Commissioned Officers: Short service commissioned officers will be allowed to exit armed forces any time between 7 and 10 years of service with a terminal gratuity equivalent of 10.5 months of reckonable emoluments. They will further be entitled to a fully funded one year executive programme or a M.Tech. programme at a premier Institute. (para 6.2.63)

Headquarters Staff: Parity in pay, up to the rank of assistants, between the field staff and headquarter staff is recommended. It is recommended that the level of assistants of CSS be brought at par with assistants in the field offices who are presently drawing GP 4200. Accordingly, in the new pay matrix the assistants of both headquarters as well as field units will come to lie in Level 6 in the pay matrix and pay fixed accordingly. This level corresponds to pre-revised GP 4200. The corresponding posts in the stenographers' cadre will also follow similar pay parity between field and headquarter staff. The pay of those assistants/ stenographers who have, in the past, been given higher grade pay would be protected. (chapter 7.1)

Recently, through a government order 'edge in pay' has been extended to the upper division clerks (UDCs) belonging to CSS in the secretariat by way of grant of non-functional selection grade to GP 4200. This is available to 30 percent of UDCs. Since the Commission is recommending placement of all assistants, field and headquarters, in Level 6 of the pay matrix, which corresponds to pre-revised GP 4200, this non-functional selection grade to GP 4200 for UDCs belonging to CSS is recommended to be withdrawn. (para 7.1.4 (j))

Two additional increments in CSS/CSSS are granted at the time of their promotion from the grade of under secretary/PPS to the grade of deputy secretary/senior PPS. The Commission finds no merit in continuation of two increments for CSS/CSSS as no such dispensation exists in any other service except the IAS and hence recommends abolition of the same. (para 7.1.6 (d))

Cadre Review: To hasten the process of cadre reviews and reduce the time taken in inter-ministerial consultations, it is recommended that the examination of the cadre restructuring proposal should be undertaken at the department level itself with one member each from DoPT and Department of Expenditure attending such meetings chaired by the concerned secretary of the cadre seeking the review, in the capacity of the cadre controlling officer. The proposal can thereafter be placed before the Cadre Review Committee chaired by the cabinet secretary where the concerned secretaries are represented. (para 7.3.17)

Common Categories: To streamline the common cadres residing in different Departments/Ministries/UTs it is recommended that the government assign specific ministries to be the nodal ministry for each such category. These nodal ministries be tasked with drafting model recruitment rules laying down the educational qualifications, job responsibilities and pay structure for all such categories. A few examples are the statistical cadres and fire fighting staff. (para 7.7.75)

Allowances: The entire structure of allowances have been examined de novo with the overall aim of transparency, simplification and rationalization, keeping amongst other things, the proposed pay structure in mind. The Commission has recommended abolishing 52 allowances altogether. Another 36 allowances have been abolished as separate identities, but subsumed either in an existing allowance or in newly proposed allowances. Particular emphasis has been placed on simplifying the process of claiming allowances. Allowances relating to risk and hardship will be governed by the proposed risk and hardship matrix. (para 8.2.5)

Most of the allowances that have been retained have been given a raise that is commensurate with the rise in DA. Allowances that are in the nature of a fixed amount but fully indexed to DA have not been given any raise. Regarding percentage based allowances, since the basic pay will rise as a result of the recommendations of this Commission, the quantum of percentage based allowances has been rationalized by a factor of 0.8. (para 8.2.3)

Risk and Hardship Allowance: Allowances relating to risk and hardship will be governed by the newly proposed nine-cell risk and hardship matrix, with one extra cell at the top, viz. RH-Max to include Siachen Allowance. This would be the ceiling for risk/hardship allowances and there would be no individual RHA with an amount higher than this allowance. (para 8.10.65 and para 8.10.66)

House Rent Allowance: In line with our general policy of rationalizing the percentage based allowances by a factor of 0.8, the Commission recommends that HRA should be rationalized to 24 percent, 16 percent and 8 percent of the basic pay for Class X, Y and Z cities respectively.

The Commission also recommends that the rate of HRA will be revised to 27 percent, 18 percent and 9 percent when DA crosses 50 percent, and further revised to 30 percent, 20 percent and 10 percent when DA crosses 100 percent. (para 8.7.15)

Currently, in the case of those drawing either NPA or MSP or both, the amounts of NPA/MSP are included with the basic pay and HRA is being paid as a percentage of the total amount. The Commission recommends that HRA should be calculated as a percentage of basic pay only and that add-ons like NPA, MSP, etc. should not be included while working out HRA. (para 8.7.16)

The Commission, in the interactions it has had with the men on the ground at all field locations it has visited, has seen first-hand that the lack of proper housing compensation is a source of discontentment among these employees.

The service rendered by PBORs of uniformed services needs to be recognized and housing provisions of PBORs of defence, CAPFs and Indian Coast Guard have been simplified and HRA coverage has been extended to them. (para 8.7.26)

Uniform related allowances have been amalgamated under a simplified dress allowance payable annually. It is thus recommended that uniform related allowances be subsumed in a single dress allowance (including shoes). (para 8.16.14)

Any allowance, not mentioned here (and hence not reported to the Commission), shall cease to exist immediately. In case there is any demand or requirement for continuation of an existing allowance which has not been deliberated upon or covered in this report, it should be re-notified by the ministry concerned after obtaining due approval of Ministry of Finance and should be put in the public domain. (para 8.2.5)

Entire CPMA will be payable to the PBORs of defence forces. Except rum allowance, other components of CPMA will be payable to PBORs of CAPFs, Indian Coast Guard, RPF and police forces of Union Territories.

Rum allowance will be granted to PBORs of CAPFs and Indian Coast Guard as per the existing guidelines. (para 8.17.25)

Night Duty Allowance: With the present weightage of 10 minutes for every hour of duty performed between the hours of 22:00 and 06:00, the present prescribed hourly rate of NDA equal to (BP+DA)/200 may be continued, the amount of NDA should be worked out separately for each employee and the existing formulation for giving same rate of NDA for all employees with a particular GP should be abolished. (para 8.17.77)

OTA should be abolished (except for operational staff and industrial employees who are governed by statutory provisions).

At the same time it is also recommended that in case the government decides to continue with OTA for those categories of staff for which it is not a statutory requirement, then the rates of OTA for such staff should be increased by 50 percent from their current levels. (para 8.17.97)

All non-interest bearing advances have been abolished. (para 9.1.4)

Regarding motor car advance and motor cycle/scooter/moped advance, since quite a few schemes for purchase of vehicles are available in the market from time to time, the employees should avail of these schemes and both these advances should be abolished. (para 9.1.7)

Regarding other interest-bearing advances, the following is recommended: (para 9.1.8)

1.	PC Advance	₹ 50,000 or actual price of PC, whichever is lower	May be allowed maximum five times in the entire service.
2.	HBA	34 times basic pay or ₹ 25 lakh or anticipated price of house, whichever is least	The requirement of minimum 10 years of continuous service to avail of HBA should be reduced to 5 years. If both spouses are government servants, HBA should be admissible to both separately. Existing employees who have already taken home loans from banks and other financial institutions should be allowed to migrate to this scheme.

The three different kinds of leave admissible to civilian/defence employees which are granted for work related illness/injuries—hospital leave, special disability leave and sick leave are being subsumed and rationalized into a composite new leave named work related illness and injury leave (WRIIL). (para 9.2.36)

1. Full pay and allowances will be granted to all employees during the entire period of hospitalization on account of WRIIL.
2. Beyond hospitalization, WRIIL will be governed as follows:

- **For Civilian Employees, RPF Employees and Personnel of Police Forces of Union Territories:** Full pay and allowances for the 6 months immediately following hospitalization and half pay only for 12 months beyond that. The half pay period may be commuted to full pay with corresponding number of days of half pay leave debited from the employee's leave account.
- **For Officers of Defence, CAPFs, Indian Coast Guard:** Full pay and allowances for the 6 months immediately following hospitalization, for the next 24 months, full pay only.
- **For PBORs of Defence, CAPFs, Indian Coast Guard:** Full pay and allowances, with no limit regarding period.

The rates of contribution as also the insurance coverage under the Central Government Employees General Insurance Scheme have remained unchanged for long. The following rates of CGEGIS are recommended: (para 9.3.6)

Level of Employee	Monthly Deduction (₹)	Insurance Amount (₹)
10 and above	5,000	50,00,000
6 to 9	2,500	25,00,000
1 to 5	1,500	15,00,000

A simplified process for cadre reviews and revamping of the screening process under central staffing scheme have been recommended. (para 7.3.41)

Health Insurance: The Commission strongly recommends the introduction of health insurance scheme for Central Government employees and pensioners. In the interregnum, for the benefit of pensioners residing outside the CGHS areas, the Commission recommends that CGHS should empanel those hospitals which are already empanelled under CS (MA)/ECHS for catering to the medical requirement of these pensioners on a cashless basis. This would involve strengthening of administrative capacity of nearest CGHS centres. The Commission recommends that the remaining 33 postal dispensaries should be merged with CGHS. The Commission further recommends that all postal pensioners, irrespective of their participation in CGHS while in service, should be covered under CGHS after making requisite subscription. The Commission recommends that possibility of such a combined network of various medical schemes should be explored through proper examination. (para 9.5.18)

Pension: The Commission recommends a revised pension formulation for civil employees including CAPF personnel and defence personnel, who have retired before January 1, 2016. This formulation will bring about complete parity of past pensioners with current retirees:

(i) All the personnel who retired prior to January 1, 2016 (expected date of implementation of the Seventh CPC recommendations) shall first be fixed in the pay matrix being recommended by this Commission, on the basis of the pay band and grade pay at which they retired, at the minimum of the corresponding level in the matrix. This amount shall be raised, to arrive at the notional pay of the retiree, by adding the number of increments he/she had earned in that level while in service, at the rate of three percent. Fifty percent of the total amount so arrived at shall be the revised pension. In the case of the defence personnel, total amount so arrived at shall be inclusive of MSP.

(ii) The second calculation to be carried out is as follows. The pension, as had been fixed at the time of implementation of the VI CPC recommendations, shall be multiplied by 2.57 to arrive at an alternate value for the revised pension.

(iii) Pensioners may be given the option of choosing whichever formulation is beneficial to them. (para 10.1.67)

Since the fixation of pension as per formulation (i) above may take a little time it is recommended that in the first instance the revised pension may be calculated as at (ii) above and the same may be paid as an interim measure. In the event calculation as per (i) above yields a higher amount the difference may be paid subsequently. (para 10.1.68)

The Commission recommends enhancement in the ceiling of gratuity from the existing ₹ 10 lakh to ₹ 20 lakh from January 1, 2016. The Commission further recommends, as has been done in the case of allowances that are partially indexed to dearness allowance, the ceiling on gratuity may increase by 25 percent whenever DA rises by 50 percent. (para 10.1.37)

Lump sum Compensation for Invalidation Due to Disability: The Commission recommends an increase in the existing lump sum compensation of ₹ 9 lakh for 100 percent disability to ₹ 20 lakh. However, it finds no justification to recommend broad banding for payment of ex-gratia award to service personnel boarded out on account of disability/war injury attributable to or aggravated by military service. (para 10.2.65)

The Commission notes that cadets are not considered on duty during training and therefore cannot be treated at par with serving defence forces personnel. The Commission, however, keeping in view the facts relating to cadets, recommends an increased ex-gratia disability award from the existing ₹ 6,300 per month to ₹ 16,200 per month for 100 percent disability. (para 10.2.67)

Disability Pension: Keeping in view the tenets of equity, the Commission is recommending reverting to a slab base system for disability element, instead of existing percentile based disability pension regime. Distinct rates separately for officers, JCOs and ORs have been prescribed. (para 10.2.55)

Ex-gratia Lump Sum Compensation to Next of Kin: The Commission is recommending the revision of rates of lump sum compensation for next-of-kin (NoK) in case of death arising in five separate circumstances, to be applied uniformly for the defence forces personnel and civilians. (para 10.2.77)

Circumstances	**Proposed (₹ lakh)**
Death occurring due to accidents in course of performance of duties.	25
Death in the course of performance of duties attribute to acts of violence by terrorists, anti-social elements etc.	25
Death occurring in border skirmishes and action against militants, terrorists, extremists, sea pirates.	35
Death occurring while on duty in the specified high altitude, inaccessible border posts, on account of natural disasters, extreme weather conditions.	35
Death occurring during enemy action in war or such war like engagements, which are specifically notified by Ministry of Defence and death occurring during evacuation of Indian nationals from a war torn zone in foreign country.	45

Indian Coast Guard: The Commission is recommending for the Indian Coast Guard:

1. Merger of pay group Z into pay group Y. (para 11.12.15)
2. X pay of ₹ 6,200 p.m. to all direct entry diploma holders. (para 11.12.18)
3. Sarang Laskars to be upgraded to pay level 4 in the civilian pay matrix. (para 11.12.21)
4. Upgradation of director general to apex level. (para 11.12.27)

Other highlights are as under:

The Edge: The edge, presently accorded to the Indian Administrative Service in the form of two additional increments @ 3 percent over their basic pay at three promotion stages i.e., promotion to the senior time scale (STS), to the junior administrative grade (JAG) and the NFSG to continue in the proposed pay matrix.

Having regard to the difficult demands placed on police officers by their jobs including long working hours, the risk of personal injury and death and the immense public responsibility they carry, the view of the Chairman has recommended that this financial edge, as given to the IAS, be extended to the IPS as also to the third all-India service, the IFoS. (para 7.2.38)

In so far as the Indian Foreign Service is concerned, the existing dispensation shall continue. (para 7.2.18 and para 7.2.19)

Shri Vivek Rae, Member, Seventh CPC is of the view that the financial edge for IAS and IFS is fully justified but has not agreed with the view that it should be extended to the IPS and the IFoS. (para 7.2.20)

Dr. Rathin Roy, Member, Seventh CPC is of the view that the financial edge accorded to the IAS and IFS should be removed. IAS officers have a multi-dimensional leadership role to play and in specific jobs such as that of DM/DC, officers occupying such positions must be able to be primus inter pares by administrative affirmation. According to him, if this position is to be reflected through superior financial remuneration, then their recruitment must be conducted separately. (para 7.2.21)

Chairman and Dr. Rathin Roy, Member are of the view that all AIS and Central Services Group A officers who have completed 17 years of service should be eligible for empanelment under the Central Staffing Scheme and the "two year edge", presently enjoyed by the IAS should be withdrawn. Shri Vivek Rae, Member, has not agreed with this view and has recommended review of the Central Staff Scheme guidelines. (para 7.2.23 and para 7.2.24)

Non-Functional Upgradation for Organised Group 'A' Services: The Chairman is of the considered opinion that since NFU has been in existence for the last ten years and is being availed by all the organised Group 'A' Services it should be allowed to continue. The same will be available not only to all organised Central Group 'A' Services but also members of CAPFs, ICG and defence forces. NFU will henceforth be based on the respective residency periods in the preceding substantive grade. All the prescribed eligibility criteria and promotional norms including 'benchmark' for upgradation to a particular level would have to be met at the time of grant of NFU. (para 6.2.35, para 7.3.21 and para 7.3.22)

Shri Vivek Rae, Member and Shri Rathin Roy, Member, have favoured abolition of NFU at SAG and HAG level. (para 7.2.24)

Chairman and Dr. Rathin Roy, Member, hold the view that the age of superannuation for all CAPF personnel should be 60 years uniformly. Shri Vivek Rae, Member, has not agreed with this recommendation and has endorsed the stand of the Ministry of Home Affairs. (para 11.22.33 and para 11.22.34)

Appendix

List of Abbreviations

B.E.	Bachelor of Engineering
B.Tech.	Bachelor of Technology
CAPF	Central Armed Police Force
CGHS	Central Government Health Scheme
CPC	Central Pay Commission
CSS	Central Secretariat Service
CSSS	Central Secretariat Stenographers' Service
DA	Dearness Allowance
DoPT	Department of Personnel and Training
GDP	Gross Domestic Product
GP 5400 (PB-3)	Grade Pay of ₹ 5,400 in Pay Band 3
HAG	Higher Administrative Grade
IIMA	Indian Institute of Management, Ahmedabad
IIMC	Indian Institute of Management, Kolkata
JCM-Staff Side	Joint Consultative Machinery (National Council)-Staff Side
JCOs/ORs	Junior Commissioned Officers/Other Ranks
LDCE	Limited Departmental Competitive Examination
M.Tech.	Masters of Technology
MACP	Modified Assured Career Progression
MHA	Ministry of Home Affairs
MNS	Military Nursing Service
MSP	Military Service Pay
MTS	Multi-Tasking Staff
NFU	Non-functional Upgrade
NPS	National Pension System
p.a.	per annum
PBORs	Persons Below Officer's Rank
p.m.	per month
PRIS	Performance Related Incentive Scheme
SAG	Senior Administrative Grade
UPSC	Union Public Service Commission
w.e.f.	with effect from

Index

should be provided [illegible] duties or conditions of work are such that a higher [illegible] would be granted but for this concession.

Class IV staffs already enjoying the concession may continue to do so.

Railway employees who are provided with residence in future should pay rent as employees in other departments.

Present classification of localities on basis of population should continue, but grant of house rent allowance in special cases may be considered on merits.

The revised rates of house rent allowance should be as follows.

[illegible]	[illegible]	[illegible]	[illegible]
[illegible]	10	7.50	5
[illegible]	15	10	7.50
400 and above but below [illegible]	20	15	7.50 for those drawing below 150
[illegible] and above	[illegible] percent of pay	[illegible] percent of pay	Nil

Where app[illegible] rates results in [illegible] rent allowance being drawn a[illegible] may be [illegible] or so.

The condi[illegible] within the limit[illegible] facilities for the purpose of house rent allowance should be abrogated for both gazetted and non-gazetted staff.

[illegible] in the proximity of [illegible]

[illegible]	[illegible]	[illegible] 30 per cent [illegible]
150 and above but below 300	[illegible] subject to a minimum of 12.50 and a maximum of 17.50	